new zealand Medicinal Plants

new zealand
Medicinal
Plants

S.G. Brooker · R.C. Cambie · R.C. Cooper

Published by Reed Books, a division of
Reed Publishing (NZ) Ltd,
39 Rawene Rd, Birkenhead, Auckland.
Associated companies, branches and
representatives throughout the world.

This book is copyright. Except for the
purpose of fair reviewing, no part of
this publication may be reproduced or
transmitted in any form or by any
means, electronic or mechanical,
including photocopying, recording, or
any information storage and retrieval
system, without permission in writing
from the publisher. Infringers of
copyright render themselves liable to
prosecution.

ISBN 0 7900 0250 7

©1987 S.G. Brooker, R.C. Cambie, R.C. Cooper
First published 1981
Revised edition published 1987
Reprinted 1991, 1993, 1998, 2002, 2005

The authors assert their moral rights in the work.

Designed by Jane Connor/Godwit
Cover design by Sunny H. Yang
Cover painting of *Metrosiderous fulgens* by Fanny Osborne
reproduced by kind permission of the Auckland Museum.

Printed in Hong Kong

Contents

Preface to the Second Edition	7
Preface to the Third Edition	11
The New Zealand Flora	14
New Zealand's Economic Plants	19
Chemistry and Pharmacology	26
Early Maori Medicinal Plants	32
The Missionaries and Medicine	43
Literature on New Zealand Medicinal Plants	50
Seaweeds: Algae	57
Fungi	60
Mosses: Musci	62
Lichens: Lichenes	64
Ferns: Filices	65
Conifers: Coniferae	78
Flowering Plants: Angiospermae	84
References	241
Glossary	258
Index	261

Preface to the Second Edition

The purpose of this book is to bring together available reports on the medicinal use of New Zealand plants. Observations on this subject have been recorded by early voyagers, travellers and explorers, missionaries, scientists, medical men, Maoris, and Pakehas. Some had little knowledge of botany and thus there are obvious difficulties in identifying the plants to which they refer. Others did not approach the subject critically and there are even greater problems in determining the authenticity of the physiological effects reported.

We have presented all the information we have been able to find in what we hope will be a readable story. Some comments have been inserted where we have doubts regarding the identification of the plants used. We hope that our work will encourage other people to make further records while it is still possible to meet Maoris and Europeans who have experience or who have inherited knowledge of the use of New Zealand plants in medicine. We are aware that some of these herbs are still being employed by the Maori as medicines, and with success, which is all the more reason for recording all possible details on the subject. There are obvious gaps in our knowledge of the plants used for medicine in North Auckland, and there is scope for further field-work there as well as in the Waikato, Taranaki, and Rotorua-Taupo districts.

We have listed all the native plants known to us as being used, or suspected of being used, medicinally by the Maori and by European settlers. Included are the plants used as 'antiscorbutics' by Captain Cook and also a number of introduced plants, but we do not claim that the list is complete.

As well as medicinal uses we have recorded what information is available to us on the chemistry of the plants and their related species, as well as brief notes on their medicinal use overseas. Where two or more species of the same genus are listed, notes on the related pharmacology have been placed after the first entry. We have omitted full details of recipes which can be found in some of the original papers quoted, and for simplicity we have also omitted page references to books cited in the bibliography.

The lower botanical orders (seaweeds, fungi, mosses, lichens, and ferns) precede the conifers and flowering plants. Within each group the families are arranged in alphabetical order and within each family the genera and species follow in alphabetical sequence. An index of general, scientific, and Maori names and a glossary of medical and botanical terms complete the work. Most of the Maori names have been obtained from Andersen.[11]

In the great majority of cases these herbs could have at best no great medicinal value. Some of them, e.g. karaka and tutu, are violent poisons, and we must stress the advisability of using orthodox medical services in preference to these fascinating but dubious specifics.

The first edition of this book[95] was published in 1961 as a Handbook of the Auckland War Memorial Museum. Its preparation was given impetus by the fact that in 1956 the Auckland Division of the British Empire Cancer Campaign Society (now the New Zealand Cancer Society) had begun a systematic investigation of New Zealand plants, with a view to finding compounds of significance in cancer therapy. The preparation of a fresh list of the native and introduced plants used in medicine with an account of their preparation and application, as well as some indication of the chemistry involved, appeared to be opportune. Some information was added to past records, but our main task was to collect information scattered through the literature and make it available to a new circle of readers.

Since publication of the first edition we have continued to gather notes, and in preparing this second edition we have had the opportunity to correct omissions, to expand various sections, and to include the more significant chemical discoveries of recent years. In the introduction to the first edition we expressed the hope that more information might come to light to fill gaps in our knowledge of the use of plants for medicine and that competent scientists would examine some of the remedies to see if they were of real therapeutic value. As to the first of these hopes, few well-authenticated cases have come to our notice since 1961 but there has been some progress in the pharmacology of the plants named, and the worldwide increasing interest in herbal remedies has enabled us to significantly increase the information under 'Related pharmacology'. We have been encouraged by our scientific colleagues to make this information available to a new and wider circle of readers.

One of the major motivations that we have had in preparing this second edition is to re-present the record in a more attractive form and to correct errors which have appeared in the literature in recent years. Unfortunately, in transcribing our work at least one author has attributed definite medicinal use to certain plants where such use was not stated in the original. It is therefore in the public interest to point out that these amendments to our work aggravate a potentially dangerous situation. There are several notable examples of this unwarranted expansion. In the first edition we mentioned, without comment, two references to the use of an infusion of kowhai bark for broken limbs; this has been altered by one author to read '... it is regarded by many authorities as a reliable remedy.' Our guarded statement about the use of rimu juice as a hair restorer becomes 'an excellent hair restorer'. We mentioned one report about the use of fern root as a remedy during the 1918 influenza epidemic; this has been changed to read that fern root was used with good effect. Gullible readers may be led to make themselves quite ill.

We illustrated the first edition of *New Zealand Medicinal Plants* with 12 reproductions of drawings from the Banks and Solander collection and this drew favourable comment. Where possible, we have illustrated each entry in the present edition with a photograph, painting, or line drawing. The line drawings from Banks and Solander are again used and we are grateful to the Council of the Auckland Institute and Museum for permission to reproduce them and to use the hitherto unpublished paintings of Mrs F. Osborne and Miss E. Blumhardt. Most of the photographs have been taken by Dr J. E. Braggins, Botany Department, University of Auckland, and we are grateful to him for his generous assistance.

CAUTION
This book is not intended for prescribing medicines or for curing afflictions. The authors and their correspondents to whom they are indebted for assistance cannot accept any responsibility for the popular 'remedies' mentioned herein. They may be dangerous.

Preface to the Third Edition

The first edition of this book took the form of a small monograph published as an Auckland Institute and Museum Handbook in 1961.[95] In the next two decades further information came to light and was included in a more lavish second edition published in 1981.[93] Contrary to the opinion of one reviewer, who considered that the demand for the book would be 'quite limited', it has enjoyed considerable attention and both the first and second editions are now out of print. This new work gives us the opportunity to include more new material and to present it in a modified format.

Interest in native plant remedies of Pacific countries continues to increase, and some excellent compilations have appeared in recent years. For example, two major works by Cribb and Cribb (1981)[166] and by Lassak and McCarthy (1983)[322] have been published on Australian medicinal plants. An unpublished study by one of us (R. C. Cambie) of Fijian plants reveals that about 450 of the 3200 endemic, indigenous and introduced species were used for medicinal purposes.

A speaker at a DSIR technology workshop held at Massey University in February 1986 stated that 25 per cent of today's pharmaceuticals are derived from plant sources, which suggests that more could be found by investigating species in unusual floras such as those of New Zealand. Added to this is the increasing interest in 'natural' foods and remedies which has resulted in spectacular growth of the sales of these products in many countries. It is also true that despite a great deal of quality research into certain diseases, particularly cancer, the mortality rate and the stresses involved for sufferers and their relatives are still high. Another example is arthritis, which while taking a much lower place in mortality statistics causes prolonged suffering and incapacity that recognised medical procedures can do little to relieve. In these cases it is natural that there should be much interest in materials from natural sources in a usually vain hope to cure the problem or at least alleviate the pain.

In 1982[238] Dr Bruce Gregory, a Maori MP then in opposition, introduced in Parliament the Maori Affairs Amendment Bill, under which it was intended to make the Maori Affairs Department responsible for collecting information on traditional Maori medicines. In one of the mysteries of parliamentary procedure, two members who spoke in favour of the bill later voted against it going further, in a critical division where the motion was lost by a single vote. In the debate Dr Gregory and his fellow MPs seemed not to have heard of our compilation, but the Hon. Venn Young said that it was an important book. The information Dr Gregory wanted collected had already been collated by ourselves and there could be some value in such a collection being given official cognisance.

Changes introduced into the third edition will be obvious, firstly in the new format, and secondly in the new material which has come to light. For example, further information has been obtained on Mother Mary Aubert, arguably the most famous of the religious healers in New Zealand, and certainly one who claimed some surprising cures. In preparing the third edition we have corrected errors and have tried to accommodate recent advances in botany, chemistry and pharmacology. The difficulties involved in identifying species from the Maori names have been further complicated by numerous revisions of botanical nomenclature, some of which will be referred to in the following section on the New Zealand flora.

In the last edition we commented on the work of Walker and his colleagues,[375] who discovered a chemical substance in *Schefflera digitata* which is specific for ringworm, confirming a Maori medicinal use for this plant. This discovery was part of a research plan by Dr Walker which was financed by pharmaceutical interests abroad, but this support has now ceased and unfortunately the search for compounds of medicinal interest in New Zealand native plants is less actively pursued than it was. A forthcoming survey of native plants for their antibiotic activity, conducted by Walker and his co-workers, will be of value.

We have recorded medicinal uses of plants by the Maori, missionaries, early settlers and others. This has been done as a research study, and no statement in this book certifies the use of any of the species mentioned as specific for any complaint; in fact their indiscriminate use could be dangerous. The only limitation we would place on this cautionary advice is that for a traveller suffering injury in an isolated situation, some of the plants could be worth trying, for instance flax fibre to staunch the flow of blood. In more developed areas, recognised sources of medical aid should always be sought.

Again we record our indebtedness to the Council of the Auckland Institute and Museum for the use of additional line drawings from the Banks and Solander collection, and to Dr J. E. Braggins and others for many of the photographs and drawings.

The New Zealand Flora

In a discussion of the geological history of New Zealand with reference to the origin of the fauna and flora, Fleming[209] emphasised that the New Zealand area has long been a relatively isolated archipelago of islands, and considered that the frequent changes in the size and relations of the islands may have played a significant role in the formation of races or species of plants and animals. In an article on the history of life in New Zealand forests, Fleming[210] pointed out that the oldest life in our forests goes back more than 100 million years to Gondwanaland. New Zealand forests are most like the Mesozoic forests of Gondwanaland, 'and are so regarded by Northern Hemisphere biologists who visit them in pilgrimage. We are the custodians of a New Zealand heritage of world interest.' In a recent book Fleming[211] gives a detailed account of the geological history of New Zealand.

As well as geological and geographic changes to the New Zealand area, there have been marked climatic changes since the Cretaceous epoch, as evidenced by the faunal changes in the fossil record. There have also been several post-glacial climatic fluctuations, which are reflected in the sequence of pollens found by Cranwell and von Post[162] in New Zealand peats and in the soil profiles of Canterbury studied by Raeside.[417] These comparatively rapid changes in the environment have decimated or extinguished some groups, have left a few unchanged, and have enabled others to evolve at a very rapid rate. The unique character of the New Zealand flora is due then to the past history of the land and climate, and particularly to the long period in which the plants have been isolated from other floras.

Despite the small area of New Zealand, it is a distinct botanic region. In Volumes 1[9] and 2[366] of the *Flora of New Zealand*, 1796 species of plants are described, consisting of 164 ferns and fern allies, 20 gymnosperms, 1273 dicotyledons and 339 monocotyledons (excluding grasses). A volume on grasses, to complete the indigenous vascular flora, will contain descriptions of about 171 species, making the total at least 1967. A remarkably high proportion of these plants is found only in New Zealand; of the 1967 species of the indigenous vascular flora, about 80 per cent, or nearly 1600, are endemic.

As well as vascular plants, the indigenous flora consists of possibly 835 species of marine macroalgae, 15 freshwater characeae, 2826 marine and freshwater microalgae, 2500 fungi, 500 liverworts, 15 hornworts, 525 mosses and 1500 lichens. The spores of cryptogams are distributed mainly by water and wind and often are carried far afield. Consequently, many species are found in other countries, for example Australia and South America, and comparatively few are endemic.

The lichens of New Zealand have been studied by Galloway, who completed a volume of the *Flora of New Zealand* in 1985.[218] He described 966 taxa in 210 genera, and considered that they comprised 60 per cent of the lichens to be found in New Zealand. A *Moss Flora* is now proposed, and a *Desmid Flora* is in preparation, but the rest of the microalgae, the liverworts and the fungi lack definitive floras, and the numbers of species given above can only be guesswork.

Mixed with the indigenous flora, and apparently part of it, are at least 1700 species of adventive vascular plants that have been introduced since humans first came to New Zealand and have persisted as weeds. They form a large part of the vegetation covering the land and filling waterways and lakes. They have been studied by Healy and Edgar, who in 1980 completed Volume 3 of the *Flora of New Zealand*, which contains descriptions of 168 species of adventive monocotyledons (excluding grasses).[254] A further volume to deal with about 1500 species of adventive dicotyledons is in preparation at the Botany Division of the DSIR at Lincoln. Many of these adventive plants have medicinal, fragrant and culinary virtues but we have included only those plants which are recorded as having been used in Maori and/or colonial medicine.

Following publication of the second edition of this book in 1981, a Christchurch reviewer wrote that we had used 'some botanical names which had long been dropped for good reasons', and ignored 'soundly based revisions'. The main problem we had in compiling *New Zealand Medicinal Plants* was to identify native plants used in herbal medicine. Anyone who tries to relate koromiko or *Veronica salicifolia* of the *Extra Pharmacopoeia* (1895) with the species of *Hebe* in Volume 1 of the *Flora of New Zealand*, by H. H. Allan (1961), will soon realise the difficulties which we encountered. Some people pursue new names with avidity, assuming that what is new must be better, but we have tried to find names which best indicate the plants to which some particular folklore applies.

Another problem, we found, is that some authors do not accept the scientific names in Volume 1 of the *Flora*; for example, Allan in 1961[9] transferred the New Zealand species of *Leucopogon* to *Cyathodes*, but the change has not been followed in Australia where the two genera have many more species. Again, most recent writers prefer the binomial *Pteridium esculentum* as the scientific name for bracken, instead of the cumbersome *Pteridium aquilinum* var. *esculentum* of Allan's *Flora*. For *Pseudowintera*, we have chosen to use the new name, Winteraceae, but also to include the former family name Magnoliaceae, as Magnoliaceae encompasses wider relationships in chemistry and pharmacology. For *Angelica* and *Apium*, we have retained the family name Umbelliferae, as well as the alternative name, Apiaceae, as the Umbelliferae are well known for their chemical and pharmacological properties. We have adopted with some reluctance the new generic name *Scandia* for the New Zealand species of *Angelica*, as the distinguishing features of the new genus, listed by Dawson (1967),[176] seem slight and, again, the change will obscure chemical and pharmacological relationships.

The late Dr H. H. Allan finished writing Volume 1 of the *Flora* in 1956 (the printing of the manuscript was delayed until 1961), and there is a need for a new edition to restore order in the chaos of corrections and name changes which have been published since 1956. Dr E. Edgar and Dr H. Connor of the Botany Division of the DSIR have published several lists of name changes and have provided guidelines for their use, but in many cases readers must choose whether or not to adopt a new name. Interested readers who wish to learn of name changes since publication of the three volumes of the *Flora* should refer to the periodical listings.[188-190]

We are unable to accept several recent revisions; for example, we have not followed Conn (1980)[155] in relegating hangehange, *Geniostoma ligustrifolium*, to variety *crassum* of the Pacific and Indonesian *G. rupestre* because his study ignored floral and vegetative differences between the two species.

Sir Joseph Hooker of Kew was an eminent pioneer plant geographer, but he was cautious about the possible geographical relationships. He noted when a New Zealand species appeared to be closely related to an Australian or Pacific species, but he refrained from linking the two as subspecies or varieties. Sometimes, it seems to be forgotten that he received and studied thousands of specimens from collectors overseas, utilised the horticultural services of the Royal Botanic Gardens to grow seeds and cuttings, and was assisted by very competent botanical artists to illustrate new plant species. Revisions of the New Zealand flora are inevitable, but their value would be greater if modern botanists had similar facilities and showed similar caution.

A Dunedin critic of the 1981 edition noted that we live in Auckland and lack precise knowledge of southern or South Island plant distribution. This is true, but since the *Manual of the New Zealand Flora* was printed in 1925,[139] few accounts of species distribution have been published. In Volume 1 of the *Flora* (1961), Allan limited his distributional notes to symbols for major geographical areas.[9] A revision of Volume 1 might well include more adequate information regarding the distribution of native plants in New Zealand.

In recent times the clearing of land for farming, forestry, and urban development has resulted in the decimation of much of the native flora. It is a sad fact that once-common plants are now often very hard to find. For example, one of us has observed that the Maori elders at Ahipara in the far north of New Zealand have planted a garden of flax (*Phormium tenax*) at the marae, as large supplies of this once-common plant are unobtainable. A recent register of rare and endangered indigenous plants in New Zealand[228] highlights the problem.

New Zealand's Economic Plants

We have discussed in detail the economic plants of New Zealand in another book[94] and only a short review is appropriate here. Further notes on plant uses will be found in the entries on the species concerned.

Despite the distinctive nature of our native flora — or because of it — very few native plants have been exploited commercially. Early European scientists and business people in New Zealand held high hopes for the plants they found but subsequent events tell a disappointing story. Again and again introduced plants have been substituted for their native equivalents; even before 1840, the Maori in some areas had largely abandoned growing kumara and were exporting the recently introduced potato to Australia.

The captains of early visiting ships were first attracted to our native timber, particularly kauri, the long straight trunks of which were ideal for replacing broken masts and spars. Most of the kauri forests of northern New Zealand have been destroyed, and southern forests have been severely depleted of other dominant species. Rimu, totara, miro and other native conifers were milled extensively for construction purposes, as was kahikatea for butter boxes because of its lack of odour. Conservationists may rightly claim that the felling of native timber trees has gone too far, but it has not ceased. Native beech species were largely ignored because of the variable quality of the timber, but increasing use is being made of them. However, there is fierce controversy over Forest Service proposals for remaining beech forests.

New Zealand Forest Service policy for native forests is to leave second-growth areas to mature, but growth is slow compared with that of exotic species such as the radiata pine which dominates so much of our landscape. Tea-tree, or manuka, is fast growing, so much so that it is considered a weed by some farmers, but its main use is for firewood, which has been in short supply since the oil crisis of the 1970s.

As long ago as 1839 Colenso[153] observed hides tanned with native barks at Ngunguru, near Whangarei, and during the First World War Aston[21] made a survey of the tanning agents in New Zealand plants. He found that the bark of a number of native trees was suitable for tanning and commented that excellent leather had been made using the native beech bark of Nelson. Aston considered that practical tanning tests, using hides, were necessary to determine the value of native bark, but by 1918 the shortage of imported tanning materials had been met and tests were never made.

In 1817 Nicholas[386] recorded the extraction by the Maori of a black dye from 'enou' (hinau) and Aston, in papers on the dyestuffs in New Zealand plants,[23] gives references to a number of early uses. In his own work, including a paper illustrated by pieces of wool coloured with the dyes, he reported that species of *Coprosma* yield fast colours which vary greatly with the mordant employed. No commercial use of *Coprosma* has resulted, but home spinners use *Coprosma* and native lichens extensively to dye woollen goods.[276]

Of gums and resins, the only commercial representative is kauri gum, a fossil product which became an important export in the late nineteenth century, reaching a peak in 1899 of

11 000 tons, with a value of over £54 per ton; thereafter, although the price increased, the export declined slowly.[207] Unfortunately, the gum cannot be taken from live trees without killing them. It is the subject of voluminous literature, including the reports of several government commissions (for example, in 1914).[239] In 1915 there was even a short-lived special branch of the civil service, the Kauri Gum Department. Some investigations have been made into the production of oil by distillation of low-grade gum[239] to give a liquid which was at one time an article of commerce.[301] At present the main sale of the gum is for souvenirs, but there is a new plant for recovery by solvent extraction of waxes and resins from a peat swamp at Kaimaumau near Kaitaia.[292]

A lively trade in Jew's ear fungus (*Hirneola* sp.) was developed in the 1880s by a Chinese entrepreneur, who used the capital so obtained to build New Zealand's first dairy factory at Kapuni in Taranaki.[303, 407]

There is a small industry producing crude vases and garden troughs from the trunks of the mamaku (*Cyathea medullaris*) and carved or turned souvenirs of native woods for the tourist trade.

New Zealand spinach (*Tetragonia* spp.), used as an antiscorbutic by Captain Cook, is grown as a minor vegetable in many countries; and New Zealand shrubs are popular garden plants in this country and overseas. There have been some recent developments in searching for species more suited to conditions in other countries,[94] and for native plants for the mini-pot-plant export trade.

During the early stages of European penetration of this country, many plants were tried for beverages; Captain Cook brewed 'spruce beer' from rimu twigs and manuka leaves during his voyages. The early whalers relied on manuka leaves to make tea — hence the name tea-tree (sometimes miscalled 'ti-tree'), but it makes no appeal to the many people brewing teas from imported herbs such as rosemary. However, it could be worthy of further consideration. The seeds of *Coprosma*, New Zealand flax, and the roots of the native dandelion (*Taraxacum magellanicum*) have been roasted and grown to make coffee,[165] but not on a commercial scale. Laing and Blackwell[319] recorded that the rata (*Metrosideros scandens* now *M. fulgens*) yields, when cut, a liquid which tastes like dry cider, but the product from apples is not yet under threat. The only case of a native plant being used commercially in the beverage line is a titoki (*Alectryon excelsus*) flavoured liqueur developed by the DSIR at Mt Albert, Auckland.

High hopes were held for the commercial uses of New Zealand flax (*Phormium tenax*) and a great deal has been written about it, for example by Hector in 1872.[255] As early as 1836, a book[376] on the subject was printed on paper from flax leaves; it is interesting to know that New Zealand Forest Products Ltd. research staff have recently worked out the techniques for growing the plant and producing paper from it,[245] though these have not been used on a commercial scale. Early observers such as Logan Campbell[477] were impressed with the strength of ropes made from flax fibres and indeed they were used during the Second World War to extend supplies of imported sisal. But it compares unfavourably with sisal in strength and handle and is no longer used. Hand processing of flax by Maori women produces a soft fibre, which is used not only for cloaks but also for baskets and art work, the basis of a growing craft industry today. Flax had many medicinal uses, which will be discussed in the appropriate place.

The basic vegetable of the Maori was the kumara, which they brought with them in their Polynesian voyages and is still much used, but is now derived from stock imported from other places.

The fruits of many native species have distinctive but acceptable flavours, though they are generally small; some have large kernels in

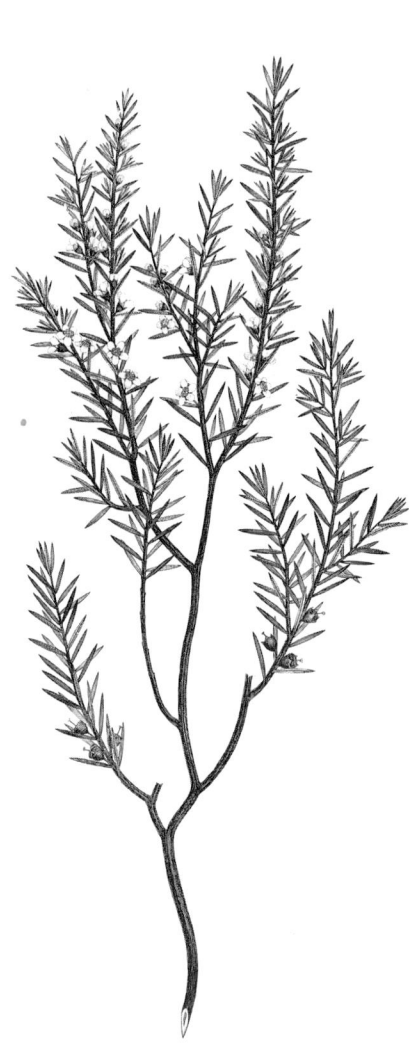

Kunzea ericoides (x 0.5) (manuka). Engraving: S. Parkinson.

relation to the amount of flesh, while others have too many seeds to be pleasant eating. Nevertheless, with modern plant-breeding techniques it may be possible to develop some fruits into acceptable products with a distinctive New Zealand flavour.

In 1878 J. A. Smith[466] suggested that seagrass (*Zostera marina* now *Zostera* spp.) might prove a fair article of export as there was an unlimited demand for it on the London market to stuff mattresses and upholstery. Nothing came of the suggestion. Todea fibre from the magnificent Prince of Wales feathers fern (*Leptopteris superba*) has been used commercially for orchid growing, but as the fern is rare, the use of tree-fern (*Dicksonia*) and sedge (*Carex*) fibres is recommended.[274]

Metrosideros fulgens (x 0.5). Engraving: S. Parkinson.

The New Zealand Geological Survey has examined a number of deposits of diatoms and some of this material has been used for insulation and filtration purposes, but an industry has not developed.[237]

Several red seaweeds belonging to the genus *Gigartina* have been used commercially since 1940 in place of imported carrageen, and two other red seaweeds belonging to the genus *Pterocladia* are collected and processed for agar jelly, which is widely used in bacteriological work and in the canning of sheep's tongues.[364, 365] For some time a factory operated in Christchurch, but New Zealand's seaweed industry is now based in the Bay of Plenty. Seaweed extracts are widely promoted as fertilisers, but most of the material used has been imported.

Edward Shortland[454] saw the Maori recovering sugar from the roots of the cabbage tree (*Cordyline* spp.) and the idea has been revived recently by Fankhauser and Brasch.[201] The root contains fructose, which is much sweeter than ordinary sugar (sucrose).

Ensuing from its use at a trade exhibition in Japan, there has recently been an increasing trade in sphagnum moss, reaching 336 tonnes with a value of $3 000 000 in 1984, but supplies could be exhausted in a decade.

Native pasture plants still play an important part in our pastoral industry, particularly on the higher and rougher sheep country, which comprises one-third of our total farmlands. Undoubtedly one of the most valuable native plants is the *Danthonia*, which forms pastures on dry hillsides. However, on easy ploughable country the change from native bush, scrub, or grasses to introduced pasture plants is far advanced, and the purpose today of most grassland research is to establish ways of obtaining the best control of introduced ryegrass-clover pastures.

The trend to study introduced rather than native plants has been strong for many years but in recent times efforts have been made to exploit the economic potential of the extractives from New Zealand plants.[116] For example, attempts have been made at the DSIR in Wellington, and by others, to use the diterpenoid manool, first isolated from the pink pine (*Dacrydium biforme*) by Hosking and Brandt,[270] as a basis for synthetic perfumes. Manool can be converted into internal acetals, which have value as fixatives in perfumery, and into ambreinolide,[444] which is derived from ambrein, the chief constituent of ambergris.

More recently, as a result of escalating costs for the production of steroidal drugs from diosgenin, which is obtained from the Mexican yam (*Dioscorea mexicana*), other sources of raw material have been investigated. These include the steroidal alkaloid solasodine, which is obtained from species of the genus *Solanum*. In New Zealand a three-company consortium set up a plant for the commercial extraction of solasodine from the indigenous species, poroporo (*S. aviculare*) and the cut-leaved nightshade (*S. laciniatum*).[125,307] Production started in 1978, but proved to be not economically viable, and the plant was closed down in 1981.

Chemistry and Pharmacology

Dr George Bennett of Sydney, who visited New Zealand in 1829, published an account of the poisonous properties of karaka (*Corynocarpus laevigatus*) and tutu (*Coriaria arborea*) which was the first discussion of New Zealand plants in the medical literature.[48] He was followed by Dr W. Lauder Lindsay of Edinburgh, who, as a result of his visit to Otago in 1861, wrote an account of the tutu which appeared in the *Pharmaceutical Journal* for 1864.[334] A Frenchman, M. Vincent, made the first chemical study of *Phormium tenax*, published in Paris in 1848.[499]

One of the first chemists to take up permanent residence in New Zealand was William Skey,[14] who joined the Otago Geological Survey in 1862 and from 1865 was Colonial Analyst until his death in 1900. He was a man of many parts, being chemist, poet and farmer. His analytical work in metallurgy was of great value to the mining industry, but in his laboratory he also composed his poems, often sitting up all night cultivating the muse, and printed them with a hand press. The first of his two books of poems, *The Pirate Chief and the Mummy's Complaint, with various Zealandian Poems*, was published to commemorate the introduction of electric light into Wellington in 1889. His poetical skill is not unimpeachable, but some of his parodies are amusing and part of one may be quoted as a digression.

To shave or not to shave? — that is the question,
Whether 'tis better on our frames to suffer
The sportive growths of flaming beard outrageous
Or to take arms against this host of troubles,
And by dispersion end them? To shave, to clip
No more and by a shave to end awhile
These pendants and the thousand natural curls,
That man is heir to: 'tis a consummation
Devoutly to be wished — To soap — to shave;
To shave! — perchance to hack! Ay, there's the rub.

Skey investigated a number of native plants — tutu,[459] karaka,[460] rangiora,[462] towai,[457] karamu,[458] and *Phormium* fibre.[461] Professor Church of the Royal Agriculture College, Cirencester, also worked on *Phormium*[143] but the techniques available in those days permitted little more than a division of the compounds found into broad groups such as bitter principles, gums, 'fixed' oils (fatty acid-glycerol esters) and essential oils.

A new chapter was begun when T. H. Easterfield,[186] first Professor of Chemistry at Victoria College, Wellington, (and later first Director of the Cawthron Institute) and B. C. Aston, first Chemist to the Department of Agriculture, collaborated (1900-1) in isolating and investigating the chemistry of tutin, the poisonous principle of tutu.[182-184] They enlisted the help of Professor Marshall of Dundee, who worked out the lethal dose of this poison. Aston deserves an important place in our story, as he was a chemist and a botanist and made useful contributions in both fields. In continued collaboration with Easterfield, he studied the chemistry of the karaka nut and rimu resin.[184] In 1910 he isolated pukateine, the poisonous principle of pukatea bark,[19 20] and later he made an extensive study of the tinctorial powers of the *Coprosma* barks[22 23] and the usefulness of some native trees in providing vegetable tannins.[21] Though circumstances compelled him in his later years to concentrate on agricultural problems, he continued to take an interest in the native plants and always had under way some item of research on them until his retirement in 1936.[24]

In more recent times the chemistry of natural products has been investigated within the DSIR and in the chemistry departments of most New Zealand universities. Of particular note is the work at Auckland University of the late Professor L. H. Briggs[117] and his co-workers, who examined a wide range of naturally occurring compounds. An interesting review of the chemistry of New Zealand plants, which touches on many aspects of their pharmacology, has been published by Briggs.[69] Murray[377] has covered the salient points of the literature up to 1949, and we have published elsewhere an extended register on the chemistry of the native flora.[118]

A brief account of the development of organic chemistry in New Zealand which largely centres on natural products has been published.[122] In later sections of this book we have indicated in the appropriate places what is significant in the chemistry, and the pharmacological possibilities of the plants coming within the scope of this work.

Later researches in this field emphasise the singular nature of our flora, already apparent to systematic botanists. Although only a relatively small number of New Zealand plants have been examined, they have yielded a diverse range of extractives which include alkaloids, toxic principles, essential oils, dyestuffs, polyphenolics, tannins, steroids, fats, etc., some of which have potential medicinal value.

Although most alkaloids are poisonous, they can have physiological and therapeutic effects when administered in low concentrations. Alkaloids usually have a bitter taste and can act as tonics as a result of their stimulating effect on the flow of saliva. Those with a mild level of toxicity can be used as purgatives or emetics. It is usually the alkaloid-containing species which attract attention for their medicinal uses.

Unfortunately, the flora of New Zealand, being a temperate-region flora, is not particularly rich in plants belonging to families such as the Apocynaceae and Rutaceae, which are well known as alkaloid-bearing, but many of the New Zealand plants do in fact contain alkaloids.

As a consequence of their potential commercial value, and as indicated in the previous section, major interest has centred on the poroporo (*Solanum aviculare*) and the cut-leaved nightshade (*S. laciniatum*). Other alkaloid studies of note include those by Briggs and his co-workers on the compounds from New Zealand *Sophora* species and from *Senecio* (now *Urostemon*) *kirkii*. Of the medicinal plants mentioned in this book the rangiora (*Brachyglottis repanda*), makomako (*Aristotelia serrata*), pukatea (*Laurelia novae-zelandiae*), and mairehau (*Phebalium nudum*) are the most noteworthy for the presence of alkaloids.

Karakin, the poisonous principle of the karaka nut, has been found by Carter[132] to contain several nitro-groups which have not been found elsewhere in constituents of the higher plants; indeed at the time of discovery this was one of the first records of compounds with this group in nature. Other non-alkaloidal toxic principles include tutin from *Coriaria* species, prostratin from the Strathmore weed (*Pimelea prostrata*), and tetraphyllins A and B from the New Zealand passionfruit (*Passiflora tetrandra*). All of these species are dealt with fully by Connor in *Poisonous Plants in New Zealand*.[156]

Among others, members of the native gymnosperms, for example *Agathis australis*, and of the family Myrtaceae, for example the manuka (*Leptospermum scoparium*), contain essential oils. Such oils can be used for respiratory ailments and many have bactericidal activity. This activity can often be traced to the presence of terpenoid compounds such as α-terpineol and cineole.

Most polyphenolic compounds possess some fungistatic and bactericidal properties. Many New Zealand plants contain tannins, which are polyphenolic compounds that act as astringents, drawing tissues together and contracting them. Among natural colouring matters, anthraquinones have laxative properties. Because of their bactericidal effects, some are used for the treatment of skin diseases. New Zealand *Coprosma* species including *C. areolata* are a rich source of hydroxylated anthraquinones. Their presence in the root of *Phormium tenax*, a well-known New Zealand medicinal plant, has been demonstrated recently. The characteristic odour of the leaves of *Coprosma foetidissima* has been found by Sutherland to be due to methyl mercaptan.[478] Mercaptans are unusual in plants, and appear to be confined to the Rubiaceae and the Cruciferae.

Some alcohols, for instance mannitol, which occurs in St John's wort (*Hypericum perforatum*), are used for their laxative or diuretic action, while medium-chain fatty acids find use as antifungal agents. Aromatic acids such as benzoic acid have antiseptic and germicidal properties and a number of natural products with diverse structures have anti-tumour activity. They include pyrrolizidine alkaloids, certain lignans, quinones, oxidised terpenoids, certain saponins, and even tannins. Examples of such compounds occur in New Zealand plants, for example senkirkine from *Urostemon kirkii*, matairesinol from *Prumnopitys taxifolia*, and prostratin from *Pimelea prostrata*.

Fastier and Laws[204] have summarised the pharmacological aspects of the native flora. However, while the New Zealand flora is rich in unique species, few native plants have been tested for medicinal properties. Some work has been carried out by Professor F. N. Fastier and his colleagues at the Department of Pharmacology, University of Otago. Many extracts from native plants have been screened for anti-cancer activity by Dr B. F. Cain and his co-workers of the Auckland Cancer Society laboratory, but few have given encouraging results. One important discovery is that the barks of the New Zealand conifers are a particularly rich source of ecdysones, or insect moulting hormones.[433] They offer some promise as useful insecticides.

More recently, Dr J. R. L. Walker, University of Canterbury, has shown that the leaves of *Schefflera digitata* contain an acetylenic alcohol which shows specific activity against common dermatophyte fungi.[375] This represents one of the few examples where the active principle has been isolated and linked with the medicinal use of a New Zealand plant, the sap having been used for ringworm.

Early Maori Medicinal Plants

Sir Joseph Banks, who accompanied Captain Cook on his first visit to New Zealand in 1769, remarked that the health of the natives was so sound that probably their need of physic was small.[269]

Captain Cook, on his second voyage of discovery, recorded in his journal for 9 November 1774 at Queen Charlotte Sound that

> in the afternoon a party of us went ashore into one of the coves, where were two families of the natives variously employed; some sleeping, some making mats, others roasting fish and fir roots, and one girl, I observed, was heating of stones. Curious to know what they were for, I remained near her. As soon as the stones were made hot, she took them out of the fire, and gave them to an old woman, who was sitting in the hut. She placed them in a heap, laid over them a handful of green cellery, and over that a coarse mat, and then squatted herself down, on her heels, on the top of all; thus making a kind of Dutch warming-pan, on which she sat as close as a hare on her seat. I should hardly have mentioned this operation, if I had thought it had no other view than to warm the old woman's backside. I rather suppose it was intended to cure some disorder she might have on her, which the steams arising from the green cellery might be specific for. I was led to think so by there being hardly any cellery in the place, we having gathered

Leptospermum scoparium (x 0.5).
Painting: F. Osborne.

Solanum aviculare (x 0.4). Painting: E. Blumhardt.

Hoheria populnea (x 0.5).
Painting: F. Osborne.

Coprosma robusta (x 0.5).
Painting: E. Blumhardt.

34

it long before; and grass, of which there was great plenty, would have kept the stones from burning the mat full as well, if that had been all that was meant. Besides, the woman looked to me sickly, and not in a good state of health.[157]

Polack[413] and others have described similar steam baths, and they seem to have been used widely.

Major Richard A. Cruise, in command of the store ship *Dromedary*, spent ten months in New Zealand in 1820 collecting a cargo of kauri spars. He was a shrewd and accurate observer of the Maori people, and remarked,

> We once observed a man, who, accidentally, inflicted a severe cut upon his leg with an axe; he immediately squeezed the juice of a potato into the wound, and tied it up, and in a few days it was quite well. There did not appear to be any particular description of persons to whom they applied in cases of sickness, but, when so circumstanced, they have recourse to different herbs and plants, with which they seem extremely well acquainted; and one of the gentlemen who was afflicted with an eruption on his lips was cured by the application of a decoction of herbs given to him by a native.[168]

An English sailor, John Rutherford, who lived in the North Island as a Maori from 1816 to 1826, recorded that he was wounded in a tribal fight by a short jagged spear which stuck in his thigh. It was afterwards cut out by two Maori women with an oyster shell and left a wound as large as a teacup. Rutherford's Maori wife applied some green herbs to the wound which immediately stopped the bleeding and also made the pain much less severe.[13]

In the section of this book on 'The Missionaries and Medicine' we refer to Father L. C. Servant, who arrived with Bishop Pompallier in 1838. His observations on the Maori of the Hokianga area[456] have been published. He noted the use as medicinal plants of pue (*Dactylanthus taylori*), nani (*Brassica campestris*), ruruhau (*Brassica* sp.), and the korau (*Cyathea medullaris*), which was cooked like the potato. All were 'refreshing remedies'. The Maori heated the root and the leaves of 'the phormium' and applied them to the affected area. The root of the rengarenga was likewise heated and applied to abscesses and tumours. Servant confirmed the views of other observers that sorcery was preferred to the use of herbs, and that sick people were abandoned to their fate without any food.

Joseph Crocome, the first European medical man in Otago, took up practice among the whalers and Maori at Waikouaiti in 1838. It is reported[216] that

> when his own scanty stock of drugs failed him he turned to the Maoris for some of their medical lore and remedies. Koromiko for internal troubles, infusion of *Phormium tenax* and the slippery gum from around the roots and leaves as a bath for severe wounds, an infusion of ngaio for severe purpose: these simples sopped into flax fibre, and teased out ribbon-wood 'jacket' packed over swellings and lumps, made useful substitutes for dressings of abscesses and tumours.

Although by the time of Crocome's arrival the Maori had been in contact with Europeans in Otago for about 40 years, and it is not certain that they did not learn the use of native plants from them, the evidence from Crocome and others quoted in Fulton's book[216] would seem to confirm that the Maori did make some use of native plants in the treatment of ailments.

Dr Ernst Dieffenbach, naturalist to the New Zealand Company, who journeyed through New Zealand in the years 1839-41, recorded[177] the use of steam rising from herbs infused in boiling water for the treatment of disease and the use of leaves of *Solanum laciniatum* as 'cataplasms for ulcers'.

Some early writers believed that the Maori had little use for herbs or other specifics in pre-European times. Colenso[150] remarked, it is highly doubtful whether the New Zealanders ever used any vegetable as an internal medicine before their intercourse with Europeans; for severe burns, however, they applied outwardly the ashes and charcoal dust of burnt fern fronds (*Pteris esculenta*), and the fine reddish dust of the large decaying fungus pukurau (*Lycoperdon fontainesii*). The blanched bases of the leaves of the harakeke (*Phormium*), and the roots of the rengarenga or maikaika (*Arthropodium cirratum*), were sometimes roasted and beaten to a pulp, and applied warm to unbroken tumours and abscesses. As a cataplasm for ulcers they used the leaves of kohoho or poroporo (*Solanum aviculare*) — and for wounds and old ulcerated sores, they used the large leaves of the pukapuka, or rangiora (*Brachyglottis repanda*), and also the hune, or pappus down of the large Bulrush, but merely as a protection against dust, etc. Layers of dry totara bark, and the lower parts of stout green flax leaves, served admirably as splints, in cases of broken bones, the New Zealanders being far better surgeons than physicians. And the leaves of several particular plants were in request for their rude steam or vapour baths, for rheumatic and other stubborn chronic complaints; but it is highly questionable whether the benefit derived from such baths did not arise entirely from the warm vapour. They sometimes rubbed the fresh juice of the ngaio (*Myoporum laetum*) over their skin, to keep off the persecuting namu (sandfly); and for several years they have used as purgative medicines, the juice of the root of the New Zealand flax (*Phormium*), and the bark of the kowhai (*Edwardsia grandiflora*); as a tonic, the leaves of the kohekohe (*Dysoxylum spectabile*); as a demulcent, in colds, etc., the bark of the houhere (*Hoheria populnea*); as a diaphoretic, *Mentha cunninghamii*; and, as slightly alterative, a decoction of the bark and stems of the pikiarero (*Clematis hexasepala*), and the root of tataraheke (*Coprosma acerosa*).

A. S. Thomson, a surgeon with the 58th Regiment during the New Zealand Wars, writing in 1859,[489] makes no mention of the use of medicines by the pre-European Maori.

Disease was attributed to evil spirits which could only be exorcised by successful incantations. Removal to other parts of the country was 'an esteemed remedy'; any beneficial effects were attributed to avoiding the powers of local evil spirits. Another remedy, which could be fatal, was to place heavy weights on the body to squeeze out evil spirits.

No account of the medicinal plants of the Maori would be complete without referring to the lengthy paper (120 pages)[233] on Maori medical lore published under the name of W. H. Goldie in 1905. Elsdon Best had been collecting information on the subject for many years but felt that it should be written up by a medical man, so he passed his notes on to Dr Goldie, who had also been a student of the subject. Unfortunately Goldie's health broke down when he was about two-thirds of his way through writing the paper, which was finished off and prepared for publication by Best. It is probably still the finest writing on Maori medicine in the setting of their beliefs about health and disease, and would justify republication.

Best, in his day the leading authority on the Maori, believed that 'the Maori of old relied principally upon his priest when attacked by sickness, and that the priests did not deal in simples, herbal remedies, etc., but believed firmly that their cryptic *karakia* and strange rites were the sole means of saving the patient's life.'[54] Various plants were used by the priests in these rites. Thus Best described how the priest would sprinkle a person who fancied himself becoming ill with a branch of karamu-ramu (*Coprosma lucida* or *robusta*), which had been dipped in water in which the priest and patient stood waist deep. In another rite a leaf of flax (*Phormium tenax*) or tutumako (*Euphrasia cuneata*), a piece of keketuwai (moss) or rarauhe (*Pteridium esculentum*) was placed on the skin of the sufferer as a way of escape (ara atua) for the demon causing the sickness. Demons were also exorcised by taking a piece of one of the plants of the generic group puwha or puha and a dead ember from a fire. These two were passed round the patient's thigh from right to left and then held high in the air so that the demon could remove himself. The term 'puha' or 'puwha' refers to a whole group of plants used by the Maori in various religious rites with the object of raising the tapu. In this connection Best specially mentions kohukohu (*Pittosporum tenuifolium*) as important for raising the tapu on sick people.

Best[54] also gave an account of various remedies used by the Maori and wrote,

> I am by no means prepared to state that all such here given were used in olden times — i.e. before the arrival of Europeans. In fact, I believe most of them to be modern, being based on the European methods of treatment of the sick. The use of simples was not encouraged in the days of old, for that would have lessened the power of the priests, who relied principally upon their absurd rites and incantations. For no Hippocrates had appeared to separate medicine (!) from theology, and shamanism was rampant.

Best[56] commented,

> there was no science of medicine in Maoriland. The native belief that all bodily ailments were caused by evil spirits, or came as punishment from the gods, effectually prevented research in even simple lines such as herbal remedies. When they at last received the knowledge of internal medicines from Europeans the natives were captivated by the new mode of exorcising evil spirits. They took to medicine as a duck takes to water, and swallowed any nostrum they could procure, be it ever so vile. Ere long they began to concoct strange herbal remedies themselves.

Again Best[56] remarked,

> In native belief illness is a condition brought about by...supernormal powers, either as a punishment for wrong committed, such as a

transgression of tapu, or such beings were the agents employed by a magician who wished to afflict or destroy him. It was this belief, firmly embedded in the native mind, that so effectually prevented anything like true medical research in Maoridom. On that account medicine was an unknown art...

It was a singular fact that, when the Maori was made acquainted with European medicines, he took to them in a manner most enthusiastic. He developed a marvellous appetite for medicine, no matter what the remedy might be, or whether he possessed any ailment or not. When camped in the byways of the land I have known natives enjoy themselves by sampling any rongoa (medicine) that might be accessible within my lowly 8 x 10 mansion. Thus when my worthy friend "The Rainy Day" came to apply for a bush-felling contract, his wife solaced herself by swallowing half a bottle of fluid cascara sagrada that she espied upon the shelf. This seductive beverage might not have seriously disturbed her accommodating interior had she not supplemented it with a dose of Mr Davis' superfine painkiller! In the scene that ensued I did not take a hand; it is sufficient to say that things happened! This, however, is a digression.

We have quoted extensively from Best, the most widely accepted authority, but we consider that his later views are incorrect. Professor R. N. H. Bulmer[101] has commented that New Guinea tribal elders give similar magical explanations of illness and death rather than describe the everyday herbal remedies used by the women of the tribe. We think that the reports of Cook, Cruise, Rutherford, Dieffenbach, and Colenso are evidence that the old-time Maori used external remedies. The use of internal medicines may have followed European settlement, although Buck indicated that some were taken for constipation and diarrhoea. Buck[100] discussed ailments caused by sorcery and continued,

> Minor ailments which were obvious to the sight were regarded in a more rational manner. Warts

(tonatona) were pared down and medicinal leaves applied after heating. Boils (whewhe) were incised and the core (whatu) expressed (whete) by squeezing between the thumbs [Possibly this refers to carbuncles]. Goitre (tenga) occurred in some districts, but was taken usually as a matter of course. Some such swellings were supposed to be eased by rubbing with the morning urine applied with the left hand. Toothache (tunga) was held to be due to a grub (tunga), hence the name. For children, a chant was used which gave some comfort at the time.

Heat was used to relieve the after-pains of childbirth and painful and difficult menstruation. An oven of hot stones was covered with the leaves of certain plants, a mat placed over the leaves, and the patient sat on the mat, thus receiving a medicinal steam bath.

Blood-letting was practised for the alleviation of pain such as headaches or pains in the side. A toetoe leaf was used to make parallel incisions in the skin over the site of the pain.

If drowning, the patient was held by the heels over the smoke of a fire, a procedure which not only allowed the water to run out, but caused sneezing which revived the patient.

Herbal purgatives were used for constipation, the best known being an infusion of the root of the flax plant. The taste is bitter but the action effective. For diarrhoea, the common remedy was to chew the young unopened leaf ends of the koromiko (*Veronica* spp.) or the mature seeds of the manuka.

The astringent sap of some plants, particularly the rata vine, was used for flesh wounds.

Beyond the few plants used for minor ailments, the possibilities of herbal remedies were not explored by the Maoris because of the accepted theory of the causation of the disease. After European contact, however, they began to use medicines more freely and to try out the native plants. The introduction of tubs led to the use of baths with various hot infusions of leaves such as kawakawa (*Piper terminalis*) [probably *Macropiper excelsum* is meant] and others. The pseudo-priests began to find curative properties in different plants which they kept secret so as to acquire more followers. They combined herbal remedies with a certain amount of native ritual and entered the same category as European quacks to such an extent that a Tohunga Suppression Act was passed by Parliament in 1907 to prevent them from imposing on the credulity and superstitions of the people.

The Tohunga Suppression Act was repealed in 1963 and the tohunga's role (for example as a faith healer in dealing with psychosomatic disorders) is now regarded with more sympathy.[504] (Readers should refer to Joan Metge's popular work on *The Maoris of New Zealand*.)

Macropiper excelsum
(x 1). Photo:
L. H. Briggs.

The Missionaries and Medicine

Marianne Williams, who came with her husband, Henry, to Paihia in 1823 with the Church Missionary Society, was a qualified midwife; her brother-in-law William Williams, who followed three years later, was trained as a surgeon, but he concentrated on his missionary duties and an exhaustive study of the Maori language, so that he is best remembered for his dictionary,[516] which was first published in 1844 and has gone through seven editions since. Gluckman[232] says that the missionaries and other European residents of those days relied largely for medical help on the providential visits of passing ships and whalers, each of which carried its own 'surgeon'.

John Wesley, the founder of Methodism, wrote a rather curious book on medicine, entitled *Primitive Physik*, which was so highly esteemed by his followers that it went through 32 editions. It is therefore not surprising that the training of the Rev. Samuel Ironside, who came to New Zealand as a Wesleyan missionary in 1839, included lectures on gynaecology and pharmacy. While stationed at Cloudy Bay in Marlborough in 1841,[278] he used his small collection of drugs and instruments to treat the Maori, operating from his study window. He dispensed such simple remedies as rhubarb, jalap, and Epsom salts. (Epsom salts was much used by the missionaries: in 1826 William Williams recorded in his diary that it was a great favourite with the natives, and he would need further supplies.) Ironside observed that some people came along, not because they needed medicine, but so that they might be on hand to share whatever good was going — 'a principle which applies pretty extensively everywhere'. The missionary got over this problem by making up pills of bread, shaking them in a magnesia bottle to give them a medicine flavour, and dispensing them to malingerers. It is evident from the published lives of other missionaries, for instance John Hobbs[518] and James Hamlin,[438] that ministering to the medical needs of the Maori was a regular part of their work, but they did not employ native plants.

Father Servant was an early member of the Marist order which sent the first Roman Catholic missionaries to Oceania. He arrived in New Zealand in 1838 and made notes on the Maori of the Hokianga region where he worked. These have recently been translated from his native French and published.[456] In a foreword it is stated that Servant had little difficulty in gaining mastery of the Maori language, in which he was able to preach within a few months. His observations on Maori medicine are discussed in the section of this book on that subject.

Also recently translated from the French is the account[428] of the experiences of Father Joseph Chouvet, another Marist missionary, who was stationed at Opotiki from 1843 to 1846. His report contains a small section entitled 'The strange medicines of the New Zealanders', which has little to add to what has been noted by others.

In 1839 Bishop Pompallier moved from Hokianga to Kororareka, where he established a hospital in 1840.[345]

G. A. Selwyn, appointed Anglican bishop of New Zealand in 1841, was responsible for bringing to the country three good medical men in E. F. Butts, C. P. Davies and A. G. Purchas. The last-named was 'one of the most gifted doctors ever to settle in New Zealand'.[232] Selwyn himself comes out as something of an enigma. He had a library of about 250 medical books; he established small hospitals at Waimate North and St Johns, Auckland, and with the well-qualified doctors he had, may be considered to have established the first medical school in the country. On the other hand he concocted a tonic from chocolate thickened with flour and water paste. He said it was 'nourishing', which would be its only medical virtue.[232]

The Rev. Richard Taylor,[484] who resided at Wanganui for many years, remarked in April 1847 that after church service he had a number of Maoris seeking medicine. He found 'that calomel combined with rhubarb in strong doses is generally very beneficial in these prevailing complaints which are pains in the head and stomach, and seems quite to have destroyed their love for Epsom salts.'

The European settlement of New Zealand resulted in the Maori people acquiring firearms with which they proceeded to decimate themselves. Diseases which came with the settlers and which were not dangerous to Europeans also took a great toll of the Maori, who had little resistance to them. Taylor described an epidemic which swept through the Wanganui Maori in 1847 when not a person was well:

> From four this morning my door was beset with anxious seekers for medicine. The doctor came over to see my patients; he found they paid so little attention to his directions and would not stay indoors that it was dangerous to give any but simple purgatives. I accordingly mixed up medicine of that character in a pail . . . and gave it to 80 patients . . . The next morning I went round . . . to visit the sick having mixed a large quantity of salts, rhubarb and magnesia in a pail. I found the number had increased and that Mr Ronaldson had to go round with another pail full for the

remainder of the pa: one poor woman I found too far gone to hope for recovery . . .

In his diary for 23 January 1844 Taylor noted that 'in every place I have been beset with applications for medicine to ensure child bearing. They said they got it from Mr Skivington. It was in vain I told them I had none. They thought me very stingy, so in self-defence I gave all the ladies a strong dose of salts as I happened to have plenty with me.' Taylor recorded in his diary for 1845 the sermon he had preached to the natives advocating the use of simples instead of foreign medicine. He wrote, 'I find the natives will not use simples, nothing but foreign medicine is used.' In the case of a Maori woman with an abscessed back he wrote, 'I ordered them when I went up the river to poultice it with pumpkin every day, but they did not do so and completely laughed at the idea of so simple a remedy, wanting linament or blister salve.'

In 1852, however, he recorded that he had excluded several natives from evening service 'for having taken their sick to a native Doctor who professed to be able to see their spirits and to learn from them the cause of their illness' and in 1860 he referred to a Maori doctor's 'filthy physic', which a Maori woman took and died.

The Rev. Thomas Chapman,[136] a missionary from 1830 to 1876, threw some light on the changes that had occurred at Rotorua. In 1857 he wrote: 'Several applications for medicine lately. Our troubles on this head have much decreased. I have passed thro' seasons when the demands were incessant — now, the natives make their own medicines — trying most extraordinary experiments. Some islanders from Tahiti first introduced the practice — many lives have been lost by using herbs which were poisonous.'

The diary of Charles Baker,[31] a member of the C.M.S. mission in New Zealand from 1827 to 1865, confirmed the changes recorded by Chapman. Baker wrote on 7 June 1854 that he went over to see the mourners and enquire into the immediate cause of George Waiohenga's death. I had been informed (and it is now confirmed) that a herb called raorika, in vinegar, had been given to him; that the former had been boiled and given to him for a drink and that the vinegar had been taken afterwards. The nature of this herb is much the same as Cantherides, hence the Natives use it in the absence of or as a substitute of blute [possibly a misprint] plaster as an application to the skin. The stimulant and corrosive properties of the raorika must have been increased from the circumstance of taking vinegar with it. The natives have been very officious in making infusions from different kinds of bark and administering to the sick. I have protested against this most strongly and have posted up notice on the Church door condemning the practice.

William Puckey, a missionary at Kaitaia from 1833 until 1878, recorded[415] similar conduct there in 1858: 'Went up the valley to visit the sick . . . found . . . that they had cast away the medicine we had sent them and were using a Maori nostrum instead . . . This I say nothing about but when they boil worms and other vile creatures and make the sick person drink the water, instead of the medicine we give them, I cannot help laughing at their incredulity . . .' Again in 1861 he commented, 'I am sorry to say that the greater part of the Maoris throughout the land seem to be infatuated. They seem to place more confidence in the Native Doctor than in their European medical attendant. They receive a mixture of certain barks and leaves and do not seem to notice the number who die under such treatment.'

Buck (Te Rangi Hiroa)[100] explained the persistence of the Maori medicine-man in a sympathetic passage:

> In individual ailments, if the patient did not derive immediate relief from the medicine prescribed by a doctor, the patient and the family concluded that the failure to respond

was due to the sickness being a Maori disease (mate Maori) and beyond the white doctor's skill. The medicine was therefore abandoned and the services of a quack tohunga were enlisted. Many quacks sprang up throughout the country, and some of them acquired a fairly large following. They were readily accessible, could speak the language, and they pandered to the superstitious fears which were awakened in times of stress . . .

Only in a few cases does the Maori usage of herbs appear to have been successful and in many of these cases evidence comes from the European settlers rather than from the Maori people. These settlers, often far from medical aid, found a number of native plants helpful in simpler complaints such as toothache, dysentery, constipation, and in wound therapy.

Mother Mary Joseph Aubert (1835-1926), a Frenchwoman who came to New Zealand early in life at the invitation of Pompallier, was remarkable in that she used native herbs extensively. She studied botany at a university in France, which did not at the time permit women students, by hiding away in the gallery. At one stage she was stationed at Meeanee in Hawke's Bay, where she became acquainted with a Dr Spencer, a well-known practitioner and at one time Mayor of Napier. There is on record[26] a letter from Mother Mary in which she recounts how she cured a Maori woman, very ill with what Spencer diagnosed as leprosy, the treatment being sodium arsenate in increasing daily doses and sponging with 'a warm, concentrated infusion or decoction of blue gum leaves or ngaio leaves' four times a day. Flax was used as a purgative where necessary. M. Aubert's letter says that Dr Spencer submitted a full account to the *Lancet*, a leading British medical journal, but it does not appear to have been published.

Combining her botanical and herbal knowledge the Reverend Mother compounded a number of remedies which were all given Maori (sic transliterated French) names such as parano, natanata, marupa, karana, etc. They were widely advertised in the 1880s and 1890s, together with unsolicited testimonials, usual at the time, from members of the Roman Catholic hierarchy, the Governor (Lord Onslow), and other dignitaries. At one stage the preparation of these nostrums was handed over to Kempthorne, Prosser & Co., the well-known manufacturing chemists of Dunedin, but there were complaints about the preparations being unsatisfactory, so Mother Mary went back to making them herself.

Later, in Wellington, she did splendid charitable work in providing homes for unmarried mothers and other needy people. She built the Home of Compassion, which is her lasting monument at Island Bay. For this work she had to enlist the support of some local doctors, and as the price of their co-operation, she had to give up her herbal remedies, and the formulas were destroyed. Her biography has been compiled by Rafter.[418]

Literature on New Zealand Medicinal Plants

Captain Cook visited New Zealand on five occasions during his three voyages of discovery to the Southern Hemisphere and his observations, made between October 1769 and February 1774, form the basis of much of our knowledge of the early Maori.[135] In a previous section, Cook's observations on a Maori 'vapour bath' have been quoted. In later sections his notes on the use of New Zealand plants as greens, and for brewing beer to offset the ravages of scurvy, are quoted extensively.

The writings of early European medicinal people in New Zealand are not very helpful to those studying medicinal plants. A doctor named Monkhouse accompanied Cook on his initial voyage in 1769,[232] and Cook made generous acknowledgement of his help in the search for antiscorbutics. The only indication of Monkhouse's contact with the Maori was a record of his shooting one, and conducting a post-mortem to trace the path of the fatal ball.

Another surgeon, John Savage, came from Australia to spend eight weeks in New Zealand in 1805, and published his impressions in 1807.[442] His view was that 'medical practice has hither to [sic] been unknown amongst them [the

Durvillaea antarctica
Photo: M. Hawkes.

Porphyra columbina
Photo: W. Nelson.

Lembophyllum clandestinum (x 0.5). Photo: J. E. Braggins.

Pseudocyphellaria coronata (x 0.3). Photo: J. Child.

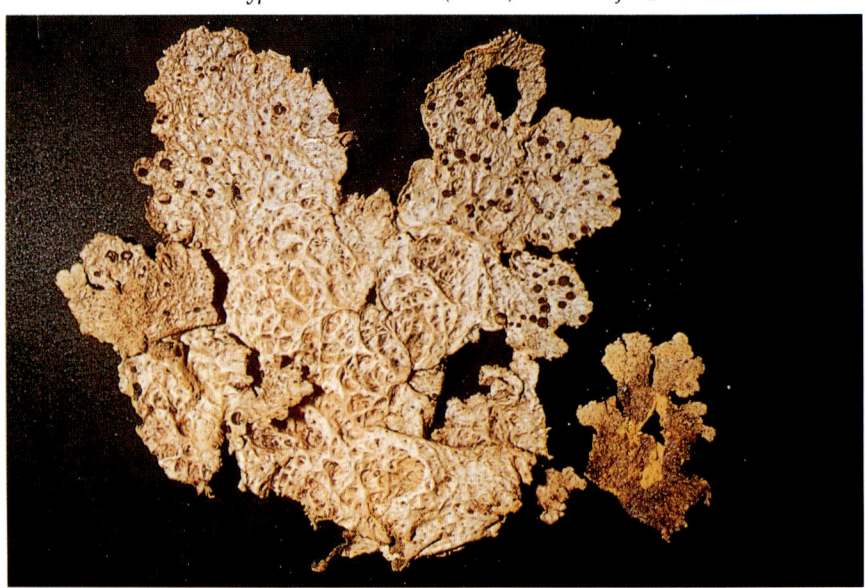

Maori]'. A. S. Thomson, Surgeon-Major to the 58th Regiment, confined his study of Maori health to a real concern about scrofula, which he attributed to inbreeding as the 'most intractable *cause of decay*' (his italics).[489]

In 1848, the Rev. Richard Taylor of Wanganui published a Maori vocabulary under the title *A leaf from the natural history of New Zealand*, containing valuable notes on the medicinal use of native plants. He revised this information in a second edition published in 1870.[485]

In the first paper delivered to the New Zealand Institute on a medical topic, Dr A. K. Newman[383] said in 1879, 'From a medical point of view, the Maoris are a singularly uninteresting race.' The only plant he mentioned was koromiko for unspecified purposes; there was a reference to a 'poultice of leaves' used in conjunction with pigeon oil and bathing in thermal springs for rheumatism. Newman said that the Maori attributed disease to the activities of evil spirits and lizards inside the body.

Dr P. J. O'N. O'Carroll, who was attached as a physician and surgeon to many expeditions against the Maori insurgents during the 1860s, published an article on Maori medicine in the *Taranaki Almanac* for 1884.[390] Some of the recipes are too elaborate to reproduce in this book and it is possible that O'Carroll was exercising his abounding Irish humour in suggesting fantastic brews to the European settlers of Taranaki.

J. H. Kerry-Nicholls, who explored the King Country in the 1880s, compiled native pharmacopoeias[293][294] which confirm and supplement the observations of other writers. Kerry-Nicholls[294] considered the Maori a singularly healthy race before the advent of the Europeans, with sickness confined to rheumatism, paipai, a skin disease, and hakihaki, the itch. However, R. Nicholl of the Anthropology Department, University of Auckland, has advised one of us that the Maori expectation of life was in the late twenties, which could have been largely due to cancer caused by carcinogens in bracken, which was an important article of diet.

A useful Maori pharmacopoeia appeared in *Brett's Colonists' Guide* of 1883.[331] In 1887 J. Baber, an Auckland civil engineer and surveyor, listed ten New Zealand plants which were used for medicine by Maori and Europeans.[27] In 1889 Dr James F. Neil of Dunedin listed 18 native plants in the *New Zealand Family Herb Doctor*, the first herbal written and produced in this country.[380] Dr Thomas W. Bell published his MD thesis on medicine in New Zealand in 1890.[37] He listed the plants used in native medicine with his own observations on their effectiveness. He was assisted by T. F. Cheeseman, curator of the Auckland Museum, in identifying the plants used. We have already referred to the paper of Elsdon Best, and Dr W. H. Goldie of Auckland, published in 1905, which contained a full account of Maori medical lore, and listed some 56 plants with medicinal uses. Their account,[233] long out of print, has been the most complete and authoritative account of native practices.

Robert Fulton's book[216] on medical practice in Otago and Southland in the early days, published in 1922, had several references to the medicinal use of plants which are dealt with in the appropriate places. Fulton quoted the first resident doctor in Otago, Joseph Crocome, about whom more is said in the section 'Early Maori Medicinal Plants'. Fulton also wrote about Dr Walter Monckton, the first doctor in Southland in 1857, who was very impressed with the healing properties of flax — so much so that he published notes about it in overseas journals.[362] This is discussed more fully in the section on that plant.

With the passing of many of the tribal elders and the tribal priest, doctor or tohunga, the lore of herbs is preserved by the older native women. Lucy Cranwell collected some notes on the subject which supplement an article in *The Botany of Auckland*.[506]

In 1954 Dr G. B. Palmer[394] described some

of the beliefs of the contemporary Maori and commented, 'native medical practices are often applied with a devotion and attention to detail worthy of sounder discipline. Some families carefully back themselves both ways, supplementing the European methods (or what they believe to be European methods) with a strong admixture of the older ways . . .'

In 1945 Olga Adams wrote a popular account of Maori medicinal plants[2] which is now out of print. Miss Adams was of Maori descent and noted many details of preparation which are not recorded elsewhere.

The drug supplies of New Zealand and other countries were threatened in 1940-41 by the war and Ruth Mason of the Botany Division of the DSIR, Wellington, searched the literature and obtained reports from Maori schoolteachers, pharmacists, and others regarding the use of native plants in medicine. We are indebted to Miss Mason and the Department for permission to use this information. The late Mr Norman Potts, who was an authority on the botany of the East Coast, collected much of the information from the Maori people for Miss Mason. Several of the informants stressed the need to prepare medicine at a fire in utensils that had not been used for cooking food. This relates to the tapu-destroying qualities of food and is probably a survival of an old-time custom.

Dr. D. MacMillan[346] had a short section on the Maori treatment of injuries and disease, and quotes Colenso on vapour baths, which were used for rheumatism and some obstinate cutaneous diseases.

Of recent years the most ambitious effort to review the interaction of Maori and Pakeha disease and medicine is that of Dr. L. Gluckman, which is referred to in several places in this book.[232] Gluckman made a study of the early medical history of New Zealand, which may be consulted for background information in this area. It deals with pre-European medical problems of the Maori. Apart from leprosy and tapeworms, most sickness arose from contact with poisonous plants such as tutu and karaka. He confirms Cook's observation on vapour baths with added herbs, but maintains that their value lay solely in the heat of the bath. Seriously ill persons, especially the elderly, were usually left to die.

Maryanne Baker, an Auckland pharmacist, contributed an interesting article[32] in 1985 on her personal experiences with Maori medicinal plants. However, since Best and Goldie's paper in 1905,[233] we believe that our book is the only work that fills the need for a compilation of the known medical uses of New Zealand plants. There have been two works which drew largely on the first edition of this book;[95] in both books there is some plagiarism compounded by incorrect quotations. In one case definite curative properties were attributed where we had been careful to emphasise that our statement did not imply any certain cures, for instance for baldness. It is often said that there is no collective work on local medicinal plants, despite the fact that the first edition of this book has been available for 25 years. We hope that this new edition will make our compilation better known.

Seaweeds
Algae

PHAEOPHYTA
Brown algae

Durvillaea antarctica (Cham.) Har.
Bull kelp
Rimurapa, rimuroa

BOTANICAL NOTES: William Colenso, a pioneer missionary and explorer, supplied Sir Joseph Hooker of Kew with the native names of many New Zealand plants, including the Maori word 'rimurapa' for the seaweed *Durvillaea utilis*. Hooker published this information in the *Handbook of the New Zealand Flora* (1864-7).[268] Lucy Cranwell, in *The Botany of Auckland*,[161] considered that 'rimurapa' was the Maori name for the bull kelp, *Durvillaea antarctica*, and Dr H. H. Allan and Lucy Moore, who assisted with the revision of the sixth edition of Williams's Maori dictionary (1957),[516] apparently accepted this identification. The Rev. Richard Taylor, in the second edition of a most interesting Maori vocabulary entitled *A leaf from the natural history of New Zealand* (1870),[485] listed 'rimuroa' as a large tubular variety of seaweed which was roasted and eaten. Dr W. H. Goldie, who wrote an important paper on Maori medical lore in 1905,[233] identified 'rimuroa' as an unknown species of *Laminaria*, but according to Chapman and Chapman[137] this species does not exist in New Zealand, and the seaweed referred to by Goldie 'may have been another *Durvillaea* species or *Ecklonia radiata*'. The species is found on the roughest coasts of New Zealand.

MEDICAL USE: The tender ends of rimuroa were roasted and eaten for itch (scabies) and intestinal worms,[233][331] and it was also roasted and eaten as an internal remedy for 'hore', a contagious eczema or dermatitis. The whiplike ends of rimurapa (bull kelp) were eaten for the itch and for expelling worms.[160]

RELATED PHARMACOLOGY: Seaweed remedies have long been used for goitre, scrofula, lymphatic and glandular disorders and stomach troubles. Both Chapman and Chapman[137] and Newton[384] have interesting summaries of these uses. For example, Chapman and Chapman recorded: 'that seaweed meal prepared from *Macrocystis*, together with milk from a seaweed-eating cow, produced a very striking speed-up in the development of a four-year-old child who, at the beginning of the treatment, was not able to sit up and talk.'

The same authors also mention that in South America stems of *Durvillaea* are known as 'goitre sticks'.

CHEMISTRY: Sannie[440] analysed this plant and found it to be rich in iodine and alginic acid. Moss and Naylor[372] have also published analyses of the two New Zealand species of *Durvillaea*.

ILLUSTRATION: See page 51

RHODOPHYTA
Red algae

Porphyra columbina Mont.
Karengo

BOTANICAL NOTES: Hooker[268] and Goldie[233] listed karengo as *Laminaria* sp. but in the latest edition of Williams's Maori dictionary[517] the name is applied to a red seaweed, *Porphyra columbina*.

MEDICAL USE: This seaweed was fermented with the juice of *Coriaria* (tutu) and used as an aperient.[233]

During the 1939-45 war quantities of the plant were gathered and sent to the Maori Battalion in the Middle East, presumably for its laxative effect. Chapman and Chapman[137] recorded that it was more thirst-quenching on desert marches than chewing gum. Quantities of koromiko (*Hebe salicifolia*) were also sent as a remedy for diarrhoea or possibly dysentery (see p. 222).

RELATED PHARMACOLOGY: *Porphyra umbilicalis* has been used in India[141] as a demulcent, alterative, and for scrofula. *Porphyra leucosticta* has been used medicinally in Hawaii.[532] *Porphyra haitanensis* is used in China for the treatment of goitre and scrofula, coughs, bronchitis, tonsilitis, asthma with excessive phlegm, urinary diseases and dropsy, and as a preventative medicine for hypertension.[494]

CHEMISTRY: *Porphyra columbina* contains polysaccharides.[68] *Porphyra tenera* contains vitamin B_{12}.[252]

ILLUSTRATION: See page 51

Fungi

Calvatia caelata (Bull.) Morg.
Puffball
Pukurau

BOTANICAL NOTES: In Hooker's *Handbook of the New Zealand Flora*,[268] the name 'pukurau' or 'pukuvau' is applied to *Lycoperdon fontanesei* Dur. & Lev., which is now known as *Calvatia caelata*. In Williams' Maori dictionary, seventh edition,[517] the name 'pukurau' is identified as *Clathrus cibarium* (Tul.) Fisch., a net-like fungus, but this is better known as 'tutae kehua' or 'tutae whetu' (faeces of ghosts or stars). *Calvatia caelata* is found in Europe, North America, India, and North Africa as well as New Zealand.

MEDICAL USE: The fine reddish dust of the large decaying fungus was applied outwardly to severe burns.[150] Several puffballs are said to possess anaesthetic properties when burnt. They have also been used as a styptic to stop bleeding of wounds.[170]

RELATED PHARMACOLOGY: *Calvatia gigantea* (giant puffball), which acts as a haemostatic, contains calvacin, a protein with activity against cancer.[167] [524] *Lycoperdon marginatum* and *L. mixtecorum* are reputed to have been used by the Mixtecs of Oaxaca, Mexico, to cause auditory hallucinations.[330] *Lycoperdon gemmatum* inactivates tobacco mosaic virus.[306]

CHEMISTRY: Many higher fungi contain vitamin C, which would aid healing.[296]

Calvatia caelata (x 0.5).

Mosses
Musci

Lembophyllum clandestinum
(H.f. et W.) Lindb.
Angiangi, kohukohu

BOTANICAL NOTES: Goldie[233] listed 'angiangi' as *Hypnum clandestinum*, a 'fern', but *H. clandestinum* is a moss, now known as *Lembophyllum clandestinum*. In Williams' Maori dictionary[517] the name 'angiangi' is identified as *Usnea barbata*, a lichen, and it is probable that the word was applied generally to soft absorbent mosses and lichens. Williams' dictionary identifies 'kohukohu' as '*Hypnum clandestinum* and other mosses, used as wrappers or absorbents.' The name is also applied to a tree, *Pittosporum tenuifolium*, the herbs *Stellaria media* and *Scleranthus biflorus*, and to lichens. Recent authors have used the name *L. divulsum* (H.f. et W.) Lindb. for this plant.

MEDICAL USE: This moss was steeped in water and applied to the affected parts in venereal disease.[54] It was also used as a diaper in menstruation[233] and the leaves, after being bruised on the hand, were lightly bandaged to a wound to check bleeding.[390] Macdonald [341] has described the use of mosses and lichens by Maori mothers in olden times for the care and nursing of babies.

'Keketuwai' was used by the Maori priest to

exorcise demons.[54] In Williams' Maori dictionary it is identified as a 'moss-like plant growing in fresh water.'

RELATED PHARMACOLOGY: *Usnea articulata* has been used in Samoa for wounds and shin bruises.[532] Old man's beard (*U. barbata*) is reputed to increase resistance to infection and to stimulate the appetite.[490]

ILLUSTRATION: **See page 52**

Lichens
Lichenes

Kohukohu

BOTANICAL NOTES: Kerry-Nicholls[294] listed 'kohukohu' as a lichen which when dried and reduced to powder was applied to cutaneous eruptions. Possibly this is an error, as Williams[517] gives 'kohukohu' as a name for mosses (see p. 62).

CHEMISTRY: *Sticta coronata*, a common native lichen, contains polyporic acid, which has some effect on leukaemia in mice.[104] Recent authors use the generic name *Pseudocyphellaria* for *Sticta*. There are numerous references in the literature to the antibiotic activity of lichens (see e.g. ref.106). Usnic acid found in lichens is strongly antibacterial[452] and is a constituent of the Chinese drug 'shi-koa' and the Japanese 'seki-ka'. The medicinal use of lichens has been reviewed by Perez-Llano.[402]

ILLUSTRATION: See page 52

Ferns
Filices

Numerous changes in the scientific names of New Zealand ferns, and the widely different practices of our leading authorities, have resulted in some confusion. We have used the list of scientific names compiled by Brownsey, Given, and Lovis.[97] Alternative names used by Allan[9] are given in the botanical notes on each species.

Asplenium bulbiferum Forst.f.
Hen and chickens fern
Mauku, mouku

BOTANICAL NOTES: 'Mauku' has been identified as *Asplenium bulbiferum*, *Cordyline pumilio*, and *Hymenophyllum* spp. by Williams[517] and as *Asplenium bulbiferum* by Best.[56] 'Mouku' has been identified as *Asplenium bulbiferum* by Williams[517] and as *Marattia salicina* by Tregear.[493] *Asplenium bulbiferum* is a common fern throughout New Zealand forests.

MEDICAL USE: An infusion of the root was used as a wash for cutaneous complaints; the juice was also drunk and the root eaten.[485] However, it is doubtful whether these uses all refer to *A. bulbiferum* as the juice would be negligible. Kerry-Nicholls, in a pharmacopoeia published in 1884,[293] listed 'mouku' with the note, 'a wash

Asplenium bulbiferum (x 0.2). Photo: J. E. Braggins.

obtained from the root is used for cutaneous complaints'. In a similar list published in 1886,[294] he noted that the wash was used for sore eyes. It is reported that new-born babies were washed with water and then wrapped in mouku, raurekau, and patete (*Schefflera digitata*).[232]

RELATED PHARMACOLOGY: A number of species of *Asplenium* are mentioned by Chopra[141] as having been used in India for various complaints, but not for cutaneous eruptions. In Fiji an infusion of *A. falcatum* fronds has been drunk for sore throat while a frond infusion of *A. laserpitiifolium* has been used for lung troubles and as a laxative. The latter species has also been used in Samoa as part of a mixture with coconut milk for headache.[532] In Tahiti *A. nidus* has been used as a vulnerary, anticatarrhal agent, and vermifuge[399] while in New Caledonia the leaves have been used as a cataplasm for rheumatism.[420]

CHEMISTRY: Briggs and Taylor[87] examined *A. bulbiferum, A. lucidum, A. flaccidum, A. falcatum,* and *A. lamprophyllum* for methyl salicylate (oil of wintergreen) and found it only in the last-named species. Methyl salicylate and its relatives produce marked analgesic effects and have antiseptic properties.[521] The amino-acids of the New Zealand *Asplenium* spp. have been investigated by Peterson[405] (see also ref. 500). The aerial parts contain diglycosides of the flavonol kaempferol.[277]

Asplenium obtusatum Forst.f.
Paretao, paretau

BOTANICAL NOTES: Taylor[485] identified 'paretau' as *'Asplenium,* large leafed fern' and later as *'Asplenium obliquum',* which is regarded now as a form of *A. obtusatum*. Hooker[268] identified 'paretao' as *A. obtusatum* on the authority of Colenso, and Cheeseman[139] listed it as a name for *A. obtusatum* and *A. lucidum* on the same authority. Both ferns occur throughout New Zealand.

MEDICAL USE: The root was used for cutaneous eruptions [294] [485] and the fern was also used in vapour baths.[233]

Asplenium obtusatum (x 0.2). Photo: J. E. Braggins.

Azolla filiculoides Lam.
Water fern
Karerarera

BOTANICAL NOTES: 'Karerarera' has been identified as *'Azolla rubra'* by Williams[517] but L. Smith[467] comments that the plants used appear to be filamentous green algae. *Azolla* is a common water plant in New Zealand; Allan[9] mentions that *Azolla* almost always harbours the blue-green alga, *Anabaena* (with which it forms a nitrogen-fixing symbiosis).

MEDICAL USE: Karerarera was rubbed on scalds of infants.[467]

Azolla filiculoides (x 2.0). Photo: J. E. Braggins.

Blechnum fluviatile (R. Br.) Salom.
Kiwikiwi

BOTANICAL NOTES: Found throughout New Zealand in damp hilly forest.

MEDICAL USE: It was chewed for sore mouth or tongue.[54]

RELATED PHARMACOLOGY: In Fiji *Blechnum procerum* has been used as a cure for strains, and for fever after childbirth.[400] In Malaysia *B. orientale* has been used as a poultice for boils[141] while in Chile the rhizome of *B. hastatum* was considered to be an emetic and abortifacient by the Araucanos Indians.[243]

CHEMISTRY: The rhizomes of *Blechnum filiforme* contain the triterpene cyclolaudenol and β-sitosterol.[124] The latter is the major component of an American proprietary drug used to lower blood cholesterol levels.[195] All New Zealand ferns which have been examined have been shown to contain the sugars xylose, arabinose, glucose, galactose, mannose, and occasionally rhamnose in the hydrolysates of extracts.[30] Twenty-four species of 64 New Zealand ferns

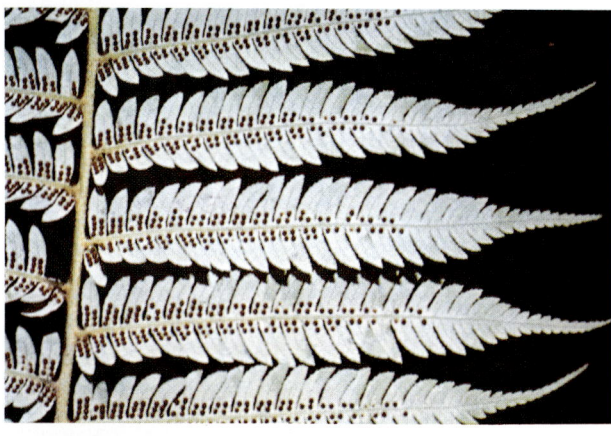

Top: *Blechnum fluviatile* (x 0.3).
Photo: J. E. Braggins.

Above: *Cyathea dealbata* (x 0.5).
Photo: J. E. Braggins.

Left: *Cyathea medullaris* (x 2.0).
Photo: J. E. Braggins.

Marattia salicina (x 4.0).
Photo: J. E. Braggins.

Pneumatopteris pennigera
(x 1.0). Photo: J. E.
Braggins.

which were examined have been shown to exhibit insect moulting hormone activity,[338] and the ecdysones responsible for this activity have been isolated from four New Zealand *Blechnum* species.[432]

ILLUSTRATION: See page 69

Cardiomanes reniforme
(Forst.f.) C. Presl
Kidney fern
Kopakopa

BOTANICAL NOTES: Unusual in the shape of the leaf. Usually to be found in wet forest, but common on the arid slopes of Rangitoto Island, Auckland. Allan[9] gives its name as *Trichomanes reniforme* Forst.f.

MEDICAL USE: The leaves were used to heal ulcers.[294] It is possible that Kerry-Nicholls misidentified the plant concerned since 'kopakopa' is a Maori name for *Plantago* spp., which had similar uses.

Cardiomanes reniforme (x 0.3). Photo: L. C. W. Jensen.

Cyathea dealbata (Forst.f.) Swartz
Silver tree-fern
Ponga

BOTANICAL NOTES: A common tree-fern, recognised easily by the white under-surface of the fronds. Found throughout New Zealand.

MEDICAL USE: The pith was used as a poultice for cutaneous eruptions.[233] A packet of 'Mrs Subritzky's Ponga powder for fever and inflammation' is kept at Wagener Museum at Houhora Heads, Northland.

RELATED PHARMACOLOGY: The leaves of *Cyathea moluccana* of Malaysia have been used to poultice sores.[102] *Cyathea usambarensis* has been used in Africa by the Chagga for tapeworm[509] while the fronds of *C. mexicana* have been used in tropical parts of Mexico to arrest haemorrhage.[330]

ILLUSTRATION: See page 69

Cyathea medullaris (Forst.f.) Swartz
Black tree-fern
Mamaku

BOTANICAL NOTES: This tall, handsome tree-fern is common throughout New Zealand and is frequently planted in collections overseas.

MEDICAL USE: The young fronds were used for poulticing inflamed mammae[45] and were also scraped and used for drawing boils.[414] The fronds were also boiled and the liquid was drunk to assist discharge of the afterbirth.[310] The hairy outer skin was peeled off the inner curled frond, or korau, and the slimy tissue was either rubbed on wounds, or was scraped and applied as a poultice either raw or boiled. It was used by bushmen and travellers and applied to sores or wounds, three applications a day being advised. It has been used with effect for saddle sore on horses, poisoned hands, swollen feet, and sore eyes.[2] The bruised pith was also used as a poultice for swollen feet and sore eyes[233,294,484] while the edible pith, applied raw, was a first-rate dressing for sores and chafings.[159] The gum was a vermifuge[423] and was also useful in attacks of diarrhoea.[27]

ILLUSTRATION: See page 69

Marattia salicina Smith
King fern, horseshoe fern
Para

BOTANICAL NOTES: Para is found in deep gullies of the Maungataniwha Ranges and southwards to Waitotara on the West Coast, and inland from

Te Puke in the Bay of Plenty. Formerly it was more plentiful and was planted by the Maori people. Cheeseman's name for it was *M. fraxinea* Smith.[139]

MEDICAL USE: The 'horseshoes' cut from the rhizome were baked or boiled and were a good remedy for diarrhoea.[389]

RELATED PHARMACOLOGY: *Marattia fraxinea* has been used as a remedy for ankylostomiasis in Usambara, Tanzania[509] and medicinally in Tahiti.[532] *Marattia attenuata* has been used in New Caledonia to induce childbirth.[420] The rhizomes of *M. salicina* have been used as a food in Tahiti.[399]

ILLUSTRATION: See page 70

Pneumatopteris pennigera
(Forst.f.) Holttum
Gully fern
Piupiu

BOTANICAL NOTES: This common fern is found in woods throughout New Zealand. It has been placed in *Polypodium, Goniopteris, Aspidium, Nephrodium, Dryopteris, Phegopteris, Polystichum, Lastrea, Cyclosorus,* and *Thelypteris*. Bell[45] wrote of the 'peu *(Polypodium pennigerum)*', but the Maori name was given as 'piupiu' by Colenso.[150] Williams[517] identified 'piupiu' as *Blechnum capense* (now *B. procerum*) and *B. discolor* as well as *Dryopteris pennigera*, while Field[206] identified it as *Lomaria discolor* (now *Blechnum discolor*).

MEDICAL USE: At Whangarei the scraped roots were used as poultices for boils. They were said to be very 'drawing'.[45]

RELATED PHARMACOLOGY: *Aspidium (Dryopteris) filix-mas* has been proposed for local applications in acne and eczema.[178] The rhizomes and stipes of *D. filix-mas* and *D. marginalis* contain an oleoresin that paralyses the voluntary muscles of the intestine as well as the analogous contractile tissue of the tapeworm.[330] *Dryopteris cyatheoides* has been used in Hawaii to ease childbirth, especially in a first pregnancy.[532]

The rhizomes of *Polypodium vulgare* have been used for the treatment of bronchial catarrh and mild constipation.[212] They have been reported to afford a low yield of a steroidal saponin, osladin, which is 300 times sweeter than sugar.[330] *Polypodium leucotomos* contains a saponin which is reported to exhibit anti-cancer activity.[330] In Tahiti *Polypodium societense* (*P. scandens*) has been used as an emollient and *P. nigrescens* as a liniment for contusions and sprains.[399] *Polypodium alternifolium* is a very popular remedy used for a great number of complaints in Tahiti. Petard[404] gives many recipes.

ILLUSTRATION: See page 70

Pteridium esculentum
(Forst.f.) Cockayne
Bracken
Rahurahu, rarahu, rarauhe, marohi, takaka

BOTANICAL NOTES: This cosmopolitan fern is found throughout New Zealand. It has been placed in *Pteris* and also treated as var. *esculentum* of *Pteridium aquilinum* (L.) Kuhn. The root was a principal food of the Maori. Johnson[285] described its use in the following note:

> The Waipa country is noted for its fine fern root, which is generally found in rich alluvial soil, on the banks of rivers, or in deep valleys: some of the choicest spots are tapued to ensure a supply, and fierce quarrels have happened between different tribes, from these spots having been set on fire. Much pain is taken in selecting it, the roots are dug up in August and September, and only those are taken which are eighteen inches below the ground. The small fibres are stript off and they are roasted

at a fire, and become very palatable, not unlike, in taste, to the Cassava bread used by the negroes in the West Indies.

MEDICAL USE: The root was used as food for invalids and was eaten before a sea voyage to prevent sea sickness.[233] Ashes and charcoal dust of burnt fronds were applied to severe burns.[150] The frond was used by the Maori priest to expel a demon from a sick person[54] and the tender shoot was eaten to cure dysentery.[294] Fern root was also masticated for dysentery.[412] It has been reported that a decoction of fern root prepared by the Maori was effective in the influenza epidemic of 1918-19.[338]

Poisoning of cattle by bracken is frequent in New Zealand, serious losses occurring in the King Country even now.[156] Evans[197] reported that 'young actively growing bracken contains a toxin(s) which reproduces many of the effects of radiation' and that carcinogenicity can be induced in laboratory animals.[198] Human stomach cancer has a high incidence in Japan, where the young fronds of bracken are eaten in a variety of ways.[156] The method of preparation reduces, but does not eliminate, the carcinogenic activity.[263] Fresh young shoots of bracken were eaten by the Maori[150] but there is no record of stomach cancer in pre-European times although it has been suggested that the low expectation of life of the Maori could have been due to the consumption of bracken.[387] Hodge[265] recommends that young fronds of bracken should not be eaten at all.

RELATED PHARMACOLOGY: *Pteridium esculentum* has been used by the Aborigines in Australia for insect bites.[322] *Pteridium aquilinum* has been used in India for disorders arising from obstruction of the viscera or spleen.[141] The fleshy parts of the fronds have also been used in Hawaii for bronchitis, diarrhoea, and as a laxative.[532] In Japan *P. aquilinum* var. *latiusculum* Underwood causes 'cattle bracken poisoning', an acute toxicity characterised by haemorrhage, ano-

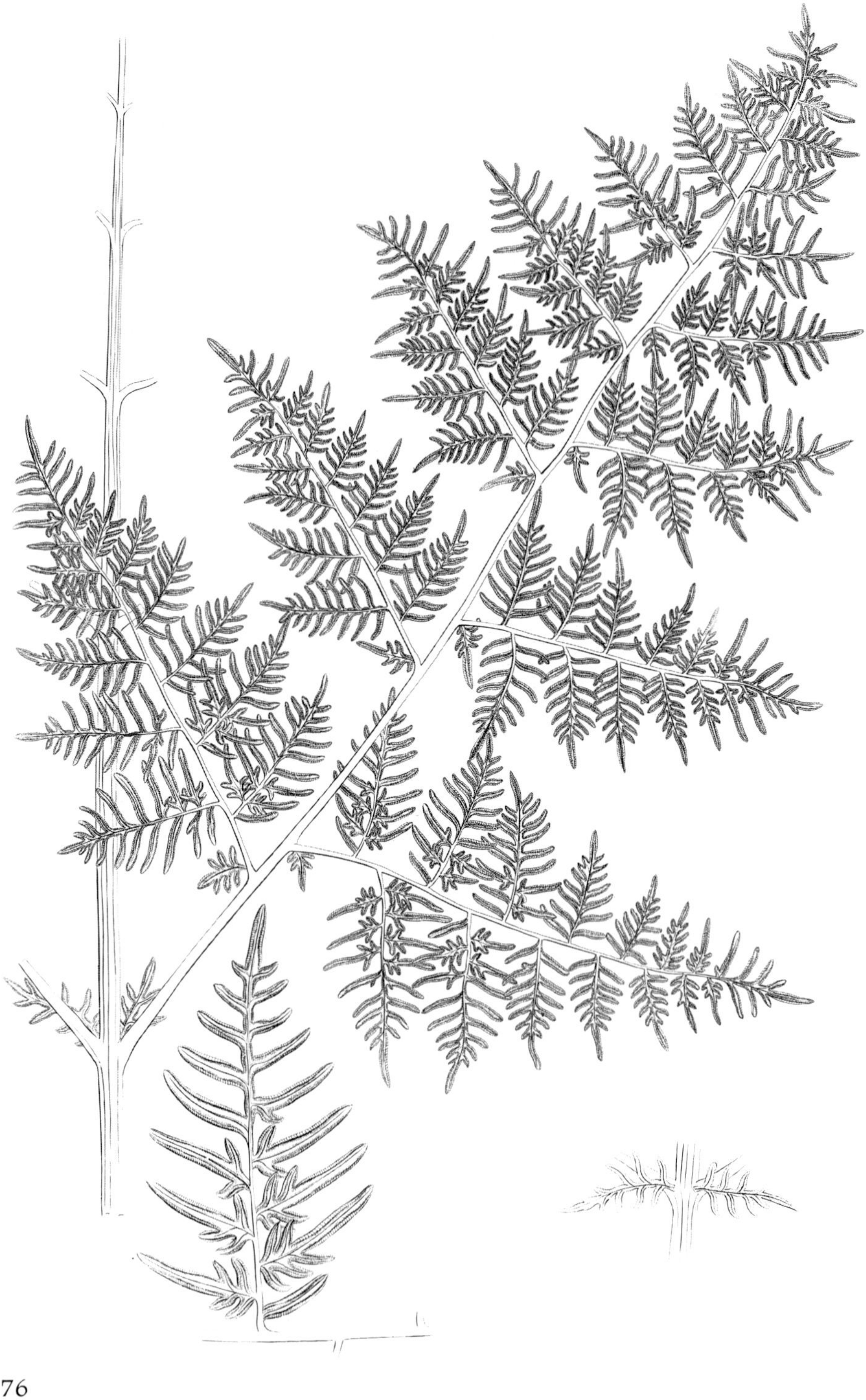

rexia, and destruction of the bone marrow, leading to leukaemia and thrombocytopenia.[214]

Pteris irregularis has been used medicinally in Hawaii and *P. tripartita* has been used in Fiji for boils.[532] In Pahang, the juice of young leaves of *P. ensiformis* has been used as a preparation for cleaning unhealthy tongues of children and in Perak the juice of the root has been applied to glandular swellings of the neck.[102] The active principle of *P. ensiformis* has been found in clinical trials to be effective in curing bacillary dysentery where standard treatments failed.[403] In Fiji *Pteris crenata* leaves and young shoots were chewed and held in the mouth for toothache.[400] Further information is given in refs. 219 and 510.

CHEMISTRY: Bennett[49] has shown that the native bracken *Pteridium esculentum* contains prunasin (β-D-glucopyranosyl-D-mandelonitrile), a cyanogenic glycoside which has also been obtained from the European plant.[309] However, prunasin does not appear to be the toxic principle of bracken. Evans and Osman[199] isolated shikimic acid from bracken and attributed to it carcinogenic and mutagenic properties. They also indicated that bracken contains another carcinogen stronger than shikimic acid which is capable of inducing the acute bracken poisoning syndrome. Evans has shown that the cancer-producing factor can be carried into the milk of grazing animals and thus find its way into human food.[166]

Bracken also contains the enzyme thiaminase which destroys thiamine. This results in a vitamin B deficiency which causes serious poisoning, particularly in horses and cattle.[330] Berüter[53] and Somogyi[469] have reported the isolation of caffeic acid, which has anti-thiamine activity. The rhizomes of *P. aquilinum* var. *latiusculum* contain a number of pterosins (illudoid sesquiterpenes) and their glucosides. However, these do not seem to be carcinogenic to rats.[215] [317] The plant contains antithiamine factors dactylifric acid (5-0-caffeoylshikimic acid), which causes depression of leucocytes and thrombocytes in calves, and astralagin.[214]

Opposite: *Pteridium esculentum* (x 0.5; detail x 1). Engraving: S. Parkinson.

Conifers
Coniferae

Agathis australis Hort. ex Lindl.
Kauri

BOTANICAL NOTES: The kauri pine forests of the northern half of the North Island were milled last century and only small areas remain. There is an extensive literature on the forests, kauri timber, and kauri gum.

MEDICAL USE: The gum was scraped to a powder, mixed with olive oil and applied to burns.[2] The fresh gum-resin from the kauri was commonly chewed as a masticatory[150][485] and was formerly an ingredient of Dental Compo, used for taking impressions for dentures.[194]

RELATED PHARMACOLOGY: *Agathis lanceolata, A. ovata,* and *A. moorei* of New Caledonia yield a resin (dammar) and an antiseptic, vulnerary essence, utilised for the dressing of wounds and ulcers and the bandaging of fractures.[419] The Malays used the resin of *A. alba* in a liniment and sometimes applied small bits of resin to the feet to prevent attacks of leeches.[102] *Agathis* spp. are included in the *Philippine National Formulary*,[406] the resin as a remedy for arthritis, and the smoke from the burning resin for asthma.

CHEMISTRY: Kauri resin contains agathic acid with a carbon skeleton similar to that of vitamin

A.[69] The constituents of both the resin and the wood have been extensively examined (see ref. 118 for a summary).

ILLUSTRATION: See page 87

Dacrycarpus dacrydioides
(A. Rich.) de Laubenf.
White pine
Kahikatea

BOTANICAL NOTES: A timber tree, found in swamp forest throughout New Zealand. Colenso, Williams, and others list 'kahikatoa' as the Maori name of *Leptospermum scoparium*, and it is possible that some of the uses listed here refer to that plant. This species was formerly placed in *Podocarpus*.

MEDICAL USE: The leaves were used in vapour baths[233] and a decoction of the leaves was taken for urinary and other internal complaints.[233][294] It has been reported that the bark, if chewed, causes tingling of the lips followed by slight numbness and that it should possess therapeutic properties.[45] The bark was used in an elaborate recipe for bruises, and chips of the wood infused in boiling water were a good tonic medicine.[390]

RELATED PHARMACOLOGY: In Malaysia a decoction of the leaves of a species of *Podocarpus* has been used as an alterative and for rheumatism and painful joints.[102]

CHEMISTRY: *Dacrycarpus dacrydioides* contains podocarpic acid (see *Dacrydium*) and other diterpenoids (see ref. 118 for a summary).

ILLUSTRATION: See page 87

Dacrydium cupressinum Lamb.
Red pine
Rimu

BOTANICAL NOTES: This tree occurs throughout New Zealand forests and was largely used for building purposes.

MEDICAL USE: Spruce beer made from young branches by Captain Cook proved an excellent remedy for scurvy.[319] Writing of their stay in Pickersgill Harbour in May 1773, Cook[157] said:

> Our people, who were daily exposed to the rain, felt no ill effects from it; on the contrary, such as were sick and ailing when we came in, recovered daily, and the whole crew soon became strong and vigorous; which can only be attributed to the healthiness of the place, and the fresh provisions it afforded. The beer certainly contributed not a little. As I have already observed, we at first made it of a decoction of the spruce leaves; but finding that this alone made the beer too astringent, we afterwards mixed with it an equal quantity of the tea plant (a name it obtained in my former voyage from our using it as tea then, as we also did now) which partly destroyed the astringency of the other, and made the beer exceedingly palatable, and esteemed by everyone on board.

During a three-week stay at Dusky Bay (now Sound) in 1791, the explorer George Vancouver recuperated his crew with fish and spruce beer. 'The good effects ... were evident in the appearance of every individual on board.'[231]

The juice from a cut stem was rubbed by Europeans on bald heads. First there was a temporary smarting and then, it is said, it acted as a hair restorer.[45] The inner bark was bruised to a pulp and applied to burns.[233] A lotion for wounds was made by cutting rimu bark into pieces and scraping the bark of tawa *(Beilschmiedia),* adding some leaves of tutu *(Coriaria),* and boiling the whole with water.[54]

The very astringent gum obtained by making cuts in the bark was used to stop the flow of blood from wounds[27] [233] while a piece of red gum about the size of a walnut was dissolved in water and taken internally to allay bleeding of the stomach and lungs.[2] [390] An infusion was used to heal running ulcers[294] and the leaves were used on sores.[363]

RELATED PHARMACOLOGY: The essential oil of *D. franklinii* shows antibacterial activity.[25]

CHEMISTRY: The essential oil and heartwood are rich sources of diterpenoids (see ref. 118 for a summary). The heart-shakes are composed almost exclusively of podocarpic acid,[129] [184] an aromatic diterpenoid, the reduction product of which, viz. podocarpinol, possesses oestrogenic activity.[66] Podocarpic acid propionate is effective in promoting the flow of bile.[240] The bark of *D. cupressinum* is rich in tannins.[21] [120]

ILLUSTRATION: See page 87

Phyllocladus trichomanoides D. Don
Celery pine
Tanekaha

BOTANICAL NOTES: The bark of this forest tree, which is found in both the North and South Islands, was used by the Maori for tanning nets.

MEDICAL USE: Tannic acid of the bark was a valuable astringent in dysentery.[380] The leaves were used for scrofulous diseases.[294]

CHEMISTRY: The essential oil, leaf alkanes, and bark have all been examined (see ref. 118 for a summary). The heartwood contains (+)-inositol[3] which has been used medicinally for cirrhosis, hepatitis, fatty infiltration of the liver, and hypercholesterolaemia.[358] [521]

ILLUSTRATION: See page 88

Podocarpus totara G. Benn. ex D. Don
Totara

BOTANICAL NOTES: A lofty tree, present in forests throughout New Zealand. The principal stands of timber have been milled.

MEDICAL USE: Smoke from the burning wood was used to treat paipai (a skin complaint), venereal disease in women, and 'mate tokatoka', which Best believed to be piles.[54] The outer bark was used for splints in bone fracture.[177,233] The inner barks of totara and manuka (*Leptospermum scoparium*) were boiled and the extract was kept in a closed bottle for a week. The resulting sweetish liquid was used to reduce fever.[45]

CHEMISTRY: The bark and heartwood extractives have each been examined (see ref. 118 for a summary). They contain the aromatic diterpenoid totarol and its dimer podototarin.[128]

ILLUSTRATION: See page 88

Prumnopitys ferruginea
(D. Don) de Laubenf.
Miro, toromiro

BOTANICAL NOTES: This tall forest tree is found throughout New Zealand and was milled for building purposes. This species was formerly placed in *Podocarpus*.

MEDICAL USE: Oil expressed from drupes was given to patients recovering from fevers[2] and was applied to the skin as an insecticide.[331] The gum which exudes from bark was applied to wounds to stop the flow of blood,[161] and to ulcers. A liquor prepared from leaves and bark was taken internally for gonorrhoea[233] and an infusion of the bark was used for stomachache.[294,485] It has been used by bushmen as an antiseptic.[408]

CHEMISTRY: The bled resin[65] and the bark are a rich source of diterpenoids (see ref. 118 for a summary).

ILLUSTRATION: See page 105

Prumnopitys taxifolia
(D. Don) de Laubenf.
Black pine
Matai

BOTANICAL NOTES: This tree occurs throughout New Zealand in mixed podocarp forests. It yielded timber which was highly valued for flooring. This species was known as *Podocarpus spicatus*.

MEDICAL USE: Juice obtained by tapping the trunk was drunk to check advance of consumption.[2] The heart cracks of old matai trees frequently contain a considerable quantity of a liquid known as matai beer. The liquid can be tapped by means of an auger, and was said to be eagerly drunk by bushmen.[185] Both miro and matai have been used by bushmen as antiseptics.[408]

CHEMISTRY: Genistein, an oestrogenic isoflavone, podospicatin, an isoflavonol with possible oestrogenic properties, as well as the lignans matairesinol and conidendrin, and the flavonoids quercetin and kaempferol, have all been found in the wood.[78] [182] Matairesinol has been shown to have some beneficial effect in reducing cancer of mice.[377] Quercetin has been used to counter abnormal capillary fragility.[358]

ILLUSTRATION: See page 105

Flowering Plants
Angiospermae

We have listed the families of flowering plants in alphabetical order and have not distinguished the monocotyledons from the dicotyledons.

AGAVACEAE (Asphodelaceae)
Yucca family

The Agavaceae include the yuccas and their relatives, the century-plants *(Agave)*, the dragon tree *(Dracaena)*, the cabbage trees *(Cordyline)*, and New Zealand hemp *(Phormium)*. Formerly *Cordyline* and *Phormium* were placed in the lily family. Lately *Phormium* has been placed in the Phormiaceae, and *Cordyline* in the Asphodelaceae.

Cordyline australis (Forst.f.) Endl.
Cabbage tree
Ti kauka

BOTANICAL NOTES: The Maori name 'ti' refers to *Cordyline* generally. The epithets awe, kauka, kouka, pua, rakau, and whanake indicate *C. australis*, which is common throughout New Zealand and widely planted overseas. The inner blanched leaves and heart were eaten raw or cooked by the Maori[150][151] and by settlers and bushmen.[319][486] Beever[41] has written an interesting paper on the origin of the common name. It goes back to 1638 when a T. Verney refers to 'cabiges (sic) that grows (sic) on trees' in the West Indies.

Cordyline australis (x 0.1).

MEDICAL USE: An infusion of the leaves was used for dysentery and diarrhoea[233] [294] and for cuts.[363] The leaves were softened by rubbing, scraped, and the scrapings were applied as an ointment to cuts, cracks in the skin, and sores.[467] The young inner shoot and top of the stem were boiled and eaten by nursing mothers and were also given to children for colic.[318]

RELATED PHARMACOLOGY: *Cordyline* is related to *Dracaena* from which 'dragon's blood' is obtained. Malays treated dysentery with a decoction of *C. fruticosa* and the fern *Lygodium*, and there were other medical and magical uses.[102] *Cordyline fruticosa* has been used in New Caledonia for a variety of ailments of the mouth and stomach[420] and in India with betel as a remedy for diarrhoea.[141] *Cordyline terminalis* has been used in Tubuai and Tahiti for diarrhoea, in Tahiti for abscesses and by nursing mothers, in Samoa for skin disease, and in Hawaii for headaches. The roots have been used in Fiji for toothache.[532] For other uses of *C. terminalis* in Fiji see ref. 400. Perry[403] gives *C. fruticosa* as an alternative name for *C. terminalis*. She records its use in Sumatra for inflamed gums, and in the Solomon Islands for feverish headache and constipation.

CHEMISTRY: Morice[367] [368] found 88 per cent of linoleic acid in the fatty acids of the seed oil of *Cordyline australis*, making it one of the richest sources known. Lack of linoleic acid, an 'essential' fatty acid, can give rise to skin complaints[521] and is considered generally to be a factor in heart disease. The root contains significant quantities of fructose[201] and the leaves contain sapogenins.[62] *Cordyline terminalis* (ti) contains a compound closely related to cinchophen[482] which has antipyretic and analgesic properties similar to the salicylates. *Dracaena australis* Forst.f. (*Cordyline terminalis*) also contains the steroidal sapogenin smilagenin.[350]

Phormium cookianum Le Jolis
Mountain flax
Wharariki

BOTANICAL NOTES: The smaller varieties of *Phormium*, with yellowish flowers and twisted pendulous capsules, are known as *P. cookianum*. Many authors have used *P. colensoi* but this name is antedated by *P. cookianum*. The common name 'mountain flax' is misleading as the plant grows from the coast to the mountains throughout New Zealand. Both *P. cookianum* and *P. tenax* are popular garden plants here and overseas.

MEDICAL USE: It was used for poulticing scrofulous wens and tumours.[45]

ILLUSTRATION: See page 106

Phormium tenax J.R. et G. Forst.
New Zealand flax, New Zealand hemp
Harakeke, korari (the scape)

BOTANICAL NOTES: One of the few native plants of economic importance. It was cultivated for its fibre and was widely used by the Maori for

Above: *Agathis australis*.
Photo: L. C. W. Jensen.

Dacrycarpus dacrydioides
(x 2.0). Photo:
J. E. Braggins.

Dacrydium cupressinum
(x 2.0). Photo:
J. E. Braggins.

Phyllocladus trichomanoides (x 2.0). Photo: J. E. Braggins.

Podocarpus totara (x 3.0). Photo: J. E. Braggins.

clothing, matting, baskets, and sandals. It is found throughout New Zealand especially in lowland swamps.

MEDICAL USE: We have collected all of the numerous statements on the use of this plant in medicine, which has necessarily led to some repetition.

A leaf of flax was used by the Maori priest to enable the demon causing illness to escape from the sufferer, a magical rather than a medical use.[54][56] Broken limbs were bound with splints made of the strongest part of flax leaves.[177] The blanched base of the leaf or root was beaten to a pulp, heated or roasted, and applied hot to bring forward abscesses or tumours where matter was forming.[150][528] The poultice was also used for swollen joints.[233][331] Gum which exuded from the base of the leaves or from cut leaves was applied to burns, wounds, and old sores,[269][331][485] and was taken internally for diarrhoea.[233] New-born babies were washed with water containing a gummy substance like flax gum.[232] It has been reported to one of us that the gum is good for sunburn.

The butts of flax leaves were sliced finely and mixed with the inner bark of *Hoheria* in water and the liquid was used on burns.[287] The roots were warmed and applied to fresh cuts,[267] and were applied to ringworm and the skin of young children to prevent chafing. A decoction of root with equal parts of kohia berry juice (*Tetrapathaea tetrandra*) was used for flatulence.[233][331] The Murimotu natives boiled the portion of the stem just above the roots in a pannikin with a little water. Half an ounce of the reddish liquid was given to an adult as a purgative but the liquid became useless after a month. A decoction of the root was said to be anthelmintic.[150][233][485] A reddish juice squeezed from the scraped base of flax leaves was rubbed into limbs affected by rheumatism or sciatica after the skin had been scored with a shell. There was temporary smarting, followed by relief of pain. The juice was also used for gonorrhoea in the Rangitikei district.

The dressed fibre of the leaf made an excellent substitute for coarse tow in dressing wounds[45] and was used as a napkin for infants.[227] The centre part of a flax root, twelve leaves of kohukohu (*Pittosporum tenuifolium*), and the leaves of three branches of matoutou (?) were boiled, the liquid was strained when cool, and taken night and morning for ague and bleeding. It was also used in an elaborate recipe for bruises[390] (see also under *Typha* (Typhaceae) and *Meryta* (Araliaceae)). A strong decoction of roots and butts of leaves boiled for 12 hours was excellent for healing wounds, lacerations, and amputations.[24] An extract of root was used as an aperient and for chilblains[380] while a decoction of the roots of *P. tenax* and of *Rubus* was taken in cases of stoppage of the menses.[54] Flax-root juice, applied raw or after boiling the roots, was the favourite native cure for gunshot or bayonet wounds during the New Zealand Wars.[159]

A decoction of the root was used as a substitute for sarsaparilla[17] and for constipation[100] and stomach trouble. The gum from young shoots was applied to burns and swallowed for diarrhoea.[2] In her treatment of a case of leprosy Mother Aubert[26] used flax as a purgative. The roots were chewed for diarrhoea.[54]

The roots were skinned and boiled and the liquid was used as a mouthwash and substitute for Epsom salts. They were also soaked, roasted to a pulp, and applied to abscesses and chilblains.[467] The roots were used for colds and headaches and the leaves for stomach troubles.[363] The thick fleshy bases of the leaves were boiled and the liquid, sweetened with sugar, was drunk for constipation.[359] [389] The roots were scraped, washed thoroughly, boiled, and the resulting liquid was strained and bottled. It was a good substitute for castor oil.[414] At Ahipara, North Auckland, the flower stalks were burnt to charcoal, pounded, and dusted on burns, which apparently healed without scarring.[51] The healing properties of the gum seemed to have been well established.

RELATED PHARMACOLOGY: New Zealand flax is very helpful in rearing young calves.[344]

CHEMISTRY: Church[143] isolated a bitter principle which he considered to be a tonic, but it has not been investigated further. The chemistry of the gum has been investigated by McIlroy,[343] who found it to be built up of D-xylose and D-glucuronic acid units, which gives no clue to its healing effects. Brandt[64] has reviewed the literature of a variety of New Zealand flax called 'ngaro'. A red crystalline compound, suspected to be a purgative anthraquinone, has been obtained from the rhizomes.[282] Recent work has indeed shown that the red colour of the rhizome is due to the presence of the anthraquinones chrysophanol and emodin, and the red compounds dianellidin and stypandrone.[251] The same compounds also occur in the roots of *P. cookianum*.[251]

The seed oil is rich in linoleic acid, an 'essential' fatty acid.[367] Kupchan *et al*.[316] have isolated cytotoxic cucurbitacins from the leaves.

ILLUSTRATION: See page 106

ARACEAE
Arum family

Zantedeschia aethiopica (L.) Spreng.
Arum lily

BOTANICAL NOTES: The arum lily persists in many localities as a garden escape. It is a native of South Africa.

MEDICAL USE: The rhizome was cooked and mashed like potato and used as a cold poultice on abscesses and boils.[2]

RELATED PHARMACOLOGY: Arum lily leaves are reported to reduce inflammation[16] and they have been applied to sores and boils by

Zantedeschia aethiopica
(x 0.1). Photo:
J. E. Braggins.

Europeans and by the Xhosa in South Africa.[509] The plant is classed as poisonous by Connor,[156] who indicates that calcium oxalate is generally held responsible for the irritation of the mouth caused by this and related plants. Water accumulating in the neighbourhood of the arum lily is reputed to have a peculiar effect upon birds who drink it. They remain unconscious for some time with their wings wide open. Subcutaneous injections of an aqueous extract of the leaves into rabbits produce a short anaesthetic action.[130] Fresh *Arum maculatum* (cuckoo-pint) contains an unstable substance that is irritant to the skin and mucosa and may produce blisters; the tongue is especially sensitive to the drug and swells considerably. The dried plant and bulb are less irritant and have been used as mild expectorants for catarrh of the respiratory tract.[212]

CHEMISTRY: *Zantedeschia aethiopica* contains saponins[257] and the alkaloid etiopina.[130] Saponins are practically non-toxic to humans upon oral ingestion but act as powerful haemolytics when injected into the bloodstream, dissolving red corpuscles even at extreme dilution.[358]

ARALIACEAE
Ivy family

Meryta sinclairii (Hook.f.) Seem.
Puka

BOTANICAL NOTES: This handsome tree grows on small islands off the coast (Three Kings and Hen and Chickens Islands). It has been planted widely as an ornamental.

MEDICAL USE: Pickmere states, 'From the mystery attached to this and from remarks, I gathered that it was used to produce abortion, as was a decoction of Tataramoa and Harakeke.'[408] Tataramoa is *Rubus cissoides* and harakeke is *Phormium tenax*. The gum of the trunk was chewed as a remedy for long-standing stomach trouble.[16]

RELATED PHARMACOLOGY: In New Caledonia the crushed barks of *Meryta microcarpa* and *Piper austrocaledonicum* have been rubbed into an incision made in a broken limb before fixing a splint.[420] *Meryta lanceolata* was used in Tahiti for neuralgia.[399] American ginseng (*Panax quinquefolium*) and Chinese ginseng (*P. schensing*) are used by North American Indians and East Asians respectively, as a tonic and aphrodisiac.[193,427,487] Each species

Meryta sinclairii (x 0.1).
Photo: J. E. Braggins.

has a cure-all reputation and they are both used routinely by great numbers of more or less healthy individuals for stimulation, added energy, and a sense of well-being. In research, undertaken largely by Chinese, Japanese, and Russian scientists, physiologically active glycosides have been isolated but none have been fully characterised. The pharmacology of ginseng has been discussed in detail by Lewis.[330]

Pseudopanax edgerleyi
(Hook.f.) C. Koch
Raukawa

BOTANICAL NOTES: A small tree, with aromatic leaves, found in hilly forest throughout New Zealand.

MEDICAL USE: The raukawa was prized by the Maori for its perfume. They rubbed their limbs and bodies with the fresh leaves, which were also used for scenting oil.[150][304] They also mixed the fragrant leaves with fat or oil and then used the mixture for anointing the body.[139]

CHEMISTRY: The pleasant odour of the leaves is due to the presence of terpenes, especially myrcene, in the essential oil.[378] The related *P. colensoi* var. *ternatum* contains syringic acid and hydroxymethylfurfural.[281]

ILLUSTRATION: See page 123

Schefflera digitata J.R. et G. Forst.
Seven finger
Patete

BOTANICAL NOTES: This shrub is common in woods throughout New Zealand.

MEDICAL USE: The sap was used on scrofulous sores and ringworm.[294][485] New-born babies were wrapped in leaves of patete, raurekau,

Schefflera digitata (x 0.2). Engraving: S. Parkinson.

and mouku (*Asplenium bulbiferum*) until they perspired.[232]

RELATED PHARMACOLOGY: *Schefflera vitiensis* leaves have been used in Fiji for lung troubles.[532] Several *Schefflera* spp. are recorded as being used as drugs in China, Taiwan, Malaysia, and other parts of the Far East,[403] mainly for parturition, but not for fungal diseases. English ivy (*Hedera helix*) leaves, in the form of a decoction, were used for ulcers and skin eruptions, particularly tetter and the itch.[178] In the Mediterranean the ivy fruit has been used to produce sterility.[509]

CHEMISTRY: The leaves of *Schefflera digitata* contain falcarindiol, an acetylenic alcohol which shows remarkable specific activity against common dermatophyte fungi such as those causing ringworm.[375] [376]

CHENOPODIACEAE
Fathen family

Atriplex patula L.
Common orache

BOTANICAL NOTES: In 1927 Cockayne and Allan[148] considered that this plant had been introduced into the flora 'as it could hardly have been missed by the earlier collectors had it been present then on the coasts.' Lucy Cranwell subsequently drew Dr Allan's attention to a specimen in the Auckland Museum labelled '*A. patula*' and collected by Banks and Solander in 1769 on Cook's first voyage. In 1935 Allan commented, 'this appears to come under *A. littoralis* L.',[7] but in 1940 he wrote[8] that this was an error and that Banks and Solander had in fact collected a narrow-leaved form of *A. patula* L. However, we cannot find any mention of *A. patula* or *littoralis* in Allan's *Flora*.[9]

MEDICAL USE: Banks wrote, 'we also once or twice met with a herb like that which the country people of England call "lamb's-quarters" or "fathen," which we boiled instead of greens.' A footnote identifies the plant as *Atriplex patula* Linn.[269] but the plant does not appear in the list of antiscorbutics given by Sparrman (see p. 136).[470]

Atriplex patula (x 0.5).
Photo:
N. H. Nickerson.

RELATED PHARMACOLOGY: *Atriplex hortensis* is reported to be valuable in Vitamin A deficiency.[42] Culpeper[169] recorded that the bruised or boiled herb was applied to the throat as 'excellent good for the swelling' which with 'the decoction taken and the herb applied to the place . . . relieves the pain of gout.' The decoction was also regarded as an excellent remedy for jaundice. The leaves of *A. olida* were taken infused for relieving nervous debility, colic, and menstrual disorders but because of its very unpleasant odour and taste, the infusion was difficult to stomach.[327]

CHEMISTRY: *Atriplex patula* is a rich source of betain,[257] which is used medicinally in combination with glycocyamine for conditions characterised by muscular weaknesses or degeneration.[358] It has a relatively high sulphur content in the flowers.[397]

Chenopodium album L.
Fat-hen, lamb's-quarters
Huainanga

BOTANICAL NOTES: This weed, introduced from Europe and Asia, is common in New Zealand.

MEDICAL USE: The leaves were gathered, boiled like spinach, and eaten as a vegetable. The water was drunk three times daily as a cure for boils and blood troubles.[2]

RELATED PHARMACOLOGY: The Annual Report of the N.Z. Department of Agriculture for 1951[12] recorded three outbreaks of apparent fat-hen poisoning of dairy cattle, which were possibly due to the presence of soluble oxalates. *Chenopodium album* was used in Australia as a poultice for septic sores and breast abscesses.[166] *Chenopodium album* has been used in China for sunburn,[403] sunstroke, insect bites,[427] worms, and decayed teeth.[403] It has been used in Indonesia for blennorrhoea in women,[403] as a laxative and anthelmintic in India,[141] and along with *C. sandwicheum* as a medicine in Hawaii.[532]

In Burma *C. album* is used to treat diarrhoea of children. *Chenopodium album* var. *centrorubum* is edible but too much causes intoxication and a rash.[403] The volatile oil of American wormseed (*C. ambrosioides*) is an effective anthelmintic.[195] The species is an anti-scabies agent and is reputed to prevent ankylostomiasis but it has a toxic action on the heart, ears, and lungs. It is mainly a veterinary medicine and has been used in New Caledonia for a variety of complaints.[420] Although it is toxic, *C. ambrosioides* var. *anthelminticum* has been widely used in tropical America against roundworms, hookworms, and intestinal amoeba.[192] [330] [524] It has many uses as a medicine and is prized as an antimalarial in the Philippines.[403]

Chenopodium olidum is a nervine and emmenagogue and has been reported to be useful in hysteria of females and as a remedy for menstrual problems.[524] Lamb's tongue (*C. atriplicinum*) is poisonous to stock while the plant is in the immature stage.[299] The pharmacology of *Chenopodium* spp. has been discussed by Le Strange.[327] They are reported to be aeroallergens and to promote photodermatitis.[330]

CHEMISTRY: *Chenopodium album* contains appreciable amounts of carotene, vitamin C (ascorbic acid),[321] and β-sitosterol (see p. 68).[509] It is also reported to contain betain (see *Atriplex*), saponins (see p. 92), and the poisonous oxalic acid.[257] β-carotene is converted in the liver to vitamin A. According to Sohn[468] *C. album* contains an active principle chenopodine. Ecdysteroids have been isolated from the roots.[38] [50] [492] The vitamin C content is reported to be 13 000-15 000 IU/100 mg fresh weight.[6]

Chenopodium album (x 0.5). Drawing: V. Cassie.

COMPOSITAE
(Asteraceae)
Daisy family

Brachyglottis repanda J.R. et G. Forst.
Rangiora, pukapuka, wharangi

BOTANICAL NOTES: A shrub or small tree, common in the North Island and northern part of the South Island. It belongs to an endemic genus which is closely allied to *Senecio*.

Brachyglottis repanda (x 0.2). Engraving: S. Parkinson.

MEDICAL USE: The leaves were used for wounds and old ulcerated sores.[150] [304] The gum was chewed but was reported to be poisonous if swallowed.[149] The bark and tips of branches on the west side of the tree were cut and gum which exuded was chewed for foul breath. The

gum was dissolved in oil or kept soft in water.[233]
[331] The leaves were bruised, mixed with olive oil, and applied to boils as a poultice.[381]

RELATED PHARMACOLOGY: The leaves are poisonous to stock, causing staggers.[24] Connor[156] has discussed the effect of feeding trials with sheep and guinea pigs. The toxin is at its maximum concentration in the young growing tips, in leaf petioles, and in the cortex of thin stems. No activity was detected in extracts of the flowers or mature portions of the shrub except the leaves. Many species of the large genus *Senecio* are toxic. They contain hepatotoxic pyrrolizidine alkaloids, which result in acute illness and death of livestock in many parts of the world. Ragwort (*Senecio jacobaea*) in the form of a decoction or ointment has been applied as a wound healer.[195]

CHEMISTRY: The leaves contain low concentrations of the hepatotoxic alkaloids senkirkine, senecionine, and unidentified bases. However, a neutral resinous ester fraction appears to be the principal hepatotoxin.[371]

Celmisia coriacea (Forst.f.) Hook.f. and allied spp.
Cotton plant, horse daisy
Tikumu

BOTANICAL NOTES: Dr Joseph Hooker, in the *Handbook of the New Zealand Flora*,[268] applied the name 'tikumu' to *Celmisia coriacea*. Dr W. Lauder Lindsay,[335] who visited New Zealand in 1861 and collected extensively in Otago, said that the term 'cotton plant' applied to the more familiar species of *Celmisia*. James Buchanan[99] identified the cotton plant of Otago as 'tikumu', a species or several species of *Celmisia*. In the latest edition of Williams' dictionary[517] the term 'tikumu' is given as the native name of '*Celmisia spectabilis*, *C. coriacea* and other similar species of plants — the silky pellicle or skin of which was used for plaited fillets.' 'The Cotton plant, found growing on the ranges of Otago, has long leaves about six inches; same shape as flax; green on the upper side, white under.'[380]

In 1980, Given revised these species of *Celmisia*[229] but the revision lacked appropriate illustrations of the taxa.

MEDICAL USE: Fulton,[216] who refers to the plant as 'lint plant', reports that the leaves were used as fine cotton lint for dressing wounds.

'It has been found a good substitute for tobacco, and for relieving asthma.'[380]

RELATED PHARMACOLOGY: Dried leaves and flowering tops of the gum plant (*Grindelia camporum*) are useful in the treatment of asthma.[195]

Ageratum conyzoides, which contains hydrocyanic acid, coumarin, and an alkaloid, is poisonous to rabbits and cows[330] but is used in Fiji for any chest complaint.[400] It is used by Aborigines in Queensland to promote healing, and is also used medicinally in Nigeria, India, and South America.[322]

Coltsfoot (*Tussilago farfara*) is said to be used as tobacco in Germany and the leaves were smoked by the ancients for pulmonary complaints.[178]

CHEMISTRY: The basal part of the leaves of the related *Celmisia petrei* contains two saponins which show antifungal, haemolytic, and cholesterol-precipitating behaviour, similar to that of other known antinutritional saponins.[431]

ILLUSTRATION: See page 123

Cirsium vulgare (Savi) Ten.
Scotch thistle
Kotimana

BOTANICAL NOTES: This is a native of Europe and Western Asia. Allan[8] recorded *Onopordon*

Cirsium vulgare (x 0.2).
Photo:
N. H. Nickerson.

acanthium L. (Scotch thistle) as an introduced weed in New Zealand. However, Healy[253] subsequently identified Scotch thistle as *Cirsium vulgare* (Savi) Ten. and listed *O. acanthium* L. as a weed to which he gave the common name 'cotton thistle'.

MEDICAL USE: The stems were heated on embers and squeezed to obtain juice which was used as a quick healer for cuts and sores.[2]

RELATED PHARMACOLOGY: *Cirsium japonicum* has been used in China for the healing of wounds, and, like other *Cirsium* spp., has been used for other medicinal purposes in Southeast Asia.[403] An antibiotic has been isolated from *Onopordon tauricum*.[1]

Gnaphalium keriense A. Cunn.
River cudweed
Puatea

BOTANICAL NOTES: O'Carroll[390] refers to 'puapuatea (?) — a weed'. Possibly this weedy daisy is meant. It is common along stream banks in the North Island and the northern part of the South Island. In 1950 this species was transferred to *Anaphalioides* as *A. keriense* (A. Cunn.) Kirpiczn., but the change was not adopted in Allan's *Flora*.[9] [189]

MEDICAL USE: The juice, pressed from the leaves,

was applied to painful bruises after the skin had been scarified.[390]

RELATED PHARMACOLOGY: *Gnaphalium* species are sometimes used in the form of a tea for intestinal and pulmonary catarrhs and externally as fomentations for bruises.[178] *Gnaphalium vulgare* (*G. uliginosum*) (cudweed) was recorded by Culpeper as a sovereign remedy against mumps and quinsy and to be good for bruises.[524] *Gnaphalium luteo-album* is astringent and pectoral[420] and has been used as a general remedy by the Australian Aborigine,[509] while *G. dioicum* (cat's-foot) has been used as an infusion for coughs, as a poultice for bruises,[194] and for diarrhoea.[212]

Gnaphalium dioica (*Antennaria dioica*) is included in the Extra Pharmacopoeia (25th ed., 1967) as a 'supplementary drug' for coughs, and as a poultice for bruises.

Gnaphalium keriense (x 0.5). Drawing: V. Cassie.

Lagenifera petiolata Hook.f.
Native daisy
Parani

BOTANICAL NOTES: This little daisy is found in both main islands of New Zealand. It is variable and closely allied to the common *L. pumila* (Forst.f.) Cheesem. and other species of the genus. In 1974 Drury revised these species of *Lagenifera*,[179] but the revision lacked adequate illustrations of the plants, only leaf outlines being provided.

MEDICAL USE: The sap was used to cure an ulcerated mouth.[54] Williams[516] gave the following example of usage, 'Ko te wai tenei otaota, o te parani, he rongoa no te Maori', which may be translated as 'The water or juice of this herb, the parani, is a remedy of the Maori people.'

ILLUSTRATION: See page 123

Senecio lagopus Raoul

BOTANICAL NOTES: A mountain herb, found in both islands.

MEDICAL USE: The silky hairs of the plant were used as a type of lint for dressing wounds.[421]

RELATED PHARMACOLOGY: *Senecio scandens* has various medicinal uses in Southeast Asia.[403] See also under *Brachyglottis repanda* (p. 100).

Sonchus oleraceus L.
Sow thistle
Rauriki, pororua, puwha

BOTANICAL NOTES: Goldie[233] gives 'tawheke' as a Maori name for this plant, but it is usually applied as 'taweke' to *S. asper* (L.) Hill. In 1927 Cockayne and Allan[148] considered that the coastal thistle collected by Banks and Solander

Senecio lagopus (x 0.2).
Drawing: V. Cassie.

Prumnopitys ferruginea. Photo: J. E. Braggins.

Prumnopitys taxifolia. Photo: J. E. Braggins.

Phormium cookianum
(x 2.0). Photo:
J. E. Braggins:

Phormium tenax (x 2.0).
Photo: J. E. Braggins.

on Cook's first voyage in 1769 was *S. littoralis* (Kirk) Ckn. and that the true *S. oleraceus* and *S. asper* had been introduced since European settlement began. In 1961 Allan[9] identified the *Sonchus* collected by Banks and Solander and preserved in the British Museum (Natural History) as *S. asper* (L.) Hill, and remarked that 'it probably came to New Zealand with the Maori, is found only as a ruderal and in cultivated ground, and there have been later introductions.' The suggestion that *S. asper* came to New Zealand with the Maori has not been made by other authors. Colenso informed J. D. Hooker that the Maori people formerly used *S. asper* for food, but preferred the introduced *S. oleraceus* as it was less bitter.[268] Sparrman,[470] who accompanied Cook on his second voyage, identified the *Sonchus* used for greens as *S. oleraceus* (see *Tetragonia*, Ficoidaceae).

In the second edition we commented that Banks and Solander, the Forsters, and Sparrman left collections of dried specimens, and these should be examined before further oracular pronouncements are made. However, in 1976 Hamlin[248] noted that *S. littoralis* (Kirk) Ckn. 1907 was antedated by *S. littoralis* Reichb. 1831, and substituted the name *S. kirkii* for it. Again in 1985 Gardner discussed the nativity of *S. asper* and suggested that it originated in the upland gardens of New Guinea (as *S. hydrophilus*) and reached New Zealand without Maori aid.[222]

MEDICAL USE: *Sonchus oleraceus* was one of the plants used by Captain Cook as an antiscorbutic.[470] It was used for cutaneous eruptions and as a drink for stomach complaints[376] and a decoction made from the rauriki plant was used for boils and 'to cure carbuncles and that sort of thing.'[54] The leaves were crushed until they were wet with milky fluid and then applied or bound onto cuts to prevent poisoning.[2] A decoction made by boiling together the leaves of kopakopa (*Plantago major*), clover, and pororua (*Sonchus oleraceus*) with some salt, was drunk by women in order to cause the placenta to be expelled.[233] The juice of the wild turnip (pohatu) and the sow thistle (puwha) was expressed and drunk for haemorrhage after childbirth.[47] It was a blood purifier, a slight laxative,[408] and the juice was used to cure warts.[144]

RELATED PHARMACOLOGY: The gum produced by drying the juice is a powerful purgative.[178] *Sonchus asper* and *oleraceus* were medicinal plants of the Araucanos Indians[243] and *S. oleraceus* has been used medicinally in Hawaii and the Marquesas,[532] by settlers in Cape Colony for wounds and ulcers, and in Tanzania as a vermicide.[509] Reports indicate that in ancient times *S. oleraceus* was given for a burning stomach and was useful for scorpion bites.[234] In Indonesia *S. arvensis* leaves have been applied to swellings.[152]

CHEMISTRY: *Sonchus oleraceus* contains vitamin C [283] [326] and the triterpene taraxasterol.[257] The vitamin C content has been determined at the DSIR in Palmerston North.[501] The phenolic constituents of *Sonchus* spp. have been examined.[349]

ILLUSTRATION: See page 124

Taraxacum magellanicum
Comm. ex Sch. Bip.
Native dandelion

BOTANICAL NOTES: This dandelion is found mainly in mountain districts and is very similar to the common introduced dandelion, *T. vulgare*, now known as *T. officinale*.

MEDICAL USE: The roots were used as an alterative.[150]

RELATED PHARMACOLOGY: The extract or juice of common dandelion (*Taraxacum officinale*) is well known in older pharmacy where it was used as a bitter in atonic dyspepsia and as a mild laxative in chronic constipation.[195] [327] It is said to be one of the best plants for inducing the flow of bile.[443] The whole plant is used as an alterative in China and is made into a poultice with distillers' grains for cancer and abscesses of the breast.[403] The roots were used to treat chronic diseases of the liver[330] and the white latex is a popular remedy for wart removal.

CHEMISTRY: The chemical constituents of *T. officinale* have been listed by Thomson.[490] They include a bitter principle taraxacin, choline, and vitamins A and B. Choline is a component of lecithin, a constituent of nervous tissue and the brain. *Taraxacum stevenii* has a high vitamin C content.[297]

ILLUSTRATION: See page 124

CONVOLVULACEAE
Convolvulus family

Calystegia sepium (L.) R.Br.
Bindweed
Pohue, pohuhe

BOTANICAL NOTES: A common weed of many forms, found in most temperate countries.

MEDICAL USE: The roots or rhizomes were boiled and eaten by nursing mothers[318] to promote the flow of milk.[160]

RELATED PHARMACOLOGY: The roots of this plant were used by the Maori as food[485] but English plants of the same species are purgative and there are many references in the literature to their purgative properties, e.g. ref. 419. The Chinese used the plant as a tonic.[427] In Fiji, a cut leaf of *Calystegia affinis* has been rubbed on the forehead for headache.[532] *Calystegia soldanella* exerts a diuretic effect.[330]

The roots of *C. sepium* var. *japonicum* have tonic properties which are made use of in many countries in the Far East.[403]

CHEMISTRY: There is scope for chemical investigation of the apparent difference between the New Zealand plant and its relatives overseas.

Calystegia sepium
(x 0.5). Engraving:
S. Parkinson.

Ipomoea batatas (L.) Lamk.
Sweet potato
Kumara

BOTANICAL NOTES: This root crop was introduced into New Zealand by the old-time Maori, who recognised and cultivated many varieties.

MEDICAL USE: The whole plant and the liquor made from it were used internally for low fever and externally for various skin diseases. [233] [331]

A recent case of the use of the kumara for treating external ulcers has come to the attention of one of the authors.[450]

RELATED PHARMACOLOGY: For a good review of the pharmacology of *Ipomoea* see ref. 509. Perry[403] lists many uses of *Ipomoea* spp. in medicine. In Hawaii *I. batatas* has been used for stomach-ache in children, for phlegm in the throat, to loosen mucus in the chest, to stop vomiting, for asthma, for trouble with the womb, to induce pregnancy, and for seasickness.[532] In Malaysia the tops were used for poulticing. The Chinese sliced the tubers, scalded and dried the slices, and made a tea to allay thirst.[102] In New Caledonia the leaves have been used to draw boils and abscesses.[419] Many references are given by Rageau[420] to the medicinal use of *Ipomoea* spp. in New Caledonia; by Zepernick[532] to their use in Hawaii, Samoa, and Fiji; and by Papy[399] to their use in Tahiti.

Many *Ipomoea* spp. are well-known purgatives.[195,524] For example, resin from scammony root (*I. orizabensis*) is described in the British Pharmaceutical Codex[89] as purgative. Santesson[441] has described 'piule', an interesting narcotic from a Mexican species. *Ipomoea violacea* and *I. tricolor* contain lysergic and isolysergic acid amides, which are degradation products of the ergot alkaloids and which produce hallucinations.[266] *Ipomoea violacea* seeds and those of the related *Rivea corymbosa* were associated by the Aztecs and other Mexican Indians with divination and were eaten by Aztec priests to induce hallucinations when they wished to communicate with their gods.[330]

Lewis[330] has recorded that the root of *I. digitata* was used in Southern Asia as a tonic, alterative, and aphrodisiac, that Pawnee Indians drank an infusion of *I. leptophyllus* as a cardiac stimulant, and that the bark of *I. arborescens* has been used in Sinaloa, Mexico, an an antidote for rattlesnake bites. *Ipomoea pes-caprae* is used by the aborigines of Groote Eylandt for snake bite and

Ipomoea batatas (x 0.1). Drawing: V. Cassie.

spider bites.[329] Some *Ipomoea* spp. have shown promise in cancer treatment.[43]

CHEMISTRY: Various compounds present in the skin of *Ipomoea batatas* accumulate as a result of infection, injury, or chemical fungicidal treatment.[156] These include ipomeamarone, the (+)-enantiomer of ngaione which is the hepatotoxin of *Myoporum laetum*. Three unidentified antibiotics have been isolated from the plant,[98] [379] the leaves of which contain antiscorbutic vitamins.[196]

CORIARIACEAE
Coriaria family

Coriaria arborea Linds.
Toot
Tutu, tupakihi, puhou

BOTANICAL NOTES: The New Zealand species of *Coriaria* were revised by Oliver[393] and the name *C. arborea* Lindsay was applied to the common large-leaved shrub formerly regarded as identical with the South American *C. ruscifolia* L. The Maori name 'tutu' is applied to most species of the genus.[335] Taylor[484] recorded the use of the plant as a drink and jelly as follows:

> At Korinito a bowl of tutu juice boiled with the pith of the Pitau fern tree was presented to our party. It is a very palatable dish and soon disappeared. The medulla thickens it the same as the rimu. . . .
> At Tawitinui . . . the natives regaled my companions with large quantities of the juice of the tutu boiled with seaweed. This makes a jelly and I think very palatable.' A pleasant wine was often made by settlers from the juicy petals; after standing some time it resembled a light claret.[304]

MEDICAL USE: The tender shoots, when plucked at certain seasons, were taken for dysentery[294] and a decoction of leaves was also given to patients suffering from dysentery. A mixture containing juices of the pith was used for insanity. The juice of the fruit was fermented with seaweed and taken to counteract costiveness caused by eating totara, rimu, or karaka berries. From the leaves, steeped in water with other plants, a lotion was made for application to wounds.[233] The juice of the fruit and a jelly made from them were a relish and laxative.[380] The young shoots were scraped and formed into poultices for bruises, bleeding cuts, and boils.[414] They were also boiled until black, and a poultice of them was applied to sprains or bruises, the water was poured over, and the whole was bandaged up.[45,363] Pith from stems was bound onto inflamed wounds, and young leaves and shoots, boiled to form a dark liquid, were used as a herbal. Bathing with it healed cuts, sores, inflammation, etc.[2]

Broken bones were plastered with the pith and sap of *Coriaria* shoots. Broken legs and bruises were bathed in warm water in which leaves had been boiled and were plastered with the leaves. Pig's fat or oil was applied first to lessen the heat of the plaster.[467] Sam Neil[381] of Opotiki described a similar treatment of broken limbs using bark instead of leaves. A preparation named 'mauru', made from the root, was used externally for neuralgia, rheumatism, and eyestrain.[236]

RELATED PHARMACOLOGY: The Mexican drug tlolocopetl is obtained from *Coriaria* sp.[178] The Chilean tree, *C. ruscifolia*, has toxic and emetic properties and is used in witchcraft.[243] It is reported to be one of the most toxic plants in Tahiti.[399]

CHEMISTRY: The leaves and seeds contain a violent poison, tutin,[163,164,183,184] which is related to coriamyrtin from *C. myrtifolia*, a European species, and which is probably identical with coriarin isolated by Japanese workers from *C. japonica*.[302] Coriamyrtin has been used as a stimulant[357] and Shibata,[453] in discussing the characteristic symptoms induced by it, suggested its use in anti-shock therapy. Tutin has been shown to be a specific antagonist of γ-

aminobutyric acid (GABA).[315]

Tutin is similar both chemically and pharmacologically to picrotoxinin, the physiologically active moiety of picrotoxin.[284] [464] Its lethal powers are reported in papers by Easterfield and Aston[183] [184] and are described in the US Dispensatory.[178] Picrotoxin is used in the treatment of poisoning by depressants of the central nervous system. Occasional outbreaks of honey poisoning in New Zealand have been traced by Palmer-Jones[395] [396] [479] and others to hyenancin (mellitoxin), which is an oxidation product of tutin produced by the passion vine hopper, *Scolypopa australis*.[203] *Coriaria japonica* leaves contain gallic acid, ellagic acid, and kaempferol.[289] [290]

ILLUSTRATION: See page 124

CORNACEAE
Dogwood family

Corokia buddleioides A. Cunn.
Korokio, korokio taranga

BOTANICAL NOTES: The Maori name of this plant has been used as the generic name. The genus is endemic to New Zealand and Rapa Island. The plant is grown in temperate countries and is an attractive garden shrub.

MEDICAL USE: The liquid from boiled leaves is said to give instant relief from stomach-ache.[2]

RELATED PHARMACOLOGY: Dogwood (*Cornus florida*) is a feeble astringent tonic[178] and in pioneer days in the USA country doctors prescribed a bitter drink made by steeping the flowers, fruit, and bark in water for fevers and chills. The treatment had been gleaned from the many eastern American Indians, who had long used dogwood as an antipyretic.[330]

CHEMISTRY: The wood contains β-sitosterol (see p. 68) and the triterpenoids, taraxerol, lupenyl acetate, and lupeol.[73]

Corokia buddleioides (x 0.2). Drawing: V. Cassie.

Griselinia littoralis Raoul
Broadleaf
Kapuka, papauma

BOTANICAL NOTES: This shrub is found in both islands, but is rare north of East Cape. Another species, *G. lucida*, is common in the north. Bell[45] lists '*G. littoralis*, pukatea', as a medicinal plant, but other authors identify *G. littoralis* as 'kapuka' or 'papauma', and 'pukatea' as *Laurelia novae-zelandiae* (Monimiaceae).

MEDICAL USE: It was an opening medicine and the inner bark was used in scrofula and venereal disease.[45]

RELATED PHARMACOLOGY: *Griselinia ruscifolia* was a medicinal plant of the Araucanos Indians.[243]

CHEMISTRY: *Griselinia littoralis* contains the flavonoids quercetin (see p. 83) and kaempferol, *p*-coumaric and caffeic acids,[257] and the iridoids magnolioside and griselinoside.[280]

ILLUSTRATION: See page 141

CORYNOCARPACEAE
Corynocarpus family

Corynocarpus laevigatus
J. R. et G. Forst.
Karaka

BOTANICAL NOTES: The family consists of one genus and four species, three of which were discussed and described by Hemsley.[259] The four species are found in New Zealand, Queensland, and some islands of the Pacific. There is a tradition that the Maori introduced the New Zealand species when they first colonised this country. The New Zealand tree is usually found on the coast, and is common in the Kermadec Islands, the North Island, and Chatham Island, but rarer in the South Island. It is planted for its glossy foliage and handsome yellow berries.

Corynocarpus laevigatus (x 0.5). Engraving: S. Parkinson.

MEDICAL USE: The leaves were healing if applied to wounds, 'but care must be taken to place the shiny green upper surface to the wound, as the under-surface draws equally as the upper surface heals.'[390] Although they are bitter and poisonous the fruits of karaka were formerly used as a source of food by the Maori, who baked and washed them before use. This had the effect of hydrolysing the toxin, thereby reducing its activity. The toxicology of karaka is discussed by Bell,[44] and by Fastier and Laws.[204]

CHEMISTRY: Karakin [1,2,6-tri-(3-nitropropanoyl)-β-D-glucopyranose] and four related nitropropanoyl glucosides, corollin, corynocarpin, coronarian, and cibarian, have been isolated from the poisonous berries.[131] [132] [373] Nitro-compounds are rare as natural products. Karakin and its relatives are toxic to larvae of the grass grub (*Costelytra zealandica*).[275]

CRUCIFERAE (Brassicaceae) Wall-flower family

Brassica oleracea L.
Wild cabbage
Kapeti

BOTANICAL NOTES: Various forms of cabbage escape and persist. These are introduced, not native. Both *Brassica oleracea* and *B. rapa* (see below) are classified as poisonous plants by Connor.[156]

MEDICAL USE: A hot decoction was used internally in cases of colic.[233] [353]

RELATED PHARMACOLOGY: *Brassica* spp. contain sinigrin (allylisothiocyanate), an active mutagen.[257] Lewis[330] records that *B. oleracea* and *B. rapa* show experimental hypoglycemic activity and that the seeds of *B. nigra* (black mustard) are a powerful rubefacient. The volatile oils of *B. nigra* and *B. juncea* have been given in cases of colic.[178] The heated leaf of *B. oleracea* has been used in Cape Colony as a local application for the relief of biliary colic, and also for oedema and bed sores.[509]

CHEMISTRY: The wild cabbage produces a thiocyanate and (S)-5-vinyloxazolidine-2-thione, which are both goitrogenic.[481]

Brassica rapa L.
Wild turnip
Pohata

BOTANICAL NOTES: Forms of *Brassica* escape from gardens and persist for short periods in fields

Above: *Brassica oleracea* (x 0.5).

Above right: *Brassica rapa* (x 0.5). Photo: J. E. Braggins.

in both islands. They are natives of Europe.

MEDICAL USE: The juice of the wild turnip (pohatu) and the sow thistle (puwha) was expressed and drunk if there was much haemorrhage after childbirth.[45]

CHEMISTRY: Turnips contain 3-butenylglucosinolate, 4-pentenylglucosinolate, and (S)-goitrin which are known goitrogens.[156]

Lepidium oleraceum Forst.f.
Cook's scurvygrass
Nau

BOTANICAL NOTES: This herb was common on the coasts and outlying islands of New Zealand but is now rare, possibly due to destruction by cattle and sheep, or by a fungal disease.

MEDICAL USE: Captain Cook's crew collected boatloads of the plant for use as an antiscorbutic.[138,470] Chapman[135] thought that the plant concerned was kahakaha (*Astelia cunninghamii*) but this is an error.

RELATED PHARMACOLOGY: *Cardaria (Lepidium) draba* (cress) and *Rorippa nasturtium-aquaticum* (watercress) are well-known antiscorbutics. *Lepidium bidentatum* has been used in Tahiti for bruises and maladies of the skin.[399] In the Bahamas the seeds of *L. virginicum* were used to cause belching and to move the bowels.[192]

CHEMISTRY: *Lepidium* and *Rorippa* spp. contain sinapin, the choline ester of sinapic acid (see p. 109 for a note on choline).[257]

Rorippa nasturtium-aquaticum
Watercress (L.) Hayek
Kowhitiwhiti

Lepidium oleraceum (x 0.2). Engraving: S. Parkinson.

BOTANICAL NOTES: *Rorippa nasturtium-aquaticum* is an introduced water plant found in the North Island. The closely allied *R. microphylla* (Reichb.) Hylander occurs in both the main islands.

MEDICAL USE: Damp watercress was applied as a pack for headaches.[310]

RELATED PHARMACOLOGY: *R. nasturtium-aquaticum* (*Nasturtium officinale*) has been used medicinally in New Caledonia[420] and Hawaii for inflamed mouth or lips.[532] *N. sarmentosum* has been used in Tubuai for 'inner diseases', carbuncles, and neuralgia in the head and neck and in Hawaii for tuberculosis. In Samoa it has been used for rheumatic fever and the leaves for elephantiasis,[532] and in Tahiti for contusions.[399]

ILLUSTRATION: See page 141

CUNONIACEAE Weinmannia racemosa Linn.f.
Lightwood family Towai, kamahi

BOTANICAL NOTES: This tree is closely allied to *W. silvicola* Sol. ex A. Cunn. and the Maori names 'tawhero' and 'towai' have been applied to both species.

MEDICAL USE: The bark from the west side of the tree, from which the outer rind had been scraped off, was steeped in hot water, and the decoction taken internally as an aperient in cases of abdominal and thoracic pains.[233] The inner bark is laxative[45] and the bark infused in boiling water was a tonic medicine.[390]

RELATED PHARMACOLOGY: The bark of *W. blumei* was used medicinally in Java[102] and *W. richii* (?) was used in Fiji for pain in the lungs and for cough.[400] *Weinmannia trichosperma* was a medicinal plant of the Araucanos Indians.[243]

Weinmannia racemosa (x 0.3). Engraving: S. Parkinson.

CHEMISTRY: The bark contains tannins and catechin,[21] which have astringent properties.

Weinmannia silvicola Sol. ex. A. Cunn.
Tawhero

BOTANICAL NOTES: A common tree in the northern part of the North Island. *Weinmannia racemosa* replaces it further south.

MEDICAL USE: The bark from the side of the tree facing the sun was taken, and the outer bark cut away. The clean inner bark was broken up, placed in water and boiled, and the decoction, sometimes mixed with olive oil, was applied

Weinmannia silvicola (x 0.2). Engraving: S. Parkinson.

warm to burns. The treatment was said to leave no scar.[2] The inner bark was also hammered and boiled, and the extract was used to bathe cuts.[467]

CHEMISTRY: The bark contains large amounts of tannin.[21]

CYPERACEAE
Sedge family

Cyperus ustulatus A. Rich.
Cutty grass
Toetoe upokotangata

BOTANICAL NOTES: The name 'toetoe' was applied to various grasses and sedges. Toetoe upokotangata, toetoe whatumanu or whatupakau were applied particularly to *C. ustulatus*. It is a common sedge, found in damp places, swamps, and alongside streams, especially near the sea. Cheeseman's name for it was *Mariscus ustulatus* (A. Rich.) Cheesem.

MEDICAL USE: The pith, taken and boiled with water, strained and bottled, was used for kidney trouble in North Auckland.[2]

RELATED PHARMACOLOGY: *Cyperus rotundus* has been used in various parts of the world as a diuretic[404][509] and in New Caledonia for a variety of ailments.[420] *Mariscus sieberianus* was used as a vermifuge in Sumatra[102] while *Mariscus cyperinus* and *Kyllinga monocephala* are astringent and have been used for the treatment of bruises and sprains in Tahiti. The latter species has been used in New Caledonia for the same purpose.[420] *Lepidosperma perplanum* has been used in New Caledonia in infusions for liver troubles.[419]

ILLUSTRATION: See page 141

Cyperus ustulatus (x 0.1). Drawing: V. Cassie.

Scirpus lacustris L.
Lake scirpus
Wawa

BOTANICAL NOTES: A common sedge, found in swamps and alongside rivers, lakes, and ponds

Pseudopanax edgerlyi. Photo:
J. E. Braggins.

Lagenifera petiolata (x 1). Photo:
J. E. Braggins.

Celmisia sp. (x 0.2). Painting:
E. Blumhardt.

Sonchus oleraceus (x 0.3).

Taraxacum magellanicum (x 0.3).
Photo: J. E. Braggins.

Coriaria arborea (x 1.0). Photo: J. E. Braggins.

in the North Island and northern part of the South Island. Blake[61] considered that the New Zealand plant was *S. validus* Vahl.

MEDICAL USE: The leaf juice was used in attempts to cure blindness.[485]

RELATED PHARMACOLOGY: *Scirpus validus* has been used medicinally in Hawaii.[532] *Scirpus americanus* is suspected of producing pulmonary emphysema in Wyoming cattle and of poisoning cattle in Australia.[330]

CHEMISTRY: The leaves of *Scirpus lacustris* are reported to give a bitter extract and to contain a flavonoid, which is probably rutin.[257] Rutin acts as a vasopressor agent and strengthens the capillaries.[521]

ILLUSTRATION: See page 141

ELAEOCARPACEAE
Elaeocarpus family

Aristotelia serrata
(J. R. et G. Forst.) Oliv.

Wineberry
Makomako

BOTANICAL NOTES: This handsome shrub is common on bush burns and the outskirts of the forest. It is frequently planted as an ornamental tree. It was known as *A. racemosa* (A. Cunn.) Hook.f. but the Forsters' name has priority.

MEDICAL USE: The leaves were boiled with a little water, and the extract was used for burns and rheumatism. The leaves were also warmed on hot coals and then bandaged on burns.[2] [476] The liquid from boiled leaves was used for boils[467] and sore eyes[258] [286] [287] [363] while an infusion for sore eyes was also made from bark soaked in cold water.[523] The bark was boiled and the liquid was used as a bath for rheumatic cases.[414]

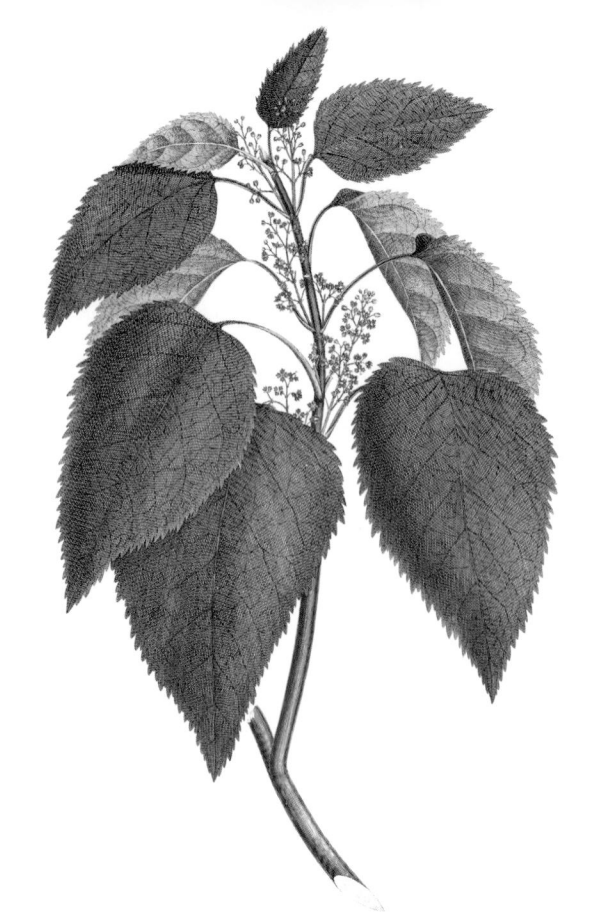

Aristotelia serrata
(x 0.5). Engraving:
S. Parkinson.

RELATED PHARMACOLOGY: *Aristotelia macqui* was a medicinal plant of the Araucanos Indians.[243] *Aristotelia chilensis* is used by the Mapoche Indians of South America, who call it 'maki', which is somewhat similar to the Maori makomako for *A. serrata*. The leaves of maki are used by various Araucarian tribes for boils, tumours, fevers, and pimples. Extracts of the leaves or the sap are used for mouth sores and throat complaints. Dried and powdered leaves or the fruit are used for wounds, cuts, and haemorrhoids, while the sap from the bark is used to ease childbirth.[58]

CHEMISTRY: The bark contains β-sitosterol (see p. 68) and the dicoumarin ellagic acid[155] which acts as a haemostatic.[358] The leaves contain the indole alkaloids, aristoteline, aristotelinone, serratoline, and serratolenone.[57] The whole plant contains 14 alkaloids related to aristoteline.[58]

Elaeocarpus dentatus
(J. R. et G. Forst.) Vahl
Hinau

BOTANICAL NOTES: Hinau is a round-headed forest tree, found in both islands. The Maori obtained a black dye from the bark, and used the fruit for food.[304]

MEDICAL USE: A decoction of the bark in a hot bath was said to cure the severest skin disease.[390]

RELATED PHARMACOLOGY: *Elaeocarpus sloanea* has bristles which cause irritant dermatitis.[330] The bark of *E. persicifolius* has been used in New Caledonia for the preparation of antidysenteric

Elaeocarpus dentatus (x 0.5). Engraving: S. Parkinson.

medications. The bark of mountain *Elaeocarpus* spp. has also been used for haemorrhoids, diarrhoea, and eczema.[420] A boiled extract of the leaves of *E. graeffei* has been used in Fiji as a cure for stomach ailments.[465]

CHEMISTRY: Morice[370] has examined the fatty acids of the seeds and fruit coat. The bark contains tannins, β-sitosterol (see p. 68), and ellagic acid (see *Aristotelia*).

EPACRIDACEAE
Epacris family

Cyathodes juniperina
(J. R. et G. Forst.) Druce

Taumingi, tumingi, mingimingi

BOTANICAL NOTES: This small-leaved shrub, formerly known as *C. acerosa* R.Br., is common and variable. Forms with numerous white or red fruit are popular for rockeries.

Cyathodes juniperina (x 0.5). Engraving: S. Parkinson.

MEDICAL USE: The prickly leaves boiled in a small quantity of water were taken for kidney trouble, asthma, and menstrual disorders[2] and for septic wounds.[15]

Leucopogon fasciculatus
(Forst.f.) A. Rich.
Mingimingi

BOTANICAL NOTES: This small tree is common in scrubland in the North Island and in the South Island as far south as Canterbury. Allan[9] transferred this species to *Cyathodes*, as *C. fasciculata* (Forst.f.) Allan, but his reduction of *Leucopogon* to a synonym of *Cyathodes* has not been adopted in Australia, where most of the species are found.

MEDICAL USE: The leaves were boiled in water and small quantities of the liquid were taken for headache and influenza.[467]

Leucopogon fasciculatus (x 0.1). Engraving: S. Parkinson.

ERICACEAE
Heath family

Gaultheria antipoda Forst.f.
Snowberry
Papapa

BOTANICAL NOTES: This little shrub is common throughout New Zealand in scrubland. Possibly it is the plant referred to by James Cowan,[159] Winifred Miller,[359] and Sam Neil,[381] although Williams[517] identifies 'papapa' as both *Pomaderris elliptica* (Rhamnaceae) and *Gaultheria antipoda*.

MEDICAL USE: The leaves, when the outer surface is rubbed off, are very soft to the touch, and the liquid obtained from boiling them was used as a strong soothing and healing agent. The uncooked leaves were also applied to wounds.[159] This was a well-known remedy for healing cuts. Either the wound was bathed with a decoction or was poulticed with the leaves.[359] An infusion of the leaves was also taken for asthma.[381]

RELATED PHARMACOLOGY: In Chile, *Gaultheria myrtilloides* was a medicinal plant of the Araucanos Indians.[243] In Java, oil of a *Gaultheria* sp. has been used for rheumatism. *Gaultheria*

Gaultheria antipoda (x 0.1). Engraving: S. Parkinson.

procumbens contains oil of wintergreen[102] and has been used as an antirheumatic, antiseptic, diuretic, rubefacient, and for the relief of pain.[330] [490] Bearberry (*Arctostaphylos uva-ursi*) is diuretic, astringent, and antiseptic for the urinary tract. The active constituent is arbutin (glycoside of hydroquinone).[195] Bearberry has also been employed for menorrhagia[178] and infections of the kidneys.[212]

CHEMISTRY: The alkanes of the leaves and stems have been examined by Eglinton.[191]

EUPHORBIACEAE
Milk-weed family

Euphorbia glauca Forst.f.
Maori spurge
Waiuokahukura, waiuatua

BOTANICAL NOTES: A herb, to 1 m tall, found sparingly on coastal sands and rocks throughout New Zealand. In 1909 it was described by Cockayne[147] as a major sand-binder, but it is now local in its occurrence.

MEDICAL USE: The weed was boiled and the water was used as a bath for skin troubles.[414]

RELATED PHARMACOLOGY: The natives of New Caledonia used *Euphorbia hirta* for dysentery. They also drank the sap of *E. kanalensis* and *E. atoto*, mixed with sea water. These saps were purgative and induced menstruation, and, in larger doses, abortion.[330 419] They have also been employed as fish poisons. The natives of Maré Island applied *E. atoto*, cooked and warm, to the breasts to induce the flow of milk.[419] The nectar of *E. atoto* was used in Australia for throat troubles.[166]

Various *Euphorbia* spp. have been used by natives of South Africa for skin troubles.[509] *Euphorbia* spp. have been used to relieve toothache while the roots of *E. ipecacuanha* and *E. corollata* have been used as emetics and purgatives. *Euphorbia hirta* (*E. pilulifera*) shows experimental hypoglycemic activity and has

Euphorbia glauca (x 0.2).
Engraving:
S. Parkinson.

been prescribed for the preparation of poultices or gargles by the Hawaiians. It relaxes the bronchioles but apparently has a depressant action on general respiration and the heart.[330] It was much esteemed in Australia as a remedy for coughs and bronchial and pulmonary disorders, but more especially for the prompt relief it afforded in paroxysmal asthma.[524] *Euphorbia pilulifera* is used in the Philippines for asthma, to stop bleeding, and for eye troubles.[406]

Euphorbia antiquorum is used in Southeast Asia for skin troubles and along with other *Euphorbia* spp. for other medicinal purposes.[403] The dried latex of *E. resinifera* was employed as a drastic purgative, but now is not used internally to any extent. It was known to ancient herbalists and Pliny mentioned its drastic purging quality.[524] The pharmacology of *Euphorbia* spp. has been discussed by Le Strange[327] (see also ref. 178).

Euphorbia peplus L.
Milkweed
Kaikaiatua[2]

BOTANICAL NOTES: A garden weed, common in both islands. Connor[156] lists it as a poisonous plant.

MEDICAL USE: The weed was boiled and the water was used as a bath for skin troubles.[2]

RELATED PHARMACOLOGY: The ingestion of *E. peplus* by domesticated animals is reported to cause painful vomiting and purgation.[447] *Euphorbia peplus* is used in Fiji for constipation and as an internal tonic for weaning infants.[465]

CHEMISTRY: *Euphorbia peplus* contains flavonoids, cyanogens, alkaloids, and glycosides.[180] [257] The two latter constituents cause dilation of blood vessels, lowering of blood pressure, and other toxic symptoms.[447] The plant contains a series of compounds called euglobals which all have remarkable anti-inflammatory activity.[175] [311] It also contains ingenane-type diterpene esters which are responsible for irritant- and tumour-promoting effects.[235] The lipid fraction contains the triterpenoids, lanosterol and ß-amyrin acetate.[426]

ILLUSTRATION: See page 142

FICOIDACEAE (AIZOACEAE)
Carpetweed family

Disphyma australe (Ait.) J. M. Black
New Zealand ice plant, round-leaved pigface
Horokaka, ruerueke

BOTANICAL NOTES: This plant, formerly known as *Mesembryanthemum australe*, is a common seashore ice plant in New Zealand, Australia, and Norfolk and Lord Howe Islands.

MEDICAL USE: The juice was expressed for boils.[485]

RELATED PHARMACOLOGY: Many species of the genus contain a cocaine-like alkaloid and are used medicinally by the Chinese.[102] The juice of the succulent leaves of *Mesembryanthemum aequilaterale* has been used for dysentery and as a diuretic. It can be taken as a gargle for sore throats and thrush, and in lotions for burns.[419] *Mesembryanthemum crystallinum* (ice plant) was considered by the early cowboys of western North America to be a sure cure for venereal diseases.[330]

CHEMISTRY: *Mesembryanthemum angulatum* leaves contain 1.72 percent oxalates;[507] *M. anatomicum* and *tortuosum* contain mesembrin $C_{17}H_{23}NO_3$, apparently belonging to the tropane group of alkaloids.[425]

ILLUSTRATION: See page 142

Tetragonia tetragonioides
(Pallas) Kuntze
New Zealand spinach, warrigal cabbage
Rengamutu, kokihi

BOTANICAL NOTES: This herb is common on sea coasts of New Zealand, Australia, Japan, New Caledonia, and South America and is cultivated as a green vegetable in many countries. The name 'kokihi' is applied by Williams[517] to this species and by Colenso[150] to the closely allied *T. trigyna*, which is also found on seashores throughout New Zealand. *Tetragonia expansa* Murr. is now treated as a synonym of *T. tetragonioides*.

MEDICAL USE: On his voyages of discovery, Captain Cook took every opportunity to collect greens for his men and dosed them with 'sour kroutt, portable soup and malt' to keep scurvy in check. Among the greens which Cook tried was the New Zealand spinach,[485] which Sir Joseph Banks later grew in England. Seldom has a vegetable been introduced under such distinguished patronage. There is a note in Cook's diary for Thursday, 13 April 1769, relating how he persuaded his men to try new foods:

> The Sour Kroutt, the men as first would not eat it, until I put it in practice — a method I never once knew to fail with seamen — and this was to have some of it dressed every day for the Cabin Table, and permitted all the Officers, without exception, to make use of it, and left it to the option of the men either to take as much as they pleased or none at all; but this practice was not continued above a week before I found it necessary to put every one on board on an allowance; for such are the Tempers and disposition of Seamen in general that whatever you give them out of the common way — altho' it be ever so much for their good — it will not go down, and you

Tetragonia tetragonioides (x 0.5). Engraving: S. Parkinson.

will hear nothing but murmurings against the Man who first invented it; but the moment they see their superiors set a value upon it, it becomes the finest stuff in the world and the inventor an honest fellow.'[513]

Dr Anders Sparrman,[470] who joined the *Resolution* at Table Bay in 1772 to assist the Forsters in their scientific work on Cook's second voyage of discovery, stated that 'the greenstuff, which was used for salad and for boiling with green peas and broth, consisted of wild celery, *Lepidium tetrandum*, *Sonchus oleraceus*, and *Tetragonia cornuta*.' The wild celery is probably *Apium prostratum*, *Lepidium tetrandum* is now known as *L. oleraceus*, and *Tetragonia cornuta* is known as *T. tetragonioides*.

The following quote from the journal of L'Horne,[332] a lieutenant on de Surville's ship the *Saint Jean Baptiste* during its voyage of 1769-73, indicated the great value of these antiscorbutics:

> This country, bare and sterile as it appeared to us, supplied us with some plants the use of which produced a wonderful effect on our sick ones. These plants were: two kinds of watercress, one of which has a straight stem and rather tall; its leaves are long, and larger at the extremity than in the centre. They are dented. This plant is not shaped like any species of cress known in Europe, but it has a very strong taste, so strong that it brings the tears to the eyes when one eats much of it raw, its milk being so acid. The other species has a rounded leaf similar to the leaf of our watercress. The stems are thick, and therefore creeping. Its taste is the same as that of our cress, but inferior in strength to the flavour of our watercress. The last species of plant of which I wish to speak is a kind of wild parsley, which appeared to me to be a sort of celery. Its root tastes like a celery, and it only requires to be cultivated as in Europe to acquire the same shape.
>
> We made great use of these three plants, [These plants are possibly *Lepidium oleraceum*

Tetragonia trigyna (x 0.5). Engraving: S. Parkinson.

(Cook's scurvygrass), *Nasturtium* or *Rorippa* sp., and *Apium australe* (Maori celery), respectively.], but our sick ones especially felt the great effects derived from the use of them. Every one of the sick ones who went ashore and ate some of these plants not only did not die, but got better remarkably quickly. One of the most desperate cases, whose body was swollen all over, and whose mouth was rotten, and who had been given up, was only fit to go to shore twice, but the use he made of these plants then and on board relieved him wonderfully, and at the end of the month he started walking, and was quite well shortly after. I found the effects of these plants so wonderful that I took some seeds of the two first mentioned. They grow in great profusion in the country. I could not gather any seed from the wild parsley, as it was not then seeding. Besides these three kinds of plants, I noticed a good number of others belonging to European species.

RELATED PHARMACOLOGY: *Tetragonia tetragonioides* has been used in New Caledonia as a laxative.[420] In Japan the whole plant of *T. tetragonioides* has been shown to be very effective against ulcer formation in mice by crude sedative drugs used in oriental medicine.[526] *Tetragonia schenkii* was found to be poisonous in South Africa.[507]

CHEMISTRY: *Tetragonia expansa* is known to contain betain (see p.97), alkaloids, much saponin,[510] and tetragonin, a yeast growth regulator;[447] it also shows carbonic anhydrase activity.[83] The active principles effective against ulcer formation are two cerebrosides, a class of compounds which are widely distributed in nature as constituents of brain, nerves, and other organs, and which are contained in milk, oysters, and some plants.

One of the cerebrosides from *T. tetragonioides* when administered intraperitoneally elongated pentobarbital-induced sleeping time and delayed the starting time of tremorine-induced tremor. The aerial parts of the plant contain water-soluble polysaccharides which have anti-inflammatory effects on carrageenan-induced oedema and adjuvant arthritis.[291]

GERANIACEAE
Geranium family

Geranium homeanum (G. australe)
Cut-leaved cranesbill
Matuakumara

BOTANICAL NOTES: This herb is found in both of the main islands of New Zealand. *Geranium dissectum* L. var. *glabratum* is probably a synonym of *G. homeanum*.

MEDICAL USE: The leaves were used for boils and sore backs.[363]

RELATED PHARMACOLOGY: The dried rhizome of *G. maculatum* has been used in chronic diarrhoea in dogs.[357] The root has a tonic and astringent action on the kidneys and an infusion of the herb is reported to be useful in infantile cholera and diarrhoea.[521] The plant shows experimental hypoglycemic activity and has been used in eastern North America for dysentery, sore gums, and pyorrhoea. *Geranium macrorrhizum* is reported to be used in Bulgaria as an aphrodisiac.[330] Seven species of *Geranium* have antibiotic effects[217] and *G. robertianum* is efficacious in haemorrhage, fevers, and other complaints.[36,212]

Geranium homeanum (x 0.5). Drawing: V. Cassie.

CHEMISTRY: *Geranium dissectum* contains tannins.[257]

Geranium microphyllum Hook.f.
Cranesbill

BOTANICAL NOTES: A slender prostrate herb, found in grassland and on rocks throughout New Zealand.

MEDICAL USE: It was a good substitute for arnica, a drug used externally for aches and pains.[423]

Geranium microphyllum
(x 0.5). Engraving:
S. Parkinson.

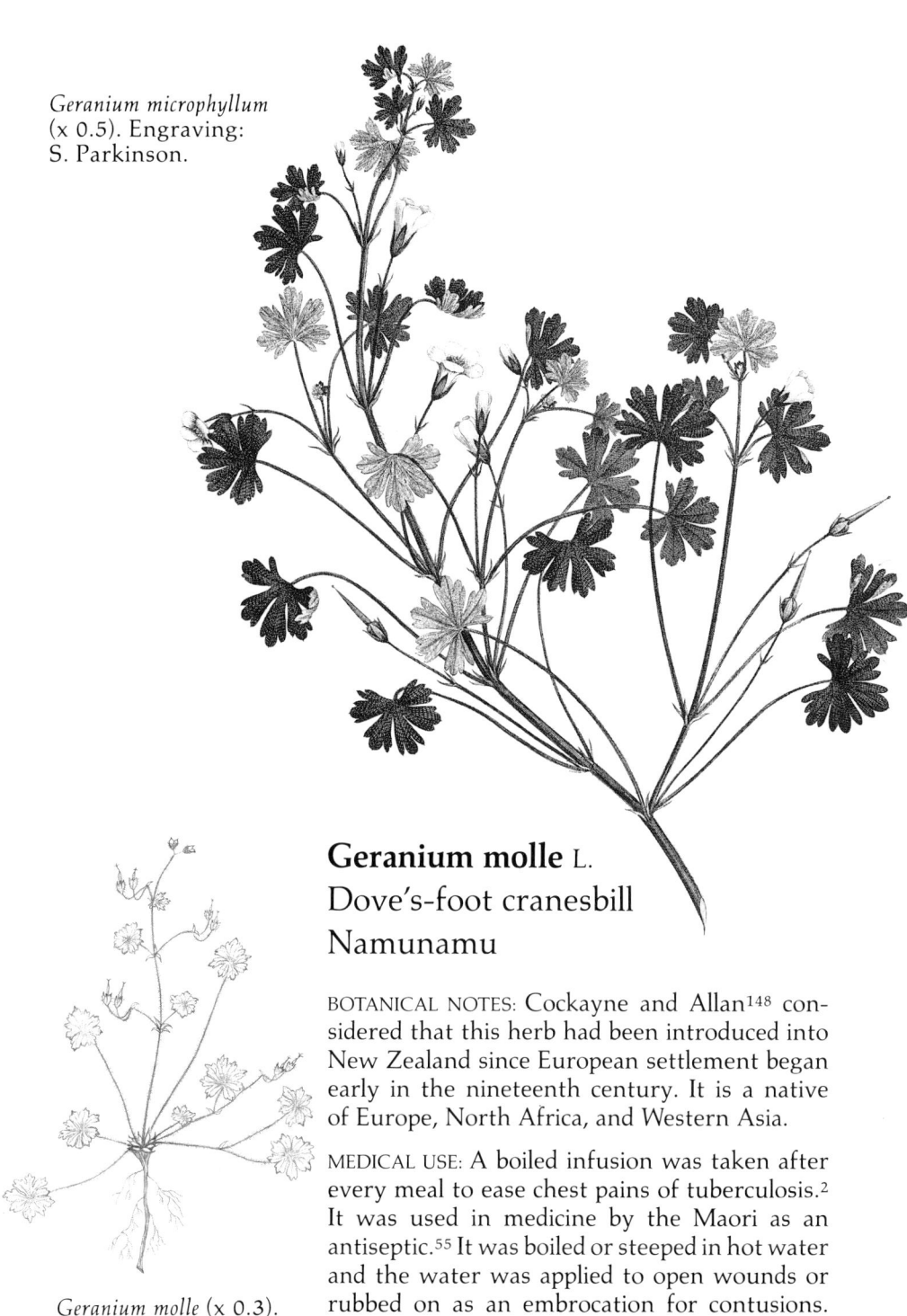

Geranium molle (x 0.3).
Drawing: V. Cassie.

Geranium molle L.
Dove's-foot cranesbill
Namunamu

BOTANICAL NOTES: Cockayne and Allan[148] considered that this herb had been introduced into New Zealand since European settlement began early in the nineteenth century. It is a native of Europe, North Africa, and Western Asia.

MEDICAL USE: A boiled infusion was taken after every meal to ease chest pains of tuberculosis.[2] It was used in medicine by the Maori as an antiseptic.[55] It was boiled or steeped in hot water and the water was applied to open wounds or rubbed on as an embrocation for contusions. The leaves were also applied as a poultice.[54 467]

Pelargonium inodorum Willd.
Kopata

BOTANICAL NOTES: This plant was identified by Sir Joseph Hooker and others as *P. australe* Willd., var. *clandestinum* (L'Her.) Hook.f., but Cheeseman placed it under *P. inodorum* Willd. It is a common weedy herb.

MEDICAL USE: A lotion from boiled leaves was used as a wash for pimples.[467] A lotion from the bruised leaves was applied to burns and scalds[233][268] and to bruises.[485] The leaves were also eaten to cure foul breath[10] and were reputed to be a good substitute for arnica.[423]

RELATED PHARMACOLOGY: *Pelargonium alchemilloides* has been applied to wounds and abscesses by the Xhosa in South Africa while *P. cucullatum* has also been used for open sores.[509] The oils of *P. odoratissimum* and *P. radula*, which are sources of geraniol, cause contact dermatitis.[330]

ILLUSTRATION: See page 142

GESNERIACEAE
African violet family

Rhabdothamnus solandri A. Cunn.
Kaikai aruhe

Goldie gave the Maori name of 'kaikai aruhe' for *R. solandri*, and Kerry-Nicholls[294] gave it the name 'kaikaiatua'. Percy Smith[139] applied the name to *Acaena sanguisorbae*. Taylor[376] listed 'kaikai aruhe' as one of the plants used by the Maori people in an oven or vapour bath, but did not otherwise identify it.

BOTANICAL NOTES: A slender twiggy shrub found only in the North Island. The colour of the striped flower ranges from almost brick-red to pale yellow.

MEDICAL USE: The leaves and twigs were used in vapour baths.[233]

RELATED PHARMACOLOGY: Extracts from species

Griselinia littoralis (x 0.2).
Photo: G. Boehnke.

Rorippa nasturtium-aquaticum (x 0.2).
Photo: N. H. Nickerson.

Cyperus ustulatus (x 0.1).
Photo: J. E. Braggins.

Scirpus lacustris.

Above: *Euphorbia peplus* (x 1). Photo: J. E. Braggins.

Disphyma australe (x 0.3). Photo: J. E. Braggins.

Pelargonium inodorum (x 1.0). Photo: C. C. Ogle.

Rhabdothamnus solandri (x 0.5). Engraving: S. Parkinson.

of this family are used in Southeast Asia to bathe wounds.[403]

CHEMISTRY: Anthocyanins have been isolated from the flowers.[337]

GRAMINEAE
(Poaceae)
Grass family

Cortaderia fulvida (Buchan.) Zotov
Cortaderia splendens Connor and allied spp.
Toetoe, kakaho

BOTANICAL NOTES: These handsome grasses form a very characteristic feature of the New Zealand landscape. The second has been known as *Arundo kakaho* Steud., *A. conspicua* Forst.f., and *Cortaderia toetoe* Zotov.

MEDICAL USE: The feathery part was used to stop the flow of blood and the ashes of the plant were applied to burns as a poultice. For diarrhoea the lower part of young undeveloped leaves was eaten.[233] Juice from the lower part of the stem was used to clean the tongues of infants and the stem was chewed and swallowed for kidney trouble.[467] This plant was also used by the Moriori of the Chatham Islands.[233]

RELATED PHARMACOLOGY: The rhizome and leaves of *Arundo donax* were given as an infusion at the end of nursing to stop the flow of milk.[419] The leaves, which contain the alkaloid gramine (donaxine), act as a vasopressor agent.[330] The dried rhizome of *Agropyron repens* is diuretic and aperient[195] and has been used for the treatment of inflammation of the kidneys and bladder, skin eruptions, and rheumatic complaints.[212]

CHEMISTRY: The leaf wax alkanes of *Arundo conspicua* have been examined by Eglinton and co-workers.[191]

ILLUSTRATION: See page 159

Hierochloe redolens
(Vahl) Roem. et Schultes
Holy grass
Karetu

BOTANICAL NOTES: This is a common native grass. Allan's name for it was *H. redolens* R. Br. but this has been revised by Zotov.[534] See Edgar and Connor[189] for subsequent taxonomic wrangles regarding this species.

MEDICAL USE: It was used in vapour baths.[484] The daisy-like flowers of the roniu (*Brachycome odorata*) and the flowering tops of the sweet-scented grass (*Hierochloe redolens*) were worn around the neck, enclosed in fibrous leaves, as a scented necklace.[150]

ILLUSTRATION: See page 159

Poa cita Edgar
Tussock grass, silver tussock
Wi

BOTANICAL NOTES: The most abundant grass of the South Island and common in the high central part of the North Island. It has been known as *Poa caespitosa*[139] and *P. laevis*[533] but neither name applies to the New Zealand plant.[519]

MEDICAL USE: A decoction of this grass, and other plants, was an internal remedy for rheumatic pains.[390] Burns were treated with ashes of 'tussac-grass'.[45]

RELATED PHARMACOLOGY: *Poa* spp. are reported to be aeroallergens.[330] *Diarrhena japonica* has been recommended by the Chinese for rheumatism.[427]

Zea mays L.
Maize, Indian corn
Kanga

BOTANICAL NOTES: This important American grain was introduced into Maori agriculture in the early days of white settlement, and is widely grown today by Maori and Pakeha.

MEDICAL USE: Maori women attributed sterility

Poa cita (x 0.1).
Drawing: V. Cassie.

to the habitual use of fermented food in the form of maize which had been steeped in water until putrid. This was purely a native idea, and one which they considered to be confirmed by the fact that fewer fertile women were found among tribes where this food was a favourite article of diet.[233]

RELATED PHARMACOLOGY: The long styles or 'silk' are diuretic and have been employed in infusions for infections of the urinary tract, gravel, and palpitations.[419] [524] *Zea mays* shows experimental hypoglycemic activity and the young stalks are reported to have antifungal properties.[330]

Peruvian Indians are reputed to inhale alkaloids in the smoke of burning maize, thereby producing intense mental excitement.[443] In Fiji a hot poultice made from the grains is used for urinary disorders.[472] The medicinal properties of *Zea mays* are discussed by Perry.[403]

CHEMISTRY: Maize contains the cytokinin zeatin, a purine derivative which induces cell division.[328] The chemical constituents of *Zea mays* have been examined extensively.[257]

ILLUSTRATION: See page 160

HALORAGACEAE
Water-milfoil family

Haloragis erecta (Murr.) Oken
Toatoa

BOTANICAL NOTES: This weedy species is common throughout New Zealand in lowland districts. The name 'toatoa' is also applied to the celery-leaved pines (*Phyllocladus*).

MEDICAL USE: The infusion of its leaves or the expressed juice was used for all scrofulous diseases.[485]

RELATED PHARMACOLOGY: *Gunnera perpensa* has been used in Africa for the skin disease known as psoriasis.[509]

Haloragis erecta (x 0.3).
Engraving:
S. Parkinson.

HYPERICACEAE
St John's wort family

Hypericum perforatum L. and allied spp.
St John's wort

BOTANICAL NOTES: This introduced weed is found in both islands and is poisonous to sheep and cattle.[156] The weed is supposed to show red spots on 29 August, the day on which St John the Baptist was beheaded — hence its name.[524]

MEDICAL USE: A preparation of *Hypericum* was taken for headaches, measles, and influenza.[467]

RELATED PHARMACOLOGY: St John's wort was used in ancient times for bruises, wounds, and a great variety of other complaints.[178] [212] [524] It has astringent and diuretic properties,[195] has proved to be antibiotic,[244] and has given good

147

results in many cases of depression.[174] It is also effective against *Mycobacterium tuberculosis*[208] and dysentery bacteria.[410] St John's wort is reported to provoke photodermatitis[330] or hypericism, a primary photosensitisation disease in many parts of the world.[146] An alcoholic decoction of the leaves of *Hypericum graminium* is astringent and heals wounds; an aqueous infusion is tonic.[420]

CHEMISTRY: The photosensitising agent is the bisanthraquinone derivative, hypericin.[355] *Hypericum perforatum* also contains rutin (see p. 125), saponins (see p. 92), mannitol, and an antibiotic in the fruit.[257] Mannitol is used medicinally.[521] Hyperforin, a compound isolated from a number of *Hypericum* spp., is active against *Staphylococcus aureus*.[241]

ILLUSTRATION: See page 160

LABIATAE
(Lamiaceae)
Mint family

Mentha cunninghamii Benth.
Maori mint
Hioi

BOTANICAL NOTES: A herb, with fragrant leaves and flowers, frequent throughout New Zealand.

MEDICAL USE: It was used to induce perspiration.[150]

RELATED PHARMACOLOGY: The mints are well known for their essential oils and stimulating or tonic properties.[327] [524] Pliny the Elder (AD 23-79) prescribed infusions of mint (*Mentha* spp.) to dissolve stones in the bladder and kidney. The dried leaves and flowering tops of *M. piperita* (peppermint) have been used to relieve spasmodic pains in the stomach and bowels and the herb has been used to treat nausea[330] and diarrhoea.[490] Lewis and Elvin-Lewis[330] include *M. piperita* in the plants used by a 'well-known European natural healer' for the preparation of cream massages which along with foot baths and vaginal douches 'apparently work miracles for the frigid female.'

Aborigines in Australia prepared a tea from *Mentha australis* which was used for coughs and colds, and to induce abortion. Early European settlers in the country used it as a tonic. *Mentha satureioides* was also used medicinally by the early settlers.[166] *Mentha* spp. are used in Southeast Asia to promote perspiration.[403]

CHEMISTRY: The essential oils of *Mentha* spp. usually contain menthol, which is used in nasal inhalers and as a mild local anaesthetic.[358]

ILLUSTRATION: See page 160

LAURACEAE
Laurel family

Beilschmiedia tawa
(A. Cunn.) T. Kirk

Tawa

BOTANICAL NOTES: A lofty forest tree, common in the North Island and northern part of the South Island.

MEDICAL USE: It was a lotion for wounds (see also under *Dacrydium*, Coniferae). The bark was used for pains in the stomach and for colds.[294] [485]

RELATED PHARMACOLOGY: The bark of 'false laurel' (*Beilschmiedia pahangensis*) is reported to have been boiled and the decoction drunk for a number of internal complaints and after childbirth.[102] Cinnamon (*Cinnamomum zeylanicum*) is antiseptic[194] and is said to relieve flatulence and nauseous vomiting.[178] *Cinnamomum* spp. are used for various medicinal purposes in Tonga.[532] An infusion of the bark of sassafras (*Sassafras variifolium*) was a popular domestic remedy for colds, and it is believed in popular superstition to have peculiar alterative properties. It is a powerful antiseptic and the mucilage from the pith is apparently useful in dysentery, catarrh, and kidney troubles.[178]

CHEMISTRY: W. E. Harvey (see ref.118) has isolated ß-sitosterol and a long-chain ester of lignoceryl alcohol from the bark of this species. ß-sitosterol is the major component of an American proprietary drug used to lower blood cholesterol levels.[195] Alkaloids have been isolated from the berries.[436]

Beilschmiedia tawa (x 0.5). Engraving: S. Parkinson.

Litsea calicaris (A. Cunn.) T. Kirk
Mangeao

BOTANICAL NOTES: A handsome tree, found sparingly from the North Cape to Rotorua, in the North Island.

MEDICAL USE: It was used in vapour baths[48][233] and in midwifery,[318] and for a number of female complaints.[322]

RELATED PHARMACOLOGY: *Litsea cubeba* root is an ingredient of a mixture administered after childbirth in China. The seeds are used by the aborigines of Taiwan as salt and the plant has other medicinal uses.[403] *Litsea cubeba* has been used in Indonesia for asthma, venereal disease, and bowel disorders.[474] *Litsea glutinosa* was used in Australia for a variety of complaints,[166] specifically for aches and pains, sores, skin infections, and eye troubles.[322] A preparation from the juice of the stems of *L. pickeringii* is said to be used in Fiji to promote menstruation,[511] and the pounded stem, strained in water, is taken internally for headache.[465] *Litsea vitiana* is noted as a medicinal plant in the Yasawa Group of Fiji where it is used to relieve swollen breasts.[465] For the chemistry and medical uses of Malaysian species, see ref.102. Two New Caledonian *Litsea* spp. have a high content of alkaloids.[420]

CHEMISTRY: Some *Litsea* spp. contain a very poisonous alkaloid laurotetanine.[468]

LEGUMINOSAE (Fabaceae)
Pea family

An extensive survey of the alkaloids of the Leguminosae in New Zealand has been made by White.[514]

Sophora microphylla Ait.
Kowhai

BOTANICAL NOTES: This tree has smaller flowers and leaflets and is more widely distributed throughout New Zealand than *S. tetraptera* with which it is frequently confused.

MEDICAL USE: An infusion of bark of *S. microphylla* and of manuka (*Leptospermum*) was drunk for internal pains and applied externally to pains in the back and side. The inner bark was used for itch[233] and an infusion of kowhai and manuka barks mixed with wood ashes was allowed to dry and then rubbed into the skin

Sophora microphylla
(x 0.3). Engraving:
S. Parkinson.

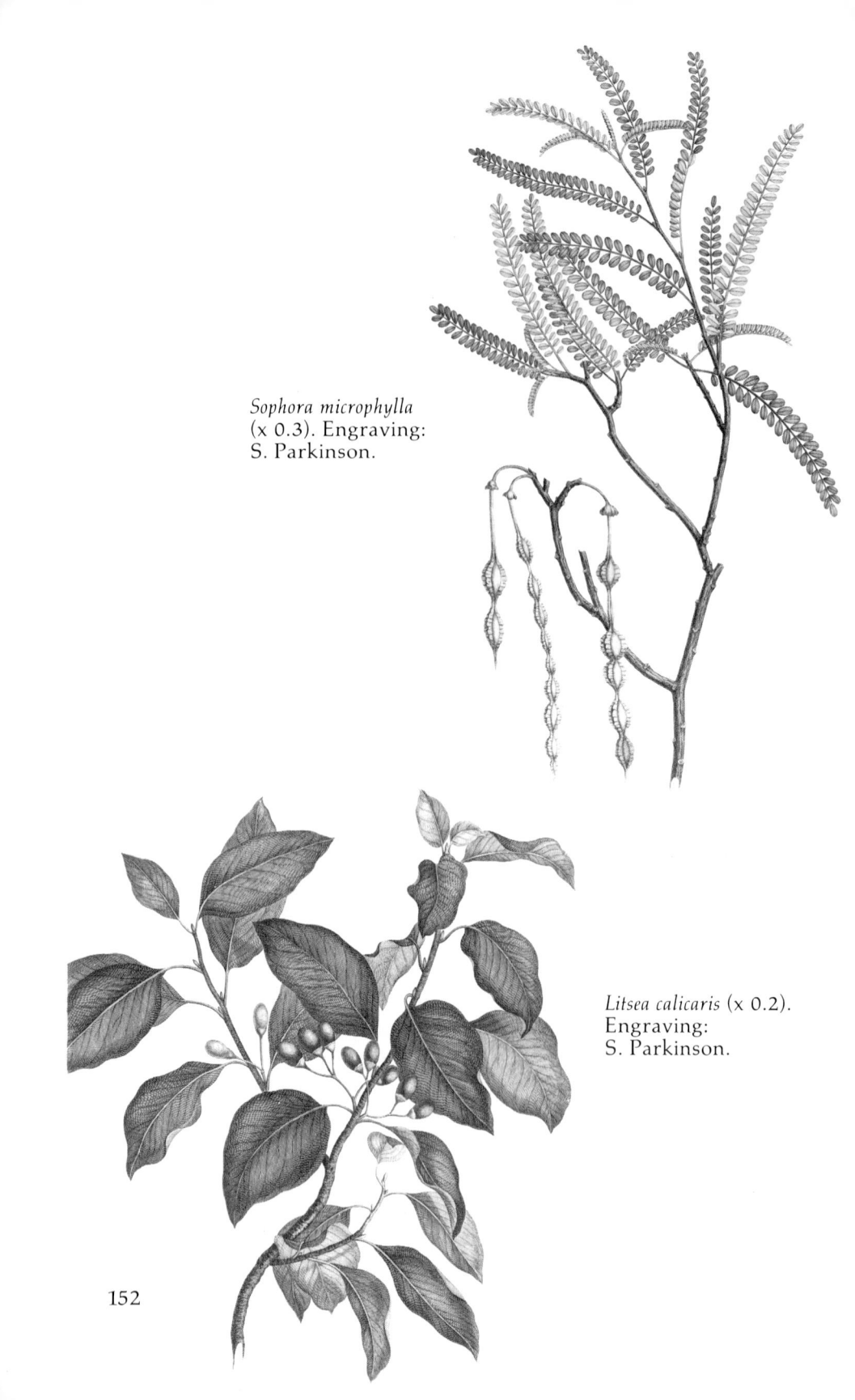

Litsea calicaris (x 0.2).
Engraving:
S. Parkinson.

Sophora tetraptera
(x 0.3). Engraving:
S. Parkinson.

Arthropodium cirratum
(x 0.2). Engraving:
S. Parkinson.

for various skin diseases.[54] The bark, crushed and steeped in boiling water, was used for bathing bruises. It was also said to help in healing fractures.[2] Monckton[216] reported that an infusion of the blossoms and leaves was well known to the older Maori as a powerful emetic. Kowhai has been used by the Maori for removing internal blood clots. In the case of the famous footballer G. Nepia, where a European doctor saw no alternative to an operation, the trouble was said to be cured by bathing in an infusion of bark taken from the side of the tree facing the sun.[382]

RELATED PHARMACOLOGY: *Sophora flavescens*, *S. japonica*, and *S. tomentosa* are reputed to be medicinal plants in the Malay Peninsula and the first two species have been sold by Chinese pharmacies for a variety of complaints.[102] *Sophora flavescens* is tonic, stomachic, and astringent; *S. japonica* was used as a vermifuge and for haemorrhoids by the Chinese.[427] It contains a glucoprotein which exhibits mitogenic activity and also contains the flavonoid rutin, which acts as a vasopressor agent.[330] The bud contains large amounts of rutin, which also strengthens the capillaries and acts as a styptic.[272,490] Extracts of the flowers of *S. japonica* are active against *Staphylococcus aureus*.[527] The plant is used in Southeast Asia for treating menstrual clots but Perry[403] records that it is used more frequently in brewing beer than medicinally.

Sophora tomentosa is a medicinal plant in New Caledonia and the seeds, which are astringent and purgative, have been used for diarrhoea, liver complaints, and fish poisoning.[419] The root bark and seeds of *S. tomentosa* have also been used for bilious vomiting and as an expectorant, and the oil has been used as an external application for bony aches.[509] The seeds have been used in Tahiti and Brazil as an emetic and cathartic.[399] The crushed leaves have been mixed with coconut oil and used in Fiji for fractures.[532] *Sophora* (*Baptisia*) *tinctoria* has been used as a febrifuge and for the treatment of ulcers.[46] Its medicinal uses have been discussed by Le Strange.[327] The red seeds of *S. secundiflora* (mescal bean) have hallucinogenic properties and have been used in southwestern states of the USA and by Mexican Indians in visionary rites.[330]

CHEMISTRY: Briggs and Ricketts[85] isolated the alkaloids cytisine, methyl cytisine, matrine, and sophochrysine from the seeds and Briggs *et al.*[75] found anagyrine and diosmin (hesperidin) in the flowers. Hesperidin is useful in haemorrhages both internal and external.[195] The pharmacology of *Sophora* alkaloids has been investigated by Georgadze.[225] The bark contains the phytoalexin 3-hydroxy-8, 9-methylenedioxy-pterocarpan[77] while the leaves contain a complex mixture of flavonoid C- and O-glycosides.[351,352]

Sophora tetraptera J. Mill.
Kowhai

BOTANICAL NOTES: The large-leaved kowhai, *S. tetraptera*, is restricted to the East Coast of New Zealand. The smaller-leaved kowhai, *S. microphylla*, is more common and is widely planted as an ornamental tree. The medical uses and other notes probably apply to both species. They have been placed in the genus *Edwardsia*.

MEDICAL USE: The bark was used as a purgative and for itch (scabies)[485] and the inner bark of the plant was often used by bushmen as a poultice for sprains, etc.[304] Poultices made of bark steeped in water were used for scrofulous wens, tumours, and for dressing wounds. A tree growing on a hillside was found and a root running towards the sun was selected. This had less juice but was stronger. The outer rind was scraped off and the second skin was removed from the central core and the juice expressed. A teaspoonful, taken internally three times daily, reputedly cured gonorrhoea in two days.[45] An infusion of the inner bark was occasionally taken as a tonic.[26]

An infusion of the barks of the kowhai and manuka trees was drunk for internal pains and applied outwardly for pains in the back or side.[54] The bark was also crushed, steeped, and boiled and applied to bruises and freshly set broken limbs.[414] K. Kahaki,[287] Honana,[267] and Collier[154] recorded the use of similar bark and leaf poultices for broken limbs and bruises, the injury being bathed first with an infusion of the bark or leaves. The ashes of kowhai were used for ringworm.[15] A recipe for colds and sore throats was to steep goai (kowhai) in boiling water and drink the infusion. It had to be taken fresh, as it would not keep, although perhaps spirits would act as a preservative. The bark was taken only from the sunny side of the tree, and thus its removal did not kill the tree.[40]

RELATED PHARMACOLOGY: *Sophora tetraptera* was a medicinal plant of the Araucanos Indians.[243] The *Sophora* of southern Chile have been known as *S. tetraptera*, *S. microphylla*, and *S. macnabiana* Grah.[352]

CHEMISTRY: The seeds have been investigated by Briggs and co-workers.[88] They contain the alkaloids cytisine, methyl cytisine, and matrine. The bark contains matrine, cytisine, and the phytoalexin 3-hydroxy-8, 9-methylenedioxy-pterocarpan.[77] More recently the alkaloids of the twigs and fruit have been examined.[300]

LILIACEAE
Lily family

Arthropodium cirratum (Forst.f.) R.Br.
Rock lily
Rengarenga, maikaika, maika ka

BOTANICAL NOTES: The rock lily is found on coastal rocks of the North Island and northern part of the South Island. It is often planted in gardens in New Zealand and overseas. The spelling *'cirratum'* is now favoured[366] instead of the original *cirrhatum*.

MEDICAL USE: The base of the leaves was used as a poultice for ulcers.[485] The roots were scraped, roasted, beaten to a pulp, and applied warm to unbroken tumours and abscesses.[150] [528]

RELATED PHARMACOLOGY: *Arthropodium paniculatum* is suspected of causing mortality in cattle.[510] Bulbs of *Lilium concolor* and *Tulipa edulis* were powdered and applied to ulcers by the Chinese.[427]

LOGANIACEAE
Nux vomica family

Geniostoma ligustrifolium A. Cunn.
Maori privet
Hangehange, papa

BOTANICAL NOTES: This shrub is common in forest in the North Island of New Zealand. See p. 17 for a note on Conn's 1980 revision.[155]

MEDICAL USE: The sap was applied to skin diseases of children[54,233] and the bark was used for the itch.[485]

RELATED PHARMACOLOGY: An infusion of the bark of *Geniostoma insulare* has been used for gastro-intestinal diseases and for stomach-ache in Tonga and Fiji. *Geniostoma vitiense* has been used in Fiji for stomach-ache and for constipation.[532] *Geniostoma ruprestre* has been used in Tahiti for neuralgia,[399] and the leaves of certain *Geniostoma* spp. have been used in New Caledonia as a poultice for boils.[420] Brucine from *Strychnos nux-vomicae* (now Strychnaceae) has been used for pruritus or itch.[178]

LORANTHACEAE
Mistletoe family

Aston[24] stated that an infusion of one of the species of mistletoe had been prepared and used by an Otago medical man as a heart tonic. Kerry-Nicholls[294] listed papa-aumu, or mistletoe, in the native pharmacopoeia and commented that the

Geniostoma ligustrifolium (x 0.2). Engraving: S. Parkinson.

bruised bark was applied for the itch by rubbing it on the skin. Papaauma or papauma was identified as *Coprosma grandifolia* by Colenso[150] and as *C. grandifolia* and *Griselinia littoralis* by Williams.[517] The plants are not mistletoes.

MALVACEAE
Mallow family

Hibiscus trionum L.
Starry hibiscus
Puarangi

BOTANICAL NOTES: In 1959 Mr A. H. Watt obtained the Maori name from older people at Te Kao, when the New Zealand Post Office wished to use an illustration of *Hibiscus* on a postage stamp. *Hibiscus trionum* is a slender erect

Hierochloe redolens (x 0.1). Photo: J. E. Braggins.

Cortaderia fulvida.

Zea mays.

Right: *Hypericum* sp. (x 0.3).

Below: *Mentha cunninghamii* (x 4).
Photo: J. E. Braggins.

or spreading herb, with a large flower, yellow with a brown centre. Both it and the allied woody prickly *H. diversifolius* Jacquin are rare and local in northern parts of the North Island. Early travellers found the two species near Maori settlements in the far north.[29] [484]

MEDICAL USE: The leaves were used to cleanse the hands.[508]

RELATED PHARMACOLOGY: For the pharmacology of *Hibiscus* see Parham,[400] Roi,[427] and Zepernick.[532] *Hibiscus cannabinus* has been used in the East Indies and Senegal for eye diseases while *H. sabdariffa* has been used in Angola and Guinea as an emollient. The flowers of *H. sabdariffa* act as a mild purgative.[490] *Hibiscus tiliaceus* has been used for congestive pulmonary conditions[509] and in Tahiti, and New Caledonia for a variety of complaints.[399] In Tahiti, where it is known as 'purau' or 'fau', it is also used for haemorrhoids, conjunctivitis, tired eyes, abscesses, tonsilitis, and bronchitis.[403] The aborigines of Groote Eylandt in the Gulf of Carpentaria use an infusion of the bark of *H. tiliaceus* to cure boils and the hot infusion is also used with salt to heal wounds which are later covered with the outer bark.[329] In Fiji the leaves of *H. tiliaceus* are wrapped on bone fractures while the stem is used as part of a remedy for treating ulcers. Juice from the leaves of *H. diversifolius* is reputed to be used in Fiji to procure an abortion.[465]

The seeds of *H. abelmoschus* have been used as an insecticide and when made into a paste with milk have been employed as a remedy for itch.[524] In New Caledonia the seeds have been used as a stimulant, antispasmodic, and diuretic. A decoction of the flowers of *H. rosa-sinensis* has been used medicinally in New Caledonia for a variety of ailments.[420] The flower buds are used in the Philippines to treat boils and abscesses. In Tahiti the tender leaves, buds, and flowers are used for convulsions, neuralgia, and painful menstruation. The plant has spasmolytic and sedative properties.[404] *Hibiscus esculentis* and other

Hibiscus spp. are used for medicinal purposes in Southeast Asia.[403]

ILLUSTRATION: See page 177

Hoheria populnea A. Cunn.
Lacebark
Hohere, houhere

BOTANICAL NOTES: The genus is endemic to New Zealand and the generic name is based on the Maori name. *Hoheria populnea* and its allied species are small forest trees which are commonly planted in gardens for their handsome foliage and white flowers.

MEDICAL USE: The bark of the houhere was used as a demulcent in colds, etc.[17] [150] Leaves, bark, and flowers were used medicinally;[233] the bark was cut into strips and soaked in cold water for two days until a thick jelly formed which was used by old people to bathe weak and sore eyes.[2] [414] The inner bark of *Hoheria* sp. was mixed with the finely cut butts of flax leaves (*Phormium*) and the exuding liquid was applied to burns.[228] The bark afforded a demulcent drink used by the Maori; Kirk[304] suggested that 'in all probability it might be advantageously used in all cases where the bark of slippery elm (*Ulmus fulva*) is employed by the druggist for demulcent drinks, cataplasms, etc.'

RELATED PHARMACOLOGY: *Althaea rosea* contains mucilage and has been used as a demulcent and emollient[487] while *A. officinalis* (marsh mallow) has been prescribed as an emollient because it contains so much healing mucilage.[212] [327] *Malva sylvestris* (common mallow) is also a demulcent and emollient.[178] *Malva parviflora* has been used in Africa for wounds, swellings, and sore eyes.[509] The mucilage of the seeds of *Abutilon avicennae* has been used as an emollient by the Chinese.[427] *Abutilon indicum* has been used in various parts of Africa for eye trouble and *A. asiaticum* and

A. hirtum have been used in India for sore eyes, ulcers, and as a demulcent.[141] The bark and root of *A. indicum* exert diuretic effects[330] and the kernels have been used in New Caledonia as an emollient and laxative.[420]

ILLUSTRATION: See page 177

MELIACEAE
Mahogany family

Dysoxylum spectabile
(Forst.f.) Hook.f.
Native cedar
Kohekohe

BOTANICAL NOTES: A handsome forest tree, usually found near the coast of the North Island and northern part of the South Island.

MEDICAL USE: The young bark is said to contain a bitter principle having tonic properties like quinine. The leaves are bitter and tonic; an infusion was occasionally used by bushmen as a stomachic.[304] A decoction of leaves and bark allayed coughing. The astringent red pulp was taken by consumptives to relieve blood-spitting.[27] [233] [294] [380] [485] An infusion of leaves in boiling water gave vapours for the treatment of colds and feverishness, and the liquid was drunk for lung haemorrhage[2] [363] and for female disorders. It was also gargled for sore throats and used as a wash and drink for boils. The boiled leaves were also applied as a poultice. The leaves had to be picked facing the sun[467] and after boiling, the liquid was drunk or used as a bath for gonorrhoea.[381]

The plant was used to cure convulsions caused by eating unprepared karaka kernels (*Corynocarpus laevigatus*) or at least to help straighten the limbs before death.[408] A decoction of the bark, macerated with water, stopped the flow of milk when applied to the breast.[10] [45] A decoction of kohekohe bark, manakura bark (*Melicytus micranthus*), puawananga vine (*Clematis paniculata*), korare stalk (*Phormium tenax*?), and kahikatoa leaves (*Leptospermum scoparium*) was taken three times a day before meals for female haemorrhage, bleeding piles, general blood disorders, kidney troubles, and skin eruptions. A decoction containing kohekohe bark and kareao roots (*Ripogonum scandens*) was taken three times daily before meals for venereal diseases.[424]

RELATED PHARMACOLOGY: The bark of *Dysoxylum decandrum* has a nauseating juice, said to be used in Java as a febrifuge and for chest complaints and colic, and also externally as an astringent. In the Philippines another species is said to be a fish poison.[102] *Dysoxylum lessertianum* has an odour of garlic and has been used as an insecticide.[420] In Fiji, *D. richii* is reputed to be a cure for most aches and pains[400] including toothache[465] and it is reported that the stomach was rubbed with a leaf of *D. richii* for sterility or frigidity in women.[532] The leaves of *D. hornei* have been used for blood in stools and for diarrhoea and *D. masta* leaves have been used in Samoa for diseases of the eye.[532] Several species of *Dysoxylum* are mentioned by Perry[403] as being used in medicine in Southeast Asia.

CHEMISTRY: Cambie[112] has investigated the heartwood and bark. β-sitosterol (see also p. 150) and much tannin have been found in both. The heartwood contains catechin, which is also found in catechu, useful in treatment of diarrhoea and throat infections.[195] The glyceride oil has been examined by Brooker[91] and found to be similar to that of *Trichilia hirta* (napahuite), used by Mexicans as a hair dressing.[187]

ILLUSTRATION: See page 177

MONIMIACEAE
Monimia family

Hedycarya arborea J. R. et G. Forst.
Pigeon wood
Porokaiwhiria, poporokaiwhiri

BOTANICAL NOTES: A small tree found in forests of the North Island and northern half of the

Hedycarya arborea (x 0.5). Engraving: S. Parkinson.

South Island. Forster's name of *Hedycarya* was supposed to have been given on account of the pleasant taste of the seeds, but Cheeseman[138] had never heard of their being eaten. The tree is classified as poisonous by Connor.[156]

MEDICAL USE: It was used in vapour baths.[233]

RELATED PHARMACOLOGY: In the Solomon Islands the leaves of *Hedycarya salomonensis* have been used to treat sores.[403]

CHEMISTRY: The leaves contain an unidentified alkaloid[118] and alkaloids have also been shown to be present in the bark[124] and berries.[119]

Laurelia novae-zelandiae A. Cunn.
Pukatea

BOTANICAL NOTES: A tall forest tree, found in swampy places, mainly in the North Island. The leaves are aromatic when crushed.

MEDICAL USE: The inner layer of bark was boiled with water and the decoction was applied to tuberculosic and chronic ulcers as well as various skin complaints. A strong decoction, or the pulped inner bark, held in the mouth, was said to relieve toothache[467][485] and was used internally and externally for syphilis.[233][331] The pulp of fresh bark steeped in hot water was taken for neuralgia.[390]

RELATED PHARMACOLOGY: *Laurelia aromatica* and *L. serrata* were medicinal plants of the Araucanos Indians.[243] The bark of *Nemuaron humboldtii* and *N. vieillardii* has been used by New Caledonian natives as a masticatory[419] while the bark of *Atherosperma moschatum* has been used by Australian Aborigines for rheumatism and syphilis.[178][330] *Nemuaron* and *Atherosperma* are now segregated in the Atherospermaceae.

CHEMISTRY: Pukatea bark contains the alkaloids pukateine and laureline. Pukateine has strong analgesic properties similar to those of morphine, but is without after-effects.[19][20][33][34][213] Bernauer and co-workers[52][512] have identified a total of ten different alkaloids in the bark, while Urzúa and Cassels have reported a further three.[495]

ILLUSTRATION: See page 178

MYOPORACEAE
Myoporum family

Myoporum laetum Forst.f.
Ngaio

BOTANICAL NOTES: A shrub, or small round-headed tree, found on the coasts of the North and South Islands. Every year ngaio takes its toll of livestock in New Zealand.[156]

MEDICAL USE: A young shoot or an infusion of the leaves was rubbed on the skin to prevent attacks of mosquito and sandfly.[2,304,485] The bark apparently healed ulcers and eruptions[485] and the inner bark was chewed for toothache, or rubbed on the gums and packed into the cavity.[2,54,233,390] However, MacMillan[346] has a reference to toothache being preferable to the cure! Twigs and leaves were used in the steam bath[233] and the leaves were used in an elaborate recipe for bruises.[390] The leaves, bruised and warmed to release the oil, made a most effective 'pack' for septic wounds. The drawing power was considerable, and veterinarians are reported to have used it in this way on horses.[408] One informant said a preparation made from ngaio leaves relieved baby eczema; another that ngaio leaves were used for sheep dip when nothing else was available.[424] Macdonald[341] reports that ngaio leaf buds were chewed for mussel poisoning. In the remarkable case of leprosy referred to in the section 'The Missionaries and Medicine' Mother Mary Aubert used a concentrated decoction of ngaio in the treatment.[418]

RELATED PHARMACOLOGY: *Myoporum deserti* of Australia is poisonous to sheep and cattle.[219] Its essential oil contains (-)-ngaione (see below) together with toxic and non-toxic sesquiterpene ketones.[247,256,480] *Myoporum sandwicense* has been used medicinally in Hawaii[532] and a decoction of the leaves of *M. tenuifolium* has been used in New Caledonia for toothache.[420] When attacked by insects *M. platycarpium* produces a manna which is sweet and slightly laxative. *Myoporum debile* was used for venereal disease in Australia,[166,322] and a decoction of *M. bontioides* is used in Taiwan as an antidote for poison.[403]

CHEMISTRY: The leaves contain mannitol[220] and ngaione.[67,342] Ngaione is an optical isomer of ipomeamarone derived from the sweet potato (cf. *Ipomoea*).[59] Ngaione is related to furfural, which has fungicidal and bactericidal powers and which has been used as a cure for athlete's foot and swimmer's itch.[491] Ngaione is toxic and causes liver damage similar to that seen in facial eczema of sheep.[173] Mannitol is used medicinally.[521]

Myoporum laetum (x 0.3). Engraving: S. Parkinson.

MYRSINACEAE
Myrsine family

Myrsine australis (A. Rich.) Allan
Red matipo
Mapau

BOTANICAL NOTES: A shrub or small tree, found throughout New Zealand in scrub and on the margins of forest. It has been known as *Suttonia australis* A. Rich. and *Rapanea australis* (A. Rich.) W.R.B. Oliver.

MEDICAL USE: The leaves were boiled and the liquid was taken for toothache.[267]

RELATED PHARMACOLOGY: *Myrsine* spp. have been used medicinally in Hawaii[532] and *M. africana* is reported to contain a saponin exhibiting chemotherapeutic action towards cancer.[330]

CHEMISTRY: Cambie and Couch[121] have found that the plant contains embelin, which also occurs in the fruits of *Embelia ribes*. This compound has been used in India as a remedy for skin disease and worms and as a general tonic.[488] The leaves of *Myrsine australis* also contain rutin,[121] which is used for the treatment of blood vessel problems (see under *Sophora*) and glucuronic acid, which is used for the relief of certain arthritic conditions.[521]

ILLUSTRATION: See page 178

MYRTACEAE
Myrtle family

Eucalyptus globulus Lab.
Blue gum

BOTANICAL NOTES: This tree has been introduced from Australia and planted widely in New Zealand.

MEDICAL USE: It was used in the post-partum bath and in post-partum haemorrhage. It was inhaled and taken internally as an infusion for asthma. Possibly missionaries taught the Maori the value of this tree.[45]

RELATED PHARMACOLOGY: *Eucalyptus globulus* is reported to cause contact dermatitis[330] and the leaves to act as an expectorant, antiseptic, and rubefacient.[490] In Australia, the leaves of the blue gum are still widely used as a household remedy in the treatment of many diseases and minor complaints. In Britain and Europe the essential oil, which is powerfully antiseptic, was given for fevers and febrile conditions, for pulmonary tuberculosis, and was applied or inhaled for relieving asthma, bronchitis, sore throat, croup, whooping cough, scarlet fever, and even diphtheria and typhoid. The dried leaves were also smoked like cigarettes for asthma while the oil in the form of an aperitif was taken as a digestive.[327] *Eucalyptus globulus* is used in the Philippines as an antiseptic and deodorant, for coughs, asthma, and as an insect repellent.[406] Numerous other *Eucalyptus* spp. are used in Australia for a variety of medicinal purposes.[166, 322, 329]

Eucalyptus spp. are reported to contain cyanogenic glycosides (capable of releasing hydrogen cyanide), to contain the vasopressor agent rutin and antidiarrhoeal agents, and to be used as expectorants.[330] *Eucalyptus rostrata* bark has an exudation (kino eucalypti[89]) which has been used for diarrhoea, sore throat, haemorrhage, and as an astringent.[178, 195]

Eucalyptus macrorhyncha and other species are a useful source of rutin, which strengthens capillary walls and may even be of use in haemophilia.[166]

CHEMISTRY: *Eucalyptus globulus* contains ellagic acid (see p. 126) in addition to many other polyphenols.[257]

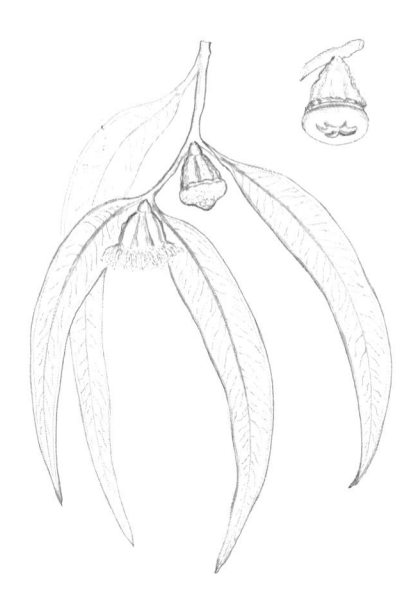

Eucalyptus globulus (x 0.3). Drawing: V. Cassie.

Leptospermum scoparium
J. R. et G. Forst.
Tea tree, red manuka
Manuka, kahikatoa

Kunzea ericoides (A. Rich) Thompson
Tree manuka, white manuka
Kanuka

BOTANICAL NOTES: *Leptospermum scoparium* is a shrub or small tree, abundant throughout New Zealand. The Maori name 'kahikatoa' is very similar to 'kahikatea' (*Dacrycarpus dacrydioides*) and it is possible that some of the uses have been assigned incorrectly. The name 'tea-plant' was given by Cook,[157] who remarked 'The leaves ... were used by many of us as tea, which has a very agreeable bitter and [sic] flavour, when they are recent, but loses some of both when they are dried. When the infusion was made strong, it proved emetic to some in the same manner as green tea.' The name 'tea-tree' was given by early settlers, who made 'tea' from the leaves.[484] ('Ti-tree' is sometimes wrongly used for this species; the name ti is properly applied to *Cordyline* spp.) Forms of this very variable species with single or double flowers, and white, pink, or red flowers, are popular shrubs in horticulture.

Kunzea ericoides, formerly *Leptospermum ericoides*, is separated from *L. scoparium* by its larger size, smaller leaves, flowers, and fruits, and is the white-wooded manuka referred to in the following notes.

MEDICAL USE: The leaves were used in vapour baths.[485] An infusion of this herb was regarded as 'peculiarly serviceable to persons in a reduced state whose previous moralities would not admit of the strictest investigation. It is very astringent.'[413] A decoction of leaves was taken for urinary and other internal complaints[485] and was also used as a febrifuge.[45] The white gum was applied to scalds and burns and given to sucklings and was also taken by adults to allay coughing. An infusion of the bark was used internally and externally as a sedative. A decoction of bark relieved diarrhoea and dysentery while a decoction of barks of manuka and kowhai (*Sophora* sp.) mixed with wood ash and dried was rubbed into the skin for various skin diseases.[54] [56] Sap drained from a length of tree trunk was used as a blood and breath purifier.

Leaves were boiled with water and the vapour was inhaled for colds. Leaves and bark were boiled and the decoction was applied for various pains such as stiff back. Seed capsules were boiled and the fluid was applied externally to reduce inflammation, e.g. in congestion of the chest. Young shoots were chewed and swallowed for dysentery.[2] The capsules were boiled and the liquid was taken for attacks of diarrhoea.[27] [505] The capsules were also chewed for dysentery[286] and a poultice of pounded capsules was used to dry an open wound or running sore.[346] Six to eight manuka capsules were chewed every ten minutes until the pains of colic subsided.[414]

The fragrant white-wooded manuka was said by natives to be the 'toa' or 'male' tree and the water in which its bark had been boiled was used as a medicine.[54] The water has also been used successfully for inflamed breasts.[522] An infusion of the barks of the kowhai (*Sophora*) and manuka trees was drunk for internal pains and applied outwardly for pains in the back and side.[54] The inner barks of manuka and totara (*Podocarpus*) were boiled and the liquid was kept in a closed bottle for a week. The liquid became sweetish and was used as a febrifuge.[45] The exudation from the tree, called pia, was collected for eating and was applied to burns and scalds; it also allayed coughing and relieved costiveness in children.[10] The bark was used to treat mouth, throat, and eye troubles[363] and the inner bark was boiled and the liquid was used as a mouthwash and gargle.[467] (See also under *Dysoxylum spectabile*, Meliaceae.)

RELATED PHARMACOLOGY: The essential oils of several species of Myrtaceae have been found to have activity against *Staphylococcus aureus*.[25] The seeds of a *Leptospermum* sp. (*ericoides* or *scoparium*) have been used in Hawaii for diarrhoea.[532] In Malaysia the leaves of *Leptospermum flavescens* have been made into a refreshing tea and used for fever, lassitude, dysmenorrhoea, to stimulate the appetite, and to relieve discomfort of the stomach. It has been applied externally for obstruction of the bowels and 'in a mysterious disease'. In the Moluccas the mountaineers distilled a little volatile aromatic oil from the plant which they inhaled for bronchitis and used as an embrocation for rheumatism.[102]

Melaleuca leucadendron has been used for healing wounds, rheumatism, stomach complaints,[474] and for toothache.[330] It was also used by the natives of Groote Eylandt in the Gulf of Carpentaria when young boys had difficulty passing urine. The penis was pricked with stiff fibres from the outer bark.[329] Steam distillation of *Melaleuca cajuputi* gives the cajuput oil of commerce, which is used for a variety of complaints.[322]

CHEMISTRY: *Leptospermum scoparium* contains leptospermone,[84] which has anthelmintic properties[79] and is closely related to compounds with similar medical properties in male fern. Leptospermone is an insecticide like valone,[298] which has a similar constitution.[69] Triterpene acids have been isolated from the bark, which also contains ursolic acid acetate not previously found in nature.[158] The bark also contains ellagic acid and O-methyl ethers of ellagic acid[108,336] (see p. 175). Pia (or manuka manna) is composed of mannitol[126] (see p. 168).

ILLUSTRATION: See page 178

Lophomyrtus bullata (A. Cunn.) Burr.
Native myrtle
Ramarama

BOTANICAL NOTES: A shrub or small tree, found in the margins of lowland forest in the North Island and northern part of the South Island. It was known as *Myrtus bullata* Sol. ex A. Cunn.

MEDICAL USE: The leaves were used in an elaborate recipe for bruises.[390]

RELATED PHARMACOLOGY: Several species of *Myrtus* were medicinal plants of the Araucanos Indians.[243] Leaves of *M. chequen* from Chile have been used for bronchitis.[357] Myrtol derived from *M. communis* is a powerful stimulant to the genito-urinary mucous membranes.[178]

CHEMISTRY: This plant contains bullatenone, which is a derivative of furfural known to have

Lophomyrtus bullata (x 0.5). Engraving: S. Parkinson.

antiseptic properties.[401] The bark contains ellagic acid and O-methyl ethers of ellagic acid[336] (see p. 175).

Lophomyrtus obcordata
(Raoul) Burr.
Rohutu

BOTANICAL NOTES: This shrub and the closely allied *Neomyrtus pedunculata* (Hook.f.) Allan are found throughout New Zealand. Both are known as 'rohutu', and it is possible that both were used for medicine. *Lophomyrtus obcordata* was known as *Myrtus obcordata* (Raoul) Hook.f. and *Neomyrtus pedunculata* was known as *Myrtus pedunculata* Hook.f.

MEDICAL USE: A preparation from bark and berries was taken for dysmenorrhoea.[54] [233]

CHEMISTRY: The bark of *Lophomyrtus obcordata* contains ellagic acid and O-methyl ethers of ellagic acid.[336] The essential oils of *L. obcordata* and *Neomyrtus pedunculata* have been examined by Briggs and co-workers.[80]

Lophomyrtus obcordata (x 1). Drawing: V. Cassie.

Metrosideros albiflora Sol. ex Gaertn.
White-flowered rata
Akatea

BOTANICAL NOTES: This handsome white-flowered climber is found only in the northern part of the North Island, usually in kauri forest. The name 'akatea' is applied to *M. albiflora* and the name 'aka' to several species of *Metrosideros*.

MEDICAL USE: For minor wounds a lotion made of the bark of fern-roots was used; for more severe wounds the inner bark of the akatea (*Metrosideros albiflora*) was used and it was reputed to be very efficacious — not merely as an antiseptic but to stop bleeding and lessen pain.[429]

It is possible that the plant discussed by Rout[429] belongs to another species of *Metrosideros* as other authors list similar uses under *M. robusta* and *M. scandens*. The sap of aka or akatea was obtained by cutting the living bark, and was used for female complaints such as uterine haemorrhage.[359]

RELATED PHARMACOLOGY: *Metrosideros collina* has been used in Hawaii for sickly children and against the pox. It contains a soporific agent.[532] Sawdust from *M. vera* is used in China to dry ulcers and the bark is used for leucorrhoea and diarrhoea.[403]

ILLUSTRATION: See page 195

Metrosideros excelsa Sol. ex Gaertn.
Christmas tree
Pohutukawa

BOTANICAL NOTES: A picturesque tree, common on northern coasts. It has been planted in temperate countries overseas and was formerly known as *M. tomentosa* A. Rich.

MEDICAL USE: An infusion of the inner bark was a valuable remedy for diarrhoea[27] [233] [294] [485] and was highly valued by bushmen as a remedy for dysentery.[304] Honey from the flowers was used for sore throat.[233]

CHEMISTRY: The flowers contain ellagic acid and gallic acid.[127] The barks of all New Zealand species which have been examined contain ellagic acid and O-methyl ethers of ellagic acid.[336] Ellagic acid has been used as an astringent in dysentery and diarrhoea. Gallic acid is weakly antiseptic and is used for a number of skin infections.[521]

ILLUSTRATION: See page 195

Metrosideros fulgens Sol. ex Gaertn.
Aka, akatawhiwhi, puatawhiwhi, aka kura

BOTANICAL NOTES: Bushmen quench thirst with the juice of the vine, which if cut and the bark left hanging exudes a large quantity of clear juice tasting somewhat like cider.[319] The identity of the various species of *Metrosideros* is discussed by Oliver[392] and prior to his paper this well-known vine was called *M. florida* Sm. Oliver identified it as *M. scandens* (J. R. et G. Forst.) Druce, but Allan[9] treats *M. scandens* and *M. florida* as synonyms of *M. fulgens*.

MEDICAL USE: The sap was used for eye troubles.[54] [233] The inner bark was used to heal sores and to stop bleeding; it had to be taken from the side on which the sun rises.[319] The inner bark was also boiled and the liquid was drunk for 'Maori sickness'.[467] The sap from short lengths of vine was blown on wounds.[2] [390] The juice of the stem was reputed to be a strengthening, slightly astringent beverage [27] which was also used as a cough mixture.[390] 'One Maori told me of a poisoned knee cured by this and karamu (*Coprosma robusta*), though the karamu seemed to feature most in the ceremonial part of the cure. Another told of a poisoned hand cured by aka. They seemed to regard it as highly as they do kumarahou (*Pomaderris elliptica*). Bushmen use it as an antiseptic.'[408]

CHEMISTRY: The bark contains ellagic acid,[336] which has been used as an astringent in dysentery and diarrhoea.

ILLUSTRATION: See page 195

Metrosideros robusta A. Cunn.
Rata

BOTANICAL NOTES: This forest tree usually

Left: *Hibiscus trionum* (x 0.5).
Painting: E. Blumhardt.

Below left: *Hoheria populnea* (x 0.3).
Painting: E. Blumhardt.

Below: *Dysoxylum spectabile* (x 0.3).
Painting: E. Blumhardt.

Myrsine australis. (x 0.3).

Laurelia novae-zelandiae (x 0.5).
Photo: J. E. Braggins.

Leptospermum scoparium (x 1.0).
Photo: J. E. Braggins.

commences life as an epiphyte. It occurs in both of the main islands and occasionally hybridises with *M. excelsa* in northern New Zealand.

MEDICAL USE: Flowers and bark as for *M. excelsa*. A lotion made from the bark was used for ringworm, aches, pains, and wounds.[54][233] Juice obtained by cutting and inverting the vine afforded a strengthening and astringent beverage — 'very wholesome';[27] however, according to Laing and Blackwell[319] this applied to *M. scandens*. The nectar was used for sore throat[160] and a decoction made by boiling pieces of bark in water was said to be an old-time lotion for wounds.[54] The bark was crushed, steeped, and boiled, and the liquid was applied externally to bruises and taken internally for colds.[414] The young leaves were chewed for toothache.[318]

CHEMISTRY: The bark contains tannin.[21] Several species of *Metrosideros* contain α-and β-pinene which are known for their antiseptic properties.[221]

ILLUSTRATION: See page 195

Syzygium maire (A. Cunn.) Sykes et Garnock-Jones
Black maire
Whawhakou, maire tawake

BOTANICAL NOTES: A lowland tree, found in swamp forest in the North Island and northern part of the South Island. This species was formerly known as *Eugenia maire* A. Cunn.

MEDICAL USE: The inner bark was used to treat ringworm.[485]

RELATED PHARMACOLOGY: *Eugenia apiculata* and *E. chequen* were medicinal plants of the Araucanos Indians.[243] The latter species is reputed to have been of value in catarrhal disorders of respiratory organs.[524] *Eugenia caryophyllata* is a Chinese tonic and digestive stimulant.[427] The oil of *E. caryophyllata* contains eugenol, which causes contact dermatitis but which has a local anaesthetic action and is mixed with zinc oxide and used as a temporary filling in order to disinfect root canals prior to permanent restoration of carious teeth.[330] The oil of cloves (*E. aromatica*) is well known for its value in dyspepsia, neuralgia, and flatulence. It also contains eugenol[195] and has bacterial and fungicidal properties.[171] A clove placed on an aching tooth is a well-known home remedy for toothache. *Eugenia jambolana* has been used as an astringent and diuretic. It has also been found to be useful in some cases of diabetes, as it reduces the amount of sugars in the urine in a very short time.[524]

In New Caledonia *E. mendute* leaves have been used as a weak laxative and vermifuge for infants and *E. uniflora* and *E. malaccensis* as a febrifuge, mouthwash for thrush, for eczema, and suppurating wounds.[420] In Tahiti *E. malaccensis* leaves have been used with those of *Terminalia catappa* for bronchitis and phthisis. The fruits of *E. jambos* have been used against biliousness and dysentery. The bark is tonic and astringent and a decoction of the root has been used for epilepsy.[399] A decoction of the bark of a *Eugenia* sp. has been used in Indonesia for diarrhoea and for the itch. In the Bahamas a decoction of *E. axillaris* has been used for diarrhoea and with *Bourreria ovata* for building blood and energy.[192] The fruits of *Eugenia* spp. are eaten in the Philippines for dysentery, while the bark is used for treating inflammation of the gums and for bathing wounds.[406]

CHEMISTRY: Dimethyl and trimethyl ethers of ellagic acid have been found in the bark of *Eugenia maire*.[76] [107] [336]

ILLUSTRATION: See page 196

ONAGRACEAE
Fuchsia family

Fuchsia excorticata
(J. R. et G. Forst.) Linn.f.
Tree fuchsia
Kotukutuku, kohutuhutu

BOTANICAL NOTES: A shrub or round-headed tree with flaking, yellow-brown bark, found in forest throughout New Zealand. It produces a large quantity of purple fruit of a rather sweet taste, somewhat astringent. According to Thomas Kirk it yielded a purple dye and afforded a good ink.[305]

MEDICAL USE: After confinement, Maori women sometimes used a vapour bath. Stones were heated and thrown in water in which various

Fuchsia excorticata (x 0.2). Engraving: S. Parkinson.

plants were steeped, such as tataramoa (*Rubus australis*), mangaeo (*Litsea calicaris*), and kotukutuku (*Fuchsia excorticata*). This bath was used twice — once on the first day and once on the second day — for an hour. If there was haemorrhage the water was taken internally.[48]

RELATED PHARMACOLOGY: *Fuchsia macrostemma* was a medicinal plant of the Araucanos Indians.[243]

PALMAE (Arecaceae) Palm family

Rhopalostylis sapida Wendl. et Drude
Nikau

BOTANICAL NOTES: The nikau palm is common in the northern part of the country and is a characteristic feature of the landscape. It was formerly known as *Areca sapida*. The central

Rhopalostylis sapida (x 0.03). Photo: J. E. Braggins.

shoot was eaten as a green vegetable on Cook's first voyage.[269]

MEDICAL USE: The slightly laxative pith was eaten by pregnant women to relax the pelvic muscles[45] [233] and the sap was also drunk to make labour in childbirth easier.[10] A packet of 'Mrs Subritzky's Nikau powder, for diarrhoea and dysentery' is kept at the Wagener Museum at Houhora Heads, Northland.

RELATED PHARMACOLOGY: *Areca catechu* (betel nut) contains the alkaloid arecoline which has some influence in muscle contraction.[391] The powdered nut is a well-known anthelmintic in Asia, especially against roundworms and tapeworms,[330] and is also used for a variety of other complaints.[403]

CHEMISTRY: The fatty acids from the seeds and fruit coat have been examined by Morice.[369] [370]

PASSIFLORACEAE
Passion-fruit family

Passiflora tetrandra
Banks et Sol. ex DC.
New Zealand passion-fruit
Kohia

BOTANICAL NOTES: A handsome climber, common in forests in the North Island and northern part of the South Island. It is also known as *Tetrapathaea tetrandra* (Sol.) Cheesem.

MEDICAL USE: The oil (called 'hinu kohia') from the seeds was applied to chronic sores, obstinate old wounds,[331] and chapped nipples[233] and was used for anointing the body.[150] The oil mixed with an equal part of a decoction of flax root (*Phormium tenax*) was used for flatulence.[233]

RELATED PHARMACOLOGY: *Passiflora foetida* has been used to cure itch. Hydrocyanic acid present might help in doing this.[102] *Passiflora incarnata* (passion-flower) was formerly prescribed as a

Passiflora tetrandra (x 0.4). Engraving: S. Parkinson.

nerve sedative, to relieve insomnia, and for treating certain types of convulsions and spasmodic disorders. It was also attributed with anodyne properties and was used in the treatment of various neuralgias and for epilepsy. Now it is an ingredient of certain types of sleeping pills.[330] In cases of overwork it is both invigorating and soothing.[443]

In the Bahamas the juice of the vine of *P. cupraea* (lizard's tail) has been applied to cuts; it burns and kills the surrounding flesh to ensure clean healing.[192] In New Caledonia *Passiflora* spp. have been used as insecticides and anthelmintics; *P. laurifolia* fruits are reported to be an excellent remedy for boils while the leaves of *P. foetida* are pectoral and have been used as an emmenagogue.[420] Small doses of the root of *P. quadrangularis* act as a vermifuge but in large amounts they are narcotic and poisonous. The leaves are used in the Philippines as a dressing for itch.[403]

CHEMISTRY: The seed oil is rich in colouring matter of unknown constitution and is unusual in containing a significant amount of margaric (heptadecanoic) acid.[92] The fruit contains the cyanoglucosides, tetraphyllin A, tetraphyllin B,[437] epitetraphyllin B, and deidaclin.[471]

PIPERACEAE
Pepper family

Macropiper excelsum (Forst.f.) Miq.
Pepper-tree
Kawakawa

BOTANICAL NOTES: The New Zealand pepper-tree is found near the coast throughout New Zealand. Formerly it was known as *Piper excelsum* Forst.f.

MEDICAL USE: The bitter root was found serviceable for urinary complaints.[413] The leaf and bark

Macropiper excelsum (x 0.2). Engraving: S. Parkinson.

were cures for cuts, wounds, and pains in the stomach; kawakawa was also used for gonorrhoea[45] and in making steam baths.[484] Its effects were reported to be stimulating; it excited the salivary glands, the kidneys, and the bowels slightly, and was an aphrodisiac. The fruit and seeds, ripe or unripe, were more powerful than the leaves although the latter were generally used.[27] It was used as an aromatic diuretic and was said to be useful as an anthelmintic, and as a counter-irritant in toothache.[45]

A decoction of the leaves was also drunk for boils[24] [54] and the leaves were also wilted over a fire to free the oil, and applied to boils.[230] The leaf was used for the paipai, a skin disease,[294] and a decoction of boiled leaves was drunk for kidney trouble and as a general tonic. Boiled with bark of onga-onga (tree nettle) it was used externally and internally for eczema and venereal disease.[2] The hot liquid from kawakawa leaves was also a treatment for serious bruises[2] [390] [463] and colds.[346] The leaves were chewed for toothache, or reduced to a pulp in hot water and applied to the face when swollen; also to any part of the body for rheumatic pains. A decoction of leaves and young twigs macerated in hot water was taken for pains in the stomach, or it might be drunk hot over a period of several days for gonorrhoea.[233] [380] The juice expressed from the roasted leaves was said to make an excellent dressing for bad wounds[159] and a decoction of the leaves was used as a blood purifier and for bladder complaints.[408] The ripe fruit and the liquid from boiled roots were applied to sore teeth.[310]

RELATED PHARMACOLOGY: The green leaves and branches were gathered by the Maori and laid in rows in the plantations of kumara or sweet potatoes, between the beds, and there burnt so that insects which injured the growing plants might be destroyed by the disagreeable bitter smoke.[151] [331] For a discussion of the Fijian species see ref. 400. Fijian 'kava' is made from the rhizome and roots of *P. methysticum*[357] (for a discussion see refs. 330 and 475). In New Caledonia the leaves of *P. austro-caledonicum* and *P. methysticum* have been chewed for bronchitis. *Piper austro-caledonicum* is also a remedy against asthma and tuberculosis. Sap from the trunk is abortifacient.[419]

In the Marind area of western New Guinea where *Piper methysticum* is known as wati[35] it has been used by natives as a tonic and soporific.[498] It is also valuable in gonorrhoea and inflammation of the uterus.[324] Numerous examples of the medicinal use of *P. methysticum* in Tahiti,[399] Hawaii, Tubuai, Fiji and other 'South Pacific Islands'[532] as well as Southeast Asia[403] have been recorded. It has been used as a panacea for a variety of common complaints. Black pepper (*P. nigrum*) contains piperine which is a febrifuge, stomachic, and antiperiodic. The rubefacient effect of *P. bantamense* and some other Malaysian spp. is so intense that they have been used by the natives as counter-irritants in poultices, for headaches and other pains. Leaves of *P. angustifolium* have served as a mild tonic, stimulant, and internal styptic. Fruits of *P. baccatum* have been used in tonics in Java and Borneo and a decoction of the root has been used for treating venereal disease in Malaysia.[102] Extracts of the fruit of *P. aurantiacum* produced strong stimulation of the uterus and intestines.[18]

The leaves of *P. puberulum*, *P. graeffei*, *P. latifolium*, and *P. tristachyon* have been used for a variety of complaints in Samoa, Fiji, Tubuai, and the Marquesas, especially for skin sores, to control menstrual bleeding, and to retard a threatened abortion.[532] Many medicinal uses, both internal and external, have been ascribed to *P. puberulum*. For example the crushed leaves are applied to wounds to promote healing, and they may be used for toothache. In Fiji the crushed leaves of *Macropiper timothianum* are sometimes used for dressing wounds, while the liquid squeezed from the leaves of *M. vitiense* is used for healing wounds.[465]

Piper novae-hollandiae is chewed by Australian Aborigines for sore gums. It is an excellent stimulant for the mucous membrane and it is also used to treat gonorrhoea. Alcoholic extracts are reputed to have shown activity against lung cancer.[166] Decoctions of the leaves, roots, stems, and fruit of *Piper* spp. have been used in Brazil and Panama for relieving toothache. *Piper medium* has been used in Costa Rica as an antidote for snake bite.[330] *Piper capense* has been used in Western Province of South Africa for stomach, heart, and kidney diseases, and *P. betle* has been used in stomach complaints and for preserving the teeth.[509] Medicinal uses of other *Piper* spp. have been listed by Perry.[403]

CHEMISTRY: *Macropiper excelsum* contains myristicin, related to eugenol, which is a mild antiseptic and is used to allay toothache[69] as a dental analgesic.[521] The leaves and wood contain a series of lignans,[74] [435] while the plant has been reported to contain an insect juvenile hormone mimic.[388]

PITTOSPORACEAE

Pittosporum family

Pittosporum eugenioides A. Cunn.
Lemonwood
Tarata

BOTANICAL NOTES: A small tree, found throughout New Zealand. It is sometimes planted in gardens as an ornamental.

MEDICAL USE: The flowers are highly fragrant and were mixed with fat and used by the Maori to anoint the body.[139] The leaves were also bruised and mixed with fat for this purpose.[304] Resinous gum, obtained by making longitudinal cuts in the bark, was eaten for foul breath.[233] The Maori mixed the resinous exudation with juice of sow thistle (*Sonchus*) and worked it into a ball which they chewed.[319] The gum was used to perfume titoki and kohia oil.[150,304] The leaves of the tarata, chewed and made into a kind of paste, have been reported to quickly cure raw places on a saddle-sore horse.[159] A case of severe allergy to the dispersed seeds and fine hairs from the related New Zealand species *P. crassifolium* (karo) has been recorded.[385]

RELATED PHARMACOLOGY: *Pittosporum ferrugineum* (Australia to Burma) was used by Malays, who made poultices from both leaves and roots for malaria.[102] *Pittosporum ferrugineum* and other species are included in the *Philippine National Formulary*[406] for fever and cough, and also as an aromatic bath following childbirth or prolonged illness. *Pittosporum resiniferum* was used as a universal remedy in the Philippines.[496] *Pittosporum* spp. have medicinal value in India[110] and have been used as fish poisons in Fiji.[224] *Pittosporum brackenridgei* leaves and an infusion of the leaves and bark of *P. rhytidocarpum* have been used in Fiji for coughs. The latter infusion of the leaves and bark of *P. rhytidocarpum* has been used in Fiji and Tonga to ease childbirth and the outer layer of the fruit of *P. hosmeri* has been used in Hawaii for abscesses.[532]

Pittosporum phylliraeoides has been used in Australia for many medicinal purposes including the encouragement of the flow of milk after childbirth. Infusions of the plant were used internally by Aborigines for pain and cramps, eczema, and colds, etc.[322] *Pittosporum venulosum* from Australia is reported to have aphrodisiac properties.[166] *Pittosporum pickeringii* is used in Fiji for stomach troubles.[465] Several *Pittosporum* spp. are listed by Perry[403] as medicinal plants in Southeast Asia. *Pittosporum tobira* has been found by Belgian workers to have strong antiviral activity.[497]

CHEMISTRY: The essential oil of *Pittosporum eugenioides* is remarkable in containing nonane as the major constituent.[133] The heartwood contains scoparone (6,7-dimethoxycoumarin).[118] The roots of the related *P. crassifolium* contain an acetylenic alcohol and ketone.[63]

ILLUSTRATION: See page 196

Pittosporum tenuifolium
Sol. ex Gaertn.
Kohukohu

BOTANICAL NOTES: Goldie[233] identified 'kohukohu' as *Pittosporum obcordatum* Raoul but this tree is rare and local in distribution. In Williams' Maori dictionary[517] and other authoritative works the name 'kohukohu' is identified as the common *Pittosporum tenuifolium*, which is found throughout New Zealand. It is planted in many countries overseas as an ornamental tree.

MEDICAL USE: It was used for itch, eczema of the scalp, and other skin diseases. Certain parts

Pittosporum tenuifolium (x 0.2). Engraving: S. Parkinson.

of the kohukohu were dried in the sun, pounded into a dust and mixed into a paste with hinu kohia (oil from the seeds of *Passiflora tetrandra*).[233] A gum-resin from the plant was used to perfume titoki and kohia oils.[150] The fresh gum-resin mixed with the thickened juice of the puwha (*Sonchus oleraceus*) was chewed as a masticatory.[150] The leaves were used in a recipe for ague[390] (see under *Phormium*). The kohukohu was used by the Maori priest to raise the tapu on sick people.[54]

CHEMISTRY: The essential oil contains α-pinene as the major constituent.[111]

PLANTAGINACEAE
Plantain family

Plantago sp.
Plantain
Kopakopa, parerarera

BOTANICAL NOTES: In Williams' Maori dictionary, fifth edition, the term 'kopakopa' was identified as *Plantago* spp. but in the seventh edition[517] it is identified as *Myosotidium hortense*, a giant forget-me-not found only in the Chatham Islands. Taylor[485] and Andersen[10] identified 'kopakopa' as plantain, and Goldie[233] and Adams[2] regarded it as *P. major* L. This is a common introduced weed. There are a number of native species and probably the term was used in a generic sense (see also *Cardiomanes reniforme*, Filices).

MEDICAL USE: Plantain leaves are supposed to take away pain.[45] Boiled leaves were used for ulcers; the upper side drew and when the wound began to heal the under-side was applied. The liquid in which leaves were boiled was used for scalds and burns and internally as a uterine stimulant.[233 380 485]

A decoction of leaves of *Plantago*, clover, and sow thistle was mixed with salt, and drunk in cases of retention of the placenta.[54] Juice obtained by bruising leaves and squeezing out

Plantago raoulii (x 0.2).
Engraving:
S. Parkinson.

juice, heating leaves and squeezing out juice, or boiling leaves with water, was used for cuts and boils, particularly when septic, and for cracked lips.[2] The leaves were bruised and used as a pack on a suppurating leg[354] and were also applied as a pack on boils and burns.[287] The plant was boiled and the liquid and steam were applied to piles.[361] Both green leaves and an infusion from boiled leaves were used for cuts.[523]

RELATED PHARMACOLOGY: *Plantago* leaves are official in many continental pharmacopoeias as an emollient and for curing inflammation of the gums. The seeds are stimulating, tonic, and antidysenteric[496] and have been used for prolapsed bowel.[36]

The wound-healing properties of *Plantago* spp. are well known (for example, see ref. 5) and ointments based on them have been patented.[260] Seeds of many species liberate abundant mucilage.[212] Le Strange[327] has discussed the pharmacology of *Plantago* spp. in detail. *Plantago major* was said by Dioscorides and Galen to be valuable internally and externally. Every part has been used since remote times. In Hawaii *P. major* leaves have been used for skin troubles, for hygiene of the female sexual organs, and for non-infectious weaknesses in children.[532] *Plantago major* has also been rubbed on the skin to relieve bee stings.[330] It is included in the *Philippine National Formulary*[406] as a remedy for inflammation of the gums and for skin irritation. Compounds isolated from the leaves of *P. major* are reputed to have healing effects[360] and some effect on reducing total lipids, triglycerides, cholesterol, and lepoproteins in blood.[348] Aqueous extracts of the plant have anti-inflammatory effects and strengthen capillary walls,[320] while plantaglucide, isolated from the leaves, showed anti-gastric ulcer activity.[502] An extract of the plant is included as a mild sedative in a patented preparation for breaking the smoking habit.[224]

The leaves of the English plantain (*P. lanceolata*) are reported to be astringent, to soothe irritation, to protect mucous membranes, and to be expectorant.[212][490] With *P. major* it is used medicinally in New Caledonia.[420] The seeds of *P. ovata* and *P. psyllium* absorb water and act as purgatives.[330][524] In Russia a small root of *P. media* has been placed in the ear of the affected side in order to relieve toothache. Fibrous strands from the petiole of *P. major* have been used in Europe in the same manner.[330] *Plantago psyllium* seeds (flea seeds) are in general used in Britain for habitual constipation.[473]

Perry[403] lists several medicinal uses for *Plantago* spp. in Southeast Asia; in other places recorded uses are for catarrh, bronchitis, asthma, sore throats, and eye complaints.[443] A review on the history and use of *Plantago* spp. as medicinal plants has been published.[308]

CHEMISTRY: The active agent in *Plantago* spp. appears to be aucubin, a glucoside derived from furfural, which is known to have bactericidal powers[102][242] (cf. ngaione under Myoporaceae). Aucubin is a potent liver-protecting agent as shown by its effect on livers damaged by carbon tetrachloride.[529] Both aucubin and a haemolytic saponin fraction from plantain leaves were active against *Micrococcus flavus* and *Staphylococcus aureus*.[483]

POLYGONACEAE
Dock family

Polygonum decipiens R. Br.
Tutunawai

BOTANICAL NOTES: O'Carroll[390] refers to 'tutuna', which Skinner[463] identified as possibly *P. serrulatum*, now known as *P. decipiens*. It is a common water plant throughout New Zealand and is also found in Tasmania and continental Australia.

MEDICAL USE: It was boiled with other plants to make an internal remedy for rheumatic pains.[390]

RELATED PHARMACOLOGY: *Polygonum decipiens* is

193

listed by Connor[156] among other poisonous *Polygonum* spp. in New Zealand but he indicates that it has not been associated with any known case of poisoning. *Polygonum glabrum* (*P. imberbe*) is reputed to be particularly useful in Tahiti for urethritis,[399] and also for heartburn in alcoholics, neuralgia, headache, amenorrhoea, dysmenorrhoea (painful menstruation), epidermomycosis, and jaundice.[403] The leaves have been used in Tubuai for gonorrhoea and 'yellow urine'.[532] It is not poisonous.[403]

Perry[403] lists several *Polygonum* spp. used medicinally in Southeast Asia but there is no specific reference to rheumatism. In Indonesia, *P. orientale* is especially recommended for arthritis of the knees.[403] An infusion of *P. aviculare* is a mild astringent[212][330] and has been used in Uruguay for rheumatism.[509] *Polygonum hydropiper* (smartweed) has styptic and diuretic effects[490] and has been used for rheumatism, generalised oedema, for amenorrhoea, and as an emmenagogue.[212] According to Culpeper, 'The juice destroys worms in the ears, being dropped into them' and 'if strewed in a chamber, it will soon kill all the fleas.'[524] It has been used in Australia as a stimulant, diuretic, and emmenagogue. The juice is haemostatic and is also used for treating sores on horses.[322] Chromatographic fractions from alcoholic extracts of *P. hydropiper* root showed antifertility effects in female rats.[223]

Polygonum punctatum (water smartweed), containing ca. seven percent calcium oxalate in the leaves, is poisonous to man and may be fatal to livestock. In England the root of *P. bistorta* was mixed equally with *Anacyclus pyrethrum* and alum, beaten into a paste with honey, and placed into carious teeth or held between the teeth.[330] The root of *P. bistorta* has also been used for diarrhoea and in veterinary medicine.[212] Knot weeds (*Polygonum* spp.) contain substances with prostaglandin-like activity.[398] *Polygonum multiflorum* significantly lowers blood cholesterol.[356]

CHEMISTRY: A number of *Polygonum* spp. contain

Polygonum decipiens (x 0.5). Drawing: V. Cassie.

Metrosideros albiflora (x 0.5). Photo: J. E. Braggins.

Left: *Metrosideros excelsa* (x 0.3). Painting: F. Osborne.

Below left: *Metrosideros fulgens* (x 0.3). Painting: F. Osborne.

Below: *Metrosideros robusta* (x 0.5). Photo: J. E. Braggins.

Above: *Syzygium maire* (x 1.0). Photo: J. E. Braggins.

Right: *Pittosporum eugenioides* (x 0.5). Photo: J. E. Braggins.

Below: *Knightia excelsa* (x 0.3). Painting: E. Blumhardt.

compounds with medicinal properties. For example, *P. coriarum* contains proanthocyanidins, which are reported to have antineoplastic properties,[142] *P. aubertii* contains the anthraquinone emodin,[525] while anthraquinones are also found in *P. ciliinerve*[249] and *P. sacchalinense*.[288] *Polygonum perfoliatum*, which shows antihypertensive effects, contains 3,3'-dimethylellagic acid, which has a significant effect on blood pressure.[333]

Rumex sp.
Dock
Paewhenua, runa

BOTANICAL NOTES: The plant concerned is probably an introduced weed. The species in New Zealand which is responsible for the poisoning of livestock is *Rumex acetosella*.[151]

MEDICAL USE: Children applied the sap of dock leaves to abrasions.[54] The dock was used in ways similar to those listed for plantain. The moist inner shoot of the dock was used on cracked lips[2] and the leaves were used on boils.[381]

RELATED PHARMACOLOGY: *Rumex* spp. are reported to be aeroallergens[330] and to act as laxatives.[212,330] The juice of dock or sorrel (*Rumex* spp.) is used in home remedies for relief from pain and itching. For example, the stinging rash obtained from stinging nettles (*Urtica* spp.) is reported to be best treated with the juice of dock. *Rumex acetosa* has been used in Transvaal and in France for boils.[509] It is reported to contain some polysaccharides which are antitumour agents.[279]

The root of *R. crispus*, which contains tannins and the anthraquinone emodin, is a purgative and the fruit is reputed to control diarrhoea.[490] *Rumex giganteus* has been used in Hawaii for leprosy and non-infectious diseases of children.[532] *Rumex verticillata* (swamp dock) was used

Rumex flexuosus (x 0.5).
Engraving:
S. Parkinson.

by North American Indians for jaundice.[330] *Rumex hymenosepalus* contains a tannin which yields leucoanthocyanidins on hydrolysis. It is reported to have chemotherapeutic properties towards cancer.[330] The root of *R. aquaticus* is an alterative, deobstruent, and detergent and has been used for cleansing ulcers in affections of the mouth. As a powder it has cleansing and detergent effects upon the teeth.[524] *Rumex crispus, R. romasa,* and *R. sanguineus* were medicinal plants of the Araucanos Indians.[243]

Polyphenols from *R. confertus* and preparations from the plant produced vasoconstriction and decreased vascular permeability. One constituent, leucodelphinidin, had inotropic effects on the heart, and anti-oedemic effects on joints following experimental inflammation.[181] A naphthatriol derivative from the root and rhizome of *R. japonicus* has strong fungicidal properties when applied in ointments and lotions.[314] The active antifungal principle nepodin has been isolated from nine *Rumex* spp., which have all been attributed to the Chinese herb medicine Yang-ti.[264] Constituents of *R. maritimus* are also toxic *in vitro* to ringworm fungi.[4] Extracts of *R. wallachii*, grown in Victoria, which contain anthracene derivatives have proved to be very efficient laxatives and purgatives.[145] An extract of the bulbs of *R. chalerpensis*, which contains the anthraquinones chrysophanol and emodin, has haemostatic properties.[202] A review on the feasibility of using *Rumex* spp. in therapy has been published.[28]

CHEMISTRY: *Rumex* spp. contain albumen tannates, which may replace ordinary tannin in skin treatment.[172] They also contain soluble oxalates, which are toxic if eaten in large quantities, particularly by sheep.[330] *Rumex acetosella* contains rutin (see p. 125), and the anthraquinones chrysophanol and emodin. The latter has cathartic properties.[358]

PROTEACEAE
Protea family

Knightia excelsa R. Br.
Honeysuckle
Rewarewa

BOTANICAL NOTES: A tall handsome tree, common in the North Island and about the northern coast of the South Island.

MEDICAL USE: The inner part of the bark was bandaged over a wound to check bleeding and heal it.[390]

CHEMISTRY: The bark contains β-sitosterol (see p. 68) and a leucocyanidin.[73]

ILLUSTRATION: See page 196

RANUNCULACEAE

Ranunculus or buttercup family

Clematis forsteri Gmel.
Pikiarero

BOTANICAL NOTES: A climber, found in the North Island and northern part of the South Island. It is separated from *C. paniculata* by its smaller stems, leaves, and flowers. It was known as *C. hexasepala* DC.

MEDICAL USE: A decoction of the bark and stems of the pikiarero and the root of the tatarahake (*Coprosma acerosa*) was taken as a mild alterative.[150] It has been reported that the sap was blown onto styes and was used for horses' chafed fetlocks.[341] Fulton[216] notes that 'the leaves were used by the Maori as a blister or counter-irritant'.

RELATED PHARMACOLOGY: *Clematis erecta* is reported to be useful in a number of skin complaints and eruptions.[246] *Clematis glycinoides* has a rubefacient and blistering sap. The root and stem are drastic, dangerous purgatives[419] and a decoction of the leaves has been used for sinusitis.[420] Referring to its use in Australia, Cribb and Cribb[166] report that 'This bush remedy for headaches gives more innocent pleasure to the person administering it than to the sufferer'. The effects are devastating but as a cure, some say it is effective. *Clematis microphylla* is also used medicinally in Australia.[322] *Clematis anthusaefolia* is used as an anti-rheumatic in China.[105]

Clematis forsteri (x 1). Photo: J. E. Braggins.

Several *Clematis* spp. are used medicinally in Southeast Asia.[403] *Clematis chinensis* has been used as an analgesic, for rheumatism, as a diuretic, laxative, and for malaria.[427] *Clematis* spp. are reported to cause contact dermatitis and to exert diuretic effects. In tropical America an ointment for skin complaints has been made from the leaves of *C. dioica*.[330] Several species of *Clematis* have been used in Africa for colds and *C. hirsuta* and *C. sinensis* have been applied to septic lesions.[509]

CHEMISTRY: See *Ranunculus*.

Clematis paniculata (x 0.5). Photo: J. E. Braggins.

Clematis paniculata Gmel.
Puawananga

BOTANICAL NOTES: A climber, found throughout New Zealand. The large white flowers are a fine sight in the springtime. It was known as *C. indivisa* Willd.

MEDICAL USE: Leaves were applied to produce blisters as a counter-irritant[233] and the sap was blown onto wounds.[2] The bark and some of the wood of puawananga were scraped and the shavings were inhaled for colds in the head.[318] (See also under *Dysoxylum spectabile*, Meliaceae.)

RELATED PHARMACOLOGY: A species named as *Clematis paniculata* but not identical with the New Zealand plant is used in China for scrofulous sores and is said to be sudorific and to be an antidote for mercuric sulphide.[403]

Ranunculus reflexus Garnock-Jones
Kopukapuka, maruru

BOTANICAL NOTES: This buttercup is abundant and variable and occurs throughout New Zealand in wet places. *Ranunculus reflexus* is listed by Connor[156] as a poisonous plant but 'in New Zealand no suspicion attaches to it.'

MEDICAL USE: The plant was used for toothache, inflamed eyes, and abrasions.[56] The soreness of the eyes was confined to redness at the corners. A certain amount of magic was connected with the treatment for toothache since the sufferer had to hold the leaves between the teeth without seeing them.[54]

RELATED PHARMACOLOGY: *Ranunculus* spp. have been used to treat abrasions, toothache, and rheumatism.[330] *Ranunculus ficaria* is astringent and has been used chiefly for piles for which it is almost a specific.[524] The Xhosa of Africa have used *R. multifidus* for sore throat and mumps.[509] The roots and leaves of *Ranunculus sceleratus* are used in China for treatment of rheumatism.[105]

CHEMISTRY: Many plants of *Clematis* and *Ranunculus* spp. contain substances which give rise to protoanemonin through enzyme action when the plant is crushed.[262] Protoanemonin has a pronounced vesicant action, is an active vermifuge, and is probably responsible for antimicrobial activity.[261] [357] [531] Hay containing *Ranunculus* is not dangerous to livestock since protoanemonin is unstable, polymerising to the inert non-toxic anemonin.

Ranunculus reflexus (x 0.3). Engraving: S. Parkinson.

Ranunculus amphitrichus
Colenso
Waoriki, raoriki

BOTANICAL NOTES: An abundant, variable little buttercup, found in wet places throughout New Zealand. Waoriki is undoubtedly the most toxic native species of *Ranunculus* and many poisonings have been attributed to it, especially in the North Island; the fact that it grows in water increases the chances of poisoning in stock.[156]

MEDICAL USE: Expressed juice has blistering properties and was used for rheumatism and other painful joint diseases.[233] The herb was boiled and the liquid gargled for quinsy.[414]

Ranunculus amphitrichus (x 0.5). Engraving: S. Parkinson.

CHEMISTRY: Connor[156] reports that ranunculin (0.7 percent of fresh weight), a glycoside which gives rise to the vesicant protoanemonin, has been isolated from the species.

RHAMNACEAE
Buckthorn family

Pomaderris kumeraho A. Cunn.
Poverty weed, gumdigger's soap
Kumarahou, papapa

BOTANICAL NOTES: A common shrub in the northern part of New Zealand. It is planted in gardens as an ornamental. Formerly it was known as *P. elliptica* Lab. Both the leaves and flowers produce a lather when rubbed between the hands in water.

MEDICAL USE: The leaves were boiled and the liquid was taken internally as a well-known relief for all chest complaints, bronchitis, and pulmonary tuberculosis. It was said to have beneficial effects on the kidneys and in heartburn,[2] to be an excellent blood purifier, and to have been used with good effect for a case of diabetes.[408] It was used for coughs and sores,[363] colds, constipation, and asthma.[414] It was sometimes used as a bath and was said to be good for the skin, especially for children.[467]

Kumarahou mixed with other herbs, particularly koromiko, was marketed by the Rev. Edgar Ward (1863-1934) under the name

'Kuranui' and claimed to be a specific for tuberculosis and asthma. Ward, who qualified as a pharmacist before entering the ministry, was at one stage Vicar of Kaitaia and it is stated by his daughter[273] that he cured many cases of tuberculosis there among the Maori using kumarahou. In his later years he operated a free clinic in Auckland from which he dispensed advice on a variety of ailments. His regular advertisements in *The Weekly News* (Auckland) had the usual claims and testimonials which were common at the time for patent medicines. An ointment made from kumarahou was sold in Auckland for skin cancer and was used as a medicine at Te Kao many years ago.[389]

RELATED PHARMACOLOGY: In New Caledonia the fresh bark of *Pomaderris* or *Alphitonia neocaledonica* was pounded and a lotion of it was applied for eczema and other skin troubles, as well as for rheumatic pains.[419] *Alphitonia ziziphoides* has been used in Fiji for earache and in Samoa for swellings and fever.[532] In Tahiti it has been used as a lotion for eczema and pityriasis, and as a febrifuge.[399]

Cascara sagrada comes from *Rhamnus purshiana* in the same family. Several *Rhamnus* spp. contain anthraquinone glycosides and thus are useful

Pomaderris kumeraho (x 0.2). Photo: J. E. Braggins.

in constipation.[195] [212] [330] *Rhamnus prinoides* has been used in Africa by the Zulu as a blood purifier, by the Sotho for pneumonia, and by the Chagga for colic. *Ziziphus micronata* has been used in Africa for chest complaints.[509]

CHEMISTRY: The leaves and flowers of *Pomaderris kumeraho* have been shown to contain the flavonols, quercetin and kaempferol, and ellagic acid (see p. 126) and its O-methyl ethers.[109]

ROSACEAE
Rose family

Acaena anserinifolia
(J. R. et G. Forst.) Druce
Bidi-bid
Hutiwai, piripiri

BOTANICAL NOTES: A creeping herb, common throughout New Zealand. The barbed fruits frequently become entangled in the wool of sheep and reduce the value of the fleece. The plant is grown in rockeries and hanging baskets as an ornamental. It was formerly known as *A. sanguisorbae* Vahl.

MEDICAL USE: Leaves, boiled or steeped in hot water, were applied to open wounds or rubbed on contusions. They were also applied to external genitals in cases of painful micturition.[54] [233] A decoction of leaves was taken internally as a tonic and as a remedy for rheumatism, kidney trouble, bladder trouble, and venereal disease.[2] [390] [467] It was used to feed young babies when the mothers could not suckle them[227] and was also used for stomach troubles.[363] An aqueous extract was used to treat an itchy skin disease known as 'hakihaki'[205] and an extract has been sold by herbalists. An infusion of the whole plant was used for gallstones[341] and as a tea both in New Zealand and Australia.[305]

RELATED PHARMACOLOGY: An infusion was used in veterinary medicine to prevent scour in calves.[24] *Acaena* spp. were medicinal plants of

Acaena anserinifolia (x 0.5). Engraving: S. Parkinson.

the Araucanos Indians.[243] Rose hips have been used as a source of vitamin C. *Prunus persica* is said to be used for instability of the bladder.[509]

CHEMISTRY: The alkanes of the stems and leaves have been examined by Eglinton and co-workers.[191]

Geum urbanum L.
Common avens, herb-bennett
Kopata

BOTANICAL NOTES: The variety of this widespread species which occurs in New Zealand and Australia is known as var. *strictum* (Ait.) Hook.f.

MEDICAL USE: The leaf is astringent and was used for diarrhoea and dysentery. It was also taken for foul breath.[233]

RELATED PHARMACOLOGY: The root of *Geum urbanum* acts as an astringent, antiseptic, and digestant and it shows anti-inflammatory and slight anaesthetic properties.[178] [212] [490] Teas or infusions of the dried herb or root are still given by herbalists as a tonic, in cases of dyspepsia, general debility, and body weakness, and as an astringent for relaxed throats.[327] [524] *Agrimonia gryposepala* contains tannin and vegetable oil and has been used as a vegetable astringent.[487] *Agrimonia eupatoria* (common agrimony) has been known as a medicinal herb since the time of the Greeks.[327] It provokes photodermatitis but also produces a mild astringent effect and has been used to treat diarrhoea as well as liver ailments.[330]

CHEMISTRY: The essential oil contains eugenol (see p. 240). The plant is rich in tannins and contains ellagic acid derivatives (see p. 126). The leaves show transglycosylase activity.[257]

Rubus cissoides A. Cunn.
Bush lawyer
Tataramoa

BOTANICAL NOTES: The common name 'bush lawyer' refers to the clinging habit of the vine. It is found in forest throughout New Zealand. Cheeseman's name for the plant was *R. australis* Forst.f.

MEDICAL USE: The bark was boiled and the liquor was taken as a purgative in cases of severe abdominal pain.[331] It was also used in vapour baths to assist in childbirth and a decoction was taken to relieve dysmenorrhoea.[233] The root bark was reputed to be of great value as a remedy for diarrhoea and dysentery.[423] An infusion of the leaves is reputed to have relieved congestion in the chest, hard cough, and sore throat. It was said that a stiff dose acted as a laxative.[359] A few leaves of senna or korokio (*Corokia buddleoides*?) were sometimes added to the infusion. For stomach-ache the young leaves of tataramoa were chewed and swallowed[467] and they were also reported to be a very good

Rubus cissoides (× 0.2).
Painting:
E. Blumhardt.

remedy for toothache.[503] (See also under *Meryta* (Araliaceae), *Typha* (Typhaceae), and *Phormium* (Agavaceae).)

RELATED PHARMACOLOGY: The French in New Caledonia have used the local species in gargles or infusions, as astringents, and as aperitifs.[419] Malays have used local species for dysentery, urinary trouble, and fever. For a period of seven days after childbirth Malaysian women used a vapour bath made from boiling water in which leaves of *Rubus* sp. had been steeped.[102] Leaves of blackberry, raspberry, and dewberry were old-world domestic remedies for mild diarrhoea on account of their tonic and astringent properties. Blackberry (*R. fruticosus*), which contains Vitamin C, was considered to be a powerful astringent and was used for all kinds of bleeding. Bruised leaves were used for gangrenous ulcers.[36] Raspberry (*R. idaeus*) contains a relaxing agent for uterine muscle.[103] *Rubus ludwigii* has been used in South Africa for relief of stomach-ache and acute pain. *Rubus pinnatus* has been used for diarrhoea, abdominal cramps, and chest conditions[509] while *R. hawaiiensis*, *R. macraeii*, and *R. rosaefolius* have been used medicinally in Hawaii.[532] An infusion of the latter species is astringent and has been used in New Caledonia as a laxative.[420]

Rubus spectabilis bark was pounded and used in northwestern United States for toothache. Tea made from the leaves of *R. macropetalus* (dewberry) has been used for general stomach troubles by Indians in western Washington while Indians from Vancouver Island, British Columbia, peeled the roots and stems of *Rubus* spp., boiled them, and drank the liquid to arrest vomiting. Root decoctions of *Rubus* spp. were a widespread North American Indian remedy against dysentery. The leaves of *R. caesius* and *R. idaeus* have been used in Europe for making tea.[330] *Rubus moluccanus* has been reported in Fiji to cause constipation.[465]

RUBIACEAE
Madder family

Coprosma australis (A. Rich.) Robins.
Manono, papauma, raurekau

Coprosma robusta Raoul
Karamu

Coprosma acerosa (A. Cunn.)
Tarakupenga, tataraheke, tatarahake

BOTANICAL NOTES: These common shrubs may be considered together. *Coprosma australis* was formerly known as *C. grandifolia* Hook.f.

MEDICAL USE: The sap from the inner bark of manono was used for scabies[233] and itch.[54] A decoction made by boiling leaves and cut twigs

Coprosma australis
(x 0.2). Engraving:
S. Parkinson.

Coprosma robusta
(x 0.2). Engraving:
S. Parkinson.

of manono was widely used for bad cuts, festered sores, and bruises, and was used with good effect on a troublesome shrapnel wound.[2] The leaves of manono were boiled and applied as a poultice for broken limbs and bruises; the liquid was also used.[267] Kahaki maintained that the bark was used for this purpose, but not the leaves.[286] The bark of manono was steeped in cold water and applied to parts where there were aches or pains.[414] The bark of manono and tips of white manuka (*Kunzea ericoides*) were boiled together and applied externally in the treatment of venereal disease.[476]

Kerry-Nicholls[299] said that the bruised bark of 'papa-aumu' or 'mistletoe' was applied for the itch, but Colenso[150] identified 'papauma' as *C. grandifolia*. Williams[517] identified 'papauma' as *Griselinia littoralis* (Cornaceae). A decoction of leaves of karamu was taken as a febrifuge[149] and the leaves were boiled in water and the extract was drunk for kidney troubles.[2] The young shoots of karamu were boiled and the liquid was drunk for bladder stoppage and inflammation.[414] The inner bark of karamu was boiled and the liquid was taken in small quantities for stomach-ache and to stop vomiting.[467] A twig of karamu was used by the Maori priest in ceremonies to dislodge an illness from a sick person.[10,54] *Coprosma acerosa* was taken as an alterative by the Maori (see *Clematis*).[150]

RELATED PHARMACOLOGY: *Coprosma persicaefolia* leaves have been used with coconut oil in Hawaii to rub on aching limbs.[532] *Coprosma tahitensis* roots have been used in Tahiti for urethritis and dysentery.[399] Ipecac comes from *Cephaelis* spp. and quinine comes from *Cinchona* sp. of the same family. In China and Southeast Asia the seeds and bark of *Gardenia florida* have been used for a variety of complaints.[427] In Fiji an infusion of *Tarenna sambucina* made with boiling water was drunk for rheumatism and swelling of the groin, and the residue used as a poultice. The leaves of *Mussaenda frondosa*, pounded up in cold water,

Coprosma acerosa (x 0.5). Drawing: V. Cassie.

Phebalium nudum (x 2.0). Photo: J. E. Braggins.

Alectryon excelsus (x 0.5).

Planchonella novo-zelandica (x 0.2).
Painting: E. Blumhardt.

Hebe sp. (x 0.3). Painting:
F. Osborne.

are said to relieve pain in the chest. *Ixora vitiensis* is also said to be used in medicine.[400]

CHEMISTRY: The colouring matters of *Coprosma* barks have been extensively investigated.[22] [23] [86] They consist of various anthraquinone derivatives related to the synthetic purgative 1,8-dihydroxyanthraquinone.[195] All New Zealand *Coprosma* spp. examined have been shown to contain the iridoid asperuloside.[83] Many contain the coumarin scopoletin, which is a growth factor for plants.[70] Wilson[520] has suggested that the quercetin and kaempferol glycosides present in the leaves could be of value in identifying the parentage of *Coprosma* hybrids.

Galium propinquum A. Cunn.
New Zealand bed-straw
Mawe, maawe

BOTANICAL NOTES: A common herb found throughout New Zealand. It was known to Cheeseman and other authors as *G. umbrosum* Sol. ex Forst.

MEDICAL USE: The plant was boiled and applied to affected parts in gonorrhoea, particularly where there was retention of urine.[54]

RELATED PHARMACOLOGY: Goose grass (*Galium aparine*) is said to be effective in all kinds of ulcers and scrofula and is antiscorbutic.[36] It is reported to dissolve stones in the bladder and has been recommended for the relief of obstruction of urinary organs, suppression of urine, and gravelly deposits.[524] An infusion of *Galium* spp. has been used in Africa for the relief of bodily and muscular pains.[509] The heated leaves and stem of *G. bungei* were placed in carious teeth to relieve toothache.[330] *Galium verum* is slightly diuretic, stimulates the metabolism, and promotes milk curdling.[212] [490] It was used as a remedy in gravel, stone, and urinary diseases, and has been used in hysteria and epilepsy.[524]

Galium propinquum (x 0.5). Engraving: S. Parkinson.

Galium odoratum acts as a sedative and an antispasmodic[490] and *G. cruciata* has been used to make a salve for wounds.[524] *Galium* spp. have been used as substitutes for coffee.[330] *Mitchella repens* tea made from its fruit reportedly aids labour and was widely used in female medicines by North American Indians.[330] It has also been used for irritation of the bladder.[178]

CHEMISTRY: *Galium* spp. contain asperuloside (see under *Coprosma*) and often flavonoid glycosides such as rutin[257] (see p. 125).

RUTACEAE
Orange family

Melicope ternata J. R. et G. Forst.
Wharangi

BOTANICAL NOTES: An aromatic shrub found in the North Island and northern part of the South Island, usually near the coast.

MEDICAL USE: The gum was chewed for foul breath.[233] [331]

RELATED PHARMACOLOGY: *Melicope cucullata* var. *cucullata* is used in Fiji for sore throats and a medicinal tea is made from *M. cucullata* var. *robusta*.[465] Pilocarpine, an imidazole alkaloid from *Pilocarpus* sp., has a powerful action in promoting perspiration and flow of saliva.[195] It has been used for initial and maintenance therapy in certain kinds of primary glaucoma.[330] The family Rutaceae includes *Cusparia febrifuga* from which angostura is obtained. It is claimed to have tonic and febrifuge effects.[46]

CHEMISTRY: Alkaloids of Australian members of the Rutaceae have been discussed by Hughes and others.[271] The bark and that of the related *Melicope simplex* contain a series of highly oxygenated flavonols.[81] [82]

Melicope ternata (x 0.5).
Engraving:
S. Parkinson.

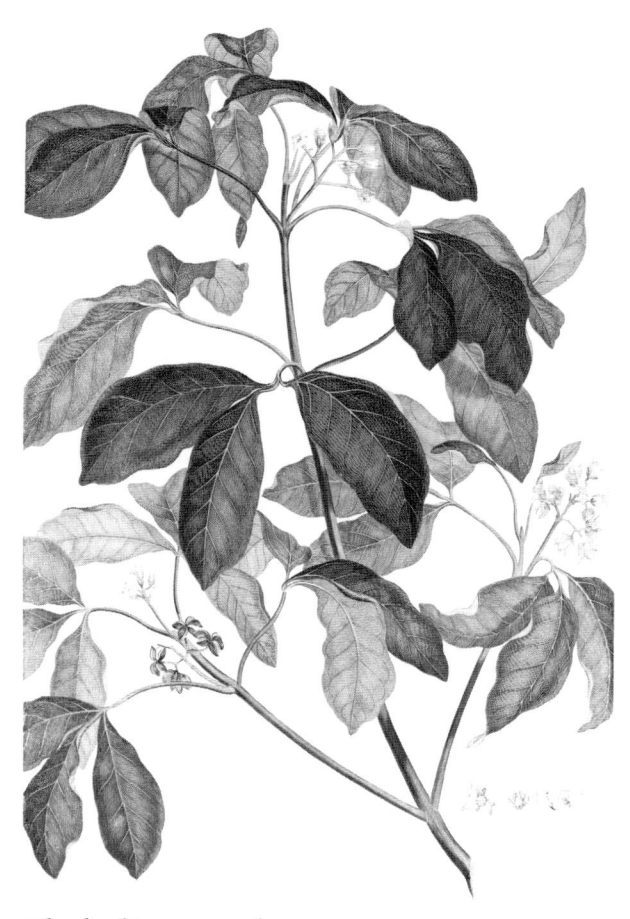

Phebalium nudum Hook.
Mairehau

BOTANICAL NOTES: This aromatic shrub is found in kauri forest and manuka scrub from Kaitaia southwards to the Coromandel Peninsula.

MEDICAL USE: The Maori rubbed their bodies with the plant and wore sachets of the fragrant leaves.[160]

RELATED PHARMACOLOGY: *Phebalium argentium* contains furocoumarins, which cause photo-sensitisation contact dermatitis.[330]

CHEMISTRY: The essential oil of the leaves contains citronellal, citral, cinnamic acid, phenol, camphene, limonene, a sesquiterpene, and a sesquiterpene alcohol.[416] From the heartwood and bark 23 compounds have been isolated, including citral, eugenol, ß-sitosterol, ellagic acid, and three furoquinoline alkaloids.[71][113]

ILLUSTRATION: See page 213

SAPINDACEAE
Litchi family

Alectryon excelsus Gaertn.
Titoki, titongi

BOTANICAL NOTES: This handsome tree is found in both of the main islands north of Banks Peninsula and Westland, frequently in stream valleys. The black seed embedded in a fleshy red aril yields an oil which was used by the old-time Maori to anoint the body.[151]

MEDICAL USE: Green oil was applied externally to weak eyes, sores, wounds, sore breasts, chapped skin in infants, bruises, painful joints, and into the ear for earache. It was taken internally as a laxative. The astringent red pulp was taken by consumptives to relieve blood-spitting.[233] A piece of soft cloth soaked in the oil was placed over the navel if it was sore or required softening in new-born children.[347]

RELATED PHARMACOLOGY: *Alectryon macrococeum* has been used in Hawaii for throat infections.[532] Burkill[102] has discussed five species of *Sapindus* which are used in Malaysian medicine for soap, insecticides, and as fish poisons. *Sapindus vitiensis* has been used in Fiji for stomach-ache[509] and *S. saponaria* var. *jardiniana* has been used in Tahiti as a fish poison.[399]

Dodonaea viscosa (akeake) has been used externally for burns and scalds in Indonesia[474] and contains quebrachitol.[411] An infusion of the leaves of *D. viscosa* has been used on Reunion Island as a sudorific, and an astringent decoction of the wood has been taken to reduce fever.[419] In New Caledonia the aromatic leaves have been used as a substitute for tea, as a febrifuge, and for a number of diseases.[420] *Dodonaea viscosa* has been used medicinally in Hawaii,[532] Australia, and other countries,[166] and in Panama the leaves are chewed for toothache.[330] The plant has an important place in Australian native medicine[322] and is used in Peru[166] in the same way as coca leaves, the source of cocaine. In Tahiti *D. viscosa* has been used as a purgative and a febrifuge. The fruit is rich in saponins and is slightly toxic.[399]

CHEMISTRY: The oil of *Alectryon excelsus* has been investigated by Brooker.[90] It has subsequently been found to contain cyanolipids,[200] which release hydrogen cyanide (HCN);[156] this appears to be a feature of the Sapindaceae family.[451 403]

ILLUSTRATION: See page 213

SAPOTACEAE
Sapodilla family

Planchonella novo-zelandica
(F. Muell.) Allan

Tawapou

BOTANICAL NOTES: A rare coastal tree found from the North Cape to Tolaga Bay on the East Coast, and to near Manukau Harbour on the West Coast. The hard, bony seeds were formerly used by the Maori as beads for necklaces.[139] The tree has been known as *Sideroxylon costatum* F. Muell. and *S. novo-zelandicum* Hemsl.

MEDICAL USE: An oily substance obtained from boiling the flesh of the berries for three hours was applied to sprains and bruises. It was said to lower blood pressure and clear bruised blood.[160]

RELATED PHARMACOLOGY: *Planchonella obovata* is said to be taken internally as a remedy for stomach-ache and chest pains, and a poultice of crushed leaves is used to treat lumbago. The heated bark may be chewed as a remedy for sprue in Southeast Asia.[403] The latex of *Sideroxylon glabrescens* has been used in Malaysia as a chewing gum and that from *S. attenuatum* as a temporary filling for prepared tooth cavities.[330]

CHEMISTRY: The wood contains triterpenes.[123]

ILLUSTRATION: See page 214

SCROPHULARIACEAE
Foxglove family

Euphrasia cuneata Forst.f.
New Zealand eyebright
Tutumako

BOTANICAL NOTES: A handsome erect herb found between East Cape and Marlborough.

MEDICAL USE: It was used by the Maori priest to expel a demon from a sick person — a magical rather than a medical use.[55]

RELATED PHARMACOLOGY: *Euphrasia officinalis* (*E. rostkoviana*) (eyebright) inhibits inflammation of mucous membranes, particularly of the eyes.[212] [323] [490] [524] *Hebenstreitia basutica* and *Sopubia scabra* have been used in South Africa for stomach troubles.[509]

CHEMISTRY: Many *Euphrasia* spp. contain the iridoid catapol which is related to aucubin[257] (see p. 193).

Hebe salicifolia (Forst.f.) Penn. and similar species
Koromiko, kokomuka

BOTANICAL NOTES: In the 1895 edition of the *Extra Pharmacopoeia*, the name 'koromiko' is identified as *Veronica salicifolia* and *V. parviflora*. In notes supplied by Miss Miller[359] to the DSIR it is identified as *V. salicifolia* and *V. speciosa*. Colenso,[150] Williams,[517] and Cheeseman[139] list the name 'koromiko' for *V. salicifolia* and other allied species. All of these authors regarded the species known as *V. salicifolia* as a population of many forms, growing in both the North and South Islands.

The New Zealand species of *Veronica* are now placed in a separate genus, *Hebe*. Allan[9] in 1961

Euphrasia cuneata (x 0.2). Engraving: S. Parkinson.

applied the name *Hebe salicifolia* to the large-leaved shrub, found in the South Island and Stewart Island, and collected, probably in Dusky Sound, by Forster on Cook's second voyage. Most of the North Island plants formerly known as *V. salicifolia* are now grouped in *Hebe stricta* (Benth.) L. B. Moore.

MEDICAL USE: The plant was used in vapour baths in early times.[233] An infusion of the leaves was a powerful astringent for dysentery and other complaints. The decoction was also taken for ulcers and for venereal disease.[380] Bruised leaves were applied as poultices for ulcers, especially for venereal disease.[331,485] A weak infusion was a tonic and a small portion of the leaf, if chewed, soon produced a keen sense of hunger.[294] Best[54] refers to 'kokomuka', a *Veronica* which was used for diarrhoea by chewing the young leaves.

Koromiko has long been valued for its beneficial effects in cases of diarrhoea and dysentery, and in 1889 Kirk predicted that it would take its place in the pharmacopoeia as a recognised remedy for diseases of this class. In 1895 it was indeed listed in the *Extra Pharmacopoeia* as an import from New Zealand, 'used there and in China as a remedy for chronic dysentery and diarrhoea. Tincture, 1 in 5 of proof spirits. Dose ½ to 1 drachm.' It was deleted from later editions. The leaves were used for sores and headaches[363] and as a pack for sore skin in infants.[523] The liquid from boiling the leaves was used as a mouthwash and gargle.[467]

Bushmen troubled with English cholera frequently treated the disease by chewing fresh leaves of the plant and swallowing the juice but usually the drug was taken in the form of an infusion. It was kept in stock by the leading druggists in the colony.[304] The leaves were chewed as a remedy for diarrhoea;[27,45,390] according to Honana[267] the leaves were not swallowed. An infusion or spirituous decoction was useful in dealing with epidemic infantile diarrhoea.[295] It stimulated evacuation of the bowels, promoted the flow of bile, and was often given to expectant mothers to facilitate rapid and easy delivery.[429] The plant was used by both settlers and Maori. Fresh young leaves were pounded and boiled with water, and the filtered decoction was effective, but an infusion of dried leaves was not.[27] The sap was used for a children's skin disease called 'hawaniwani'.[54] Top shoots and young leaves, either boiled green, dried and later boiled, or eaten raw, were a remedy for dysentery and summer sickness. They were also used for kidney and bladder troubles.[2]

During the Second World War the leaves were found effective for dysentery by the New Zealand troops in North Africa. Several authors state that Sir Peter Buck first used it during the First World War, but he had no knowledge of its use at that time (letter to DSIR). Koromiko was used as a blood purifier by the Rev. Edgar Ward[273] (see *Pomaderris kumeraho*).

RELATED PHARMACOLOGY: Brooklime (*Veronica beccabunga*) is antiscorbutic[178] and has been applied externally to ulcers, burns, and whitlows. Common speedwell (*V. officinalis*) is 'indiscriminately recommended in maladies calling for tonics and demulcents.' It is reputed to be useful in dysentery and skin diseases,[36] [330] in promoting menstruation,[524] and even in curing the poison of 'serpents'.[346] *Veronica virginica* promotes the flow of bile.[194] Picrorhiza from *Picrorhiza lindleyana* is a powerful tonic with a slight laxative action.[178]

CHEMISTRY: It has been suggested that the virtue of koromiko resides in the presence of tannins[220] but there is dispute over this. The alkanes of *Hebe stricta* have been examined by Eglinton *et al*.[191] The wood of *H. salicifolia* contains mannitol,[123] which has medicinal use.[358] [521]

ILLUSTRATION: See page 214

SMILACACEAE
Sarsaparilla family

This family is sometimes treated as a part of the Liliaceae or lily family.

Ripogonum scandens J.R. et G. Forst.
Supplejack
Kareao, pirita

BOTANICAL NOTES: Supplejack is a woody liane found in lowland forest throughout New Zealand.

MEDICAL USE: The burnt stem was used to cauterise wounds[2][54] and water exuding from a broken shoot was applied to wounds.[54] It is a demulcent,[27] and a cold infusion was used for rheumatism.[45] A decoction of the roots was reputed to be good for rheumatism, bowel complaints, fever, general debility, and skin diseases,[380] and formed a good substitute for sarsaparilla.[17][294] The decoction was also used for secondary symptoms of syphilis and for producing an abortion. Young shoots were used for the itch. A liquor made by skinning the underground rootstocks, beating them to pulp, steeping them in water, and straining, was also taken as a medicine.[233] The stems were bruised and applied for venereal disease[236] (see also *Dysoxylum spectabile*, Meliaceae).

Ripogonum scandens (x 0.5). Photo: J. E. Braggins.

RELATED PHARMACOLOGY: Aloes from various species of *Aloe* can cause abortion.[194] Many powers have been attributed to *Aloe barbadensis* but only two of the claims have persisted for centuries, viz. purgation[195] and the healing of skin.[330] The healing properties may be due to the presence of chrysophanic acid. The leaf sap has been used in Africa for burns and sunburn and as a cure for ringworm. Among the Greeks and Romans *A. barbadensis* was highly regarded as a laxative. The juice of the leaves contains the anthraquinone emodin, which acts chiefly on the large intestine.[330]

Sarsaparilla from *Smilax* spp. was formerly used in skin infections, syphilis, and chronic rheumatism.[194] *Smilax sandwicensis* has been used medicinally in Hawaii and *S. vitiensis* was given in Fiji to children whose mothers became pregnant within two months of childbirth.[532] The macerated bark from the base of the stem of a *Smilax* sp. has been used in New Guinea as a remedy for toothache. The rhizomes of *Smilax* spp. have been used in Eastern Asia and Central America as tonics, panaceas, and aphrodisiacs.

SOLANACEAE
Potato family

Solanum aviculare Forst.f.
Bullibulli
Poroporo, kohoho

Solanum laciniatum Ait.
Cut-leaved nightshade

BOTANICAL NOTES: *Solanum aviculare* is a large softwooded shrub found in lowland districts in both islands. Baylis[39] has shown that the plant population consists of two species, *S. aviculare* and *S. laciniatum*, with distinct chromosome and morphological characters. Some authors have identified 'poroporo' as *S. nigrum*, a smaller, weedy plant, and it is probable that the Maori did not distinguish the species.

MEDICAL USE: The inner skin of the leaf[485] and the bark[160] were used for the itch. The plant was used as a cataplasm for ulcers[150] [177] and the inner bark was used for scabies and the leaves as poultices for ulcers.[233] The juices expressed from the green leaves and young berries of this plant were also used for itch or scabies.[45] The pith of the dry stem was included in an elaborate recipe for bruises.[390] The juice, mixed with soot, was rubbed into the wounds produced by tattooing instruments.[515] Young leaves, mixed or boiled with lard, were applied as a healing salve[485] and were found effective for scab in sheep.[390]

RELATED PHARMACOLOGY: *Solanum nigrum* (common nightshade) has been used in New Caledonia,[420] Tahiti, Easter Island, Hawaii,[532] and the Bahamas[192] for a variety of complaints, especially for throat infections, eye troubles, and

Solanum laciniatum (x 0.5). Engraving: S. Parkinson.

the healing of wounds. It and other *Solanum* spp. were medicinal plants of the Araucanos Indians.[243] *Solanum nigrum* has also been used as a purgative,[532] for swelling of the testicles,[169] [321] and along with other *Solanum* spp. for ulcers and ringworm.[509] *Solanum nodiflorum*,[250] *S. aculeatissimum*, and *S. capense* have been used medicinally in Hawaii[532] and the Philippines,[406] *S. bahamense* and *S. erianthum* in the Bahamas,[192] *S. indicum* and *S. surattense* in India,[330] *S. merker* and *S. panduraeforme* in Africa,[330] and *S. agrarium* and *S. paniculatum* in Brazil.[330] *S. melongena* has been used in China,[427] *S. mammosum* in Costa Rica, and *S. americanum* by the Rappahannock Indians in the USA.[330]

The berries and root of *S. carolinense* are antispasmodic and act as a sedative. The plant is reported to be a remedy for infantile and hysterical convulsions, and for epilepsy and paroxysms connected with menstrual derangements.[524] Dried stems of *S. dulcamara* (bittersweet) were formerly used for rheumatism, bronchitis, and chronic skin diseases.[357] The stem is reported to stimulate the central nervous system and to be slightly diuretic.[490]

Solanum hermanii (apple of Sodom) has been used for a wide variety of diseases in South Africa and Queensland and shows promise in cancer treatment.[166] Perry[403] gives many references to the uses of *Solanum* spp. in medicine in Southeast Asia; perhaps the most remarkable discovery is that the fruits of *S. sanitwongsei* reduce sugar in the urine of diabetics. *Atropa belladonna* is in the same family. The pharmacology of *Solanum* alkaloids has been discussed by Connor.[156]

CHEMISTRY: *Solanum* alkaloids in New Zealand species have been investigated extensively by Briggs.[69] [72] A glycoside, solasonine, has been isolated and can be hydrolysed to the aglycone solasodine. This is the nitrogen analogue of diosgenin, which is used commercially as a raw material for the manufacture of several hormones. A plant for the commercial extraction of solasodine for use as a replacement for diosgenin in the production of steroidal drugs was operating in the New Plymouth area from 1978 to 1981.[307] The anti-accelerator cardiac action of solasodine and some of its chemical derivatives has been reported by Krayer and Briggs.[312] Solasodine and its glycoalkaloids show antifungal activity while antifungal stress metabolites from the leaves of *Solanum* spp. are 5ß-solasodan-3-one and solasodenone.[430]

ILLUSTRATION: See page 231

Solanum tuberosum L.
Potato
Taewa

BOTANICAL NOTES: Introduced very early in European history of New Zealand.

MEDICAL USE: Water in which potatoes had been boiled was a lotion for pimples, ague, skin eruptions, and burns.[485] Cruise[168] refers to the use of potato juice as a healing agent (see p. 35).

RELATED PHARMACOLOGY: *Solanum tuberosum* contains proteins which act as lectins.[330] It also

Solanum tuberosum (x 1).
Photo: J. E. Braggins.

contains tuberosines which are active against protozoa. The pharmacology of *S. tuberosum* has been discussed by Connor.[156]

CHEMISTRY: Green and sprouting potatoes contain the glycoalkaloids, solanine and chaconine.[446] The plant is rich in riboflavin.[439]

THYMELAEACEAE
Daphne family

Pimelea prostrata (J. R. et G. Forst.) Willd.
Strathmore weed
Pinatoro

BOTANICAL NOTES: A prostrate shrub found in both islands. Often it is the first coloniser of sandbanks left along the banks of rivers which have flooded, for example at Tangiwai following the railway disaster of 1953.

MEDICAL USE: Although it had no recorded medicinal uses by the Maori this plant was known to the early settlers as Strathmore weed, and there are many reports of it being toxic to livestock, especially horses.[24][156]

Pimelea prostrata (x 0.5).
Engraving:
S. Parkinson.

RELATED PHARMACOLOGY: *Pimelea microcephala* was used in Australia to treat colds, relieve pain, and for throat and chest complaints.[166]

CHEMISTRY: The plant contains prostratin, a tumour-inhibiting agent, and other related compounds.[134 340 530]

TYPHACEAE
Bulrush family

Typha orientalis C. B. Presl
Bulrush
Raupo

BOTANICAL NOTES: The bulrush is found in marshy places in both the main islands. Cheeseman's name for it was *T. angustifolia* L.

MEDICAL USE: The 'hune' or pappus of the seeds was applied to wounds and old ulcerated sores as a protection against dust.[151] The rhizome was boiled with flax root (*Phormium*) and tataramoa root (*Rubus*) and the liquid was drunk to assist the removal of the afterbirth.[523]

RELATED PHARMACOLOGY: *Typha angustifolia* was a medicinal plant of the Araucanos Indians.[243] The rhizomes are slightly astringent, diuretic, and antidysenteric.[419] In the Philippines the woolly inflorescence is used to treat wounds.[403] Pollen of *Typha* has been used in China as an astringent and vulnerary[427] and *Typha capensis* has been used by the Zulu in Africa to aid in the expulsion of the placenta.[509] *Typha* spp. act as aero-allergens.[330]

ILLUSTRATION: See page 231

UMBELLIFERAE (APIACEAE)
Carrot family

Apium australe Thouars
Maori celery, green celery, prostrate parsley
Tutae koau

BOTANICAL NOTES: An edible herb found near the seashore throughout New Zealand. Cheese-

Apium australe (x 0.3). Engraving: S. Parkinson.

man's name for the plant was *A. prostratum* Lab. and it has been used again for New Zealand plants.[190]

MEDICAL USE: Probably it was one of the plants employed in making vapour baths.[135] It was used by Cook as an antiscorbutic.[470]

RELATED PHARMACOLOGY: *Apium* spp. are well-known antiscorbutics. Wild celery (*A. graveolens*) is diuretic and a decoction of the whole plant is mentioned in several continental pharmacopoeias.[313] It has a variety of uses in medicine, e.g. for rheumatoid arthritis.[195,524] It provokes contact dermatitis and photodermatitis, shows hypoglycemic activity, and an extract produces contraction of the uterus.[330] It is used in the Philippines as an emetic, for asthma, and hypertension.[406] An alcoholic extract of parsley (*Petroselinum crispum*) has been used in menstrual disorders.[195,327]

Solanum aviculare (x 1.0). Photo: J. E. Braggins.

Typha orientalis.

Melicytus micranthus. Photo: J. E. Braggins.

Pseudowintera axillaris (x 1). Photo: J. E. Braggins.

Scandia rosaefolia (Hook.) Dawson
Rose-leaved anise
Koheriki, kohepiro

BOTANICAL NOTES: This coastal herb is found in the northern part of New Zealand. It was formerly known as *Angelica rosaefolia* Hook.

MEDICAL USE: The aromatic leaves were used as a diuretic, for dropsy, and as a remedy for syphilitic disease.[150]

RELATED PHARMACOLOGY: *Angelica* spp. give angelica root, which has been used as a diuretic. *Angelica anomala* var. *chinensis* has been used for uterine complaints,[178] female maladies, and skin troubles.[427] In England *A. archangelica* juice was

Scandia rosaefolia (x 0.3). Engraving: S. Parkinson.

placed into carious teeth and the oil was used in dental preparations. It was also used in Eurasia as a tonic to improve well-being and mental harmony. The ripe fruit has been used for making tea and the root has been used to flavour cigarette tobacco.[330] The root is said to stimulate digestion, to inhibit flatulence, and to be used as an expectorant.[490]

Culpeper[524] recorded that 'The root in powder, made up in plaister with a little pitch and laid on the biting of mad dogs or any other venomous creature doth wonderfully help.' The seeds stimulate the stomach, are diuretic, and diaphoretic.[490] Extracts of *A. polymorpha* var. *sinensis* have long been used in Chinese medicine to stimulate uterine contraction. *Angelica sylvestris* is one of the chief therapeutic agents in the Chinese pharmacopoeia.[403] The pharmacology of *Angelica* spp. has been discussed in detail by Le Strange.[327]

CHEMISTRY: *Angelica* spp. usually contain coumarins[257] (see p. 215).

URTICACEAE
Nettle family

Urtica ferox Forst.f.
Tree nettle
Ongaonga

BOTANICAL NOTES: A shrub with stinging hairs, found in both the main islands, usually near the coast. The nettle is dangerous to horses and dogs and a fatal poisoning in man has been recorded.[156] The extract of just five hairs can kill a guinea pig.[204]

MEDICAL USE: The bark was boiled with *Macropiper* leaves and taken internally and externally for eczema and venereal disease.[2]

RELATED PHARMACOLOGY: *Urtica dioica* and *U. urens* are efficacious in uterine and other haemorrhages.[325] *Urtica dioica* exerts a diuretic effect,[330] promotes the elimination of uric acid, is a slight hydragogue, stimulates the metabolism, is externally epispastic and antirheumatic,[212] [490] and has been used in northern temperate regions in homeopathic medicine. It is also used for dysmenorrhoea, and nose bleeding and externally for ulcers and wounds.[443] The root is an ingredient in commercial hair growth preparations, and the seeds have been used as a home remedy for hair troubles generally. The leaves contain histamine-like substances which are transferred by means of stinging hairs to the skin.[330]

CHEMISTRY: Acetylcholine, histamine, and serotonin (5-hydroxytryptamine) are all present in the hair fluid[60] [409] but in quantities no greater than those found in the hairs of the common European nettle (*U. urens*), which is not dangerous. The toxic principle, triffydin, has

Urtica ferox (x 0.3).
Engraving:
S. Parkinson.

been isolated but has yet to be characterised.[204] Acetylcholine exerts a powerful stimulation of the parasympathetic nerve system. It is also a cardiac depressant and an effective vasodilator.[521]

VERBENACEAE
Verbena family

Vitex lucens Kirk
Puriri

BOTANICAL NOTES: This attractive spreading tree is found in the northern half of the North Island, and produces valuable hardwood.

MEDICAL USE: The water from boiled leaves is reputed to be still used to bathe sprains and backache.[2] The infusion was also a remedy for

Vitex lucens (x 0.3).
Engraving:
S. Parkinson.

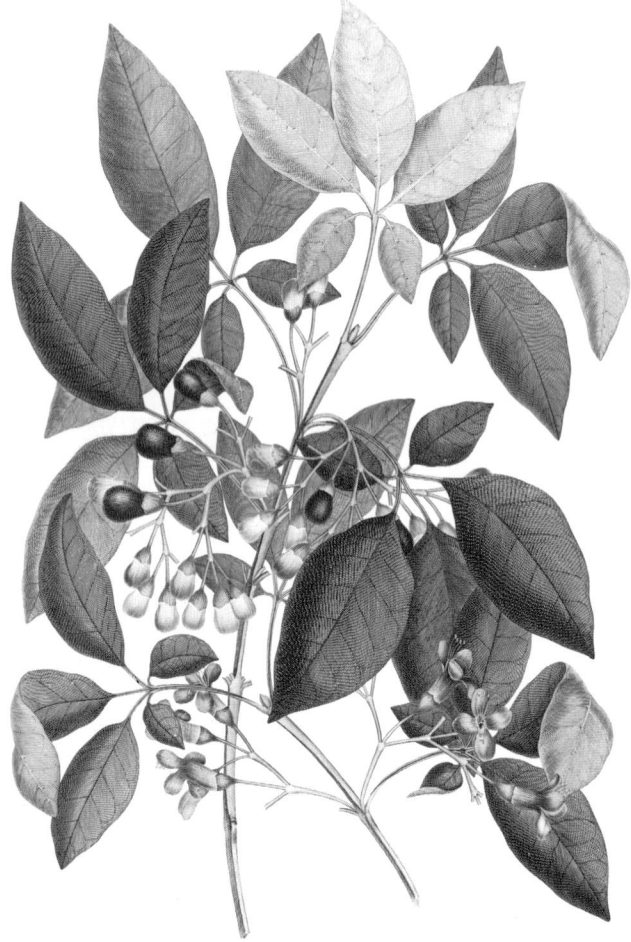

ulcers, especially under the ear,[390] and for sore throats.[363]

RELATED PHARMACOLOGY: See Burkill[102] for a note on the chemistry and medical uses of *Vitex* spp. in Malaysia. *Vitex negundo* contains vitamin C and carotene[37] and has been used for many medicinal purposes in Indonesia,[496] New Caledonia,[419] and China.[427] It is included in the *Philippine National Formulary*[406] as a remedy for coughs and fever, and for headache, wounds, and ulcers. *Vitex trifolia* has been used medicinally in Fiji,[400] India, many Southeast Asian countries,[403] and Hawaii.[532] For example, in Fiji its leaves have been used for fracture while in Samoa they have been used for fever and swellings and the stem for tuberculosis and brain disease.[532]

Vitex agnus-castus was used by the Romans and Greeks both internally and for poulticing.[102] It is a symbol of chastity; the ground fruit, substituted for pepper, was supposed to reduce libido.[330] *Vitex peduncularis* is reported to be of great therapeutic importance in India for the treatment of various fevers, particularly blackwater fever. The bark has anti-haemolytic activity and has been used against cobra venom.[448] A decoction of the bark of *V. simplicifolia* has been used on the Ivory Coast to relieve toothache.[330]

CHEMISTRY: The chemical constituents of *Vitex lucens* have been listed by Cambie.[118] The most notable is a flavonoid C-glycoside, vitexin. The heartwood contains β-sitosterol (see p. 68), while β-carotene and p-hydroxybenzoic acid occur in the leaves.[114] The methyl ester of the latter compound has been patented as a germicide.[195] β-carotene is converted in the liver to vitamin A.[521]

VIOLACEAE
Violet family

Melicytus micranthus Hook.f.
Manakura

BOTANICAL NOTES: This shrub is found in lowland forest throughout New Zealand.

MEDICAL USE: The plant was used to perfume titoki oil[517] and the bark was used in a decoction for a variety of complaints (see *Dysoxylum spectabile*, Meliaceae).

RELATED PHARMACOLOGY: The root of a species of *Viola* has emetic, laxative, emollient, and cathartic properties and has also been used as a demulcent.[178] The English violet (*V. odorata*) and pansy (*V. tricolor*) each contain saponins. The root of the former dissolves mucus and the latter is diuretic and reduces fever. Both have been used as expectorants.[212][490] Their use as medicinal plants is discussed by Le Strange.[327] *Viola kauaiensis* has been used medicinally in Hawaii.[532]

ILLUSTRATION: See page 232.

Melicytus ramiflorus J. R. et G. Forst.
Whitey wood
Mahoe

BOTANICAL NOTES: A small tree, common in scrub and forests throughout New Zealand.

MEDICAL USE: The leaves were boiled and the liquid was used to bathe parts affected by rheumatism. The boiled leaves were bandaged on surfaces affected with scabies[467] and a plaster of steamed leaves was placed over a stomach wound.[422] The inner bark was frayed and applied as a pack on burns.[154]

RELATED PHARMACOLOGY: Mahoe is reported to contain an opossum toxin.[140]

Melicytus ramiflorus (x 0.5). Engraving: S. Parkinson.

WINTERACEAE (MAGNOLIACEAE)

Wintera or magnolia family

The Winteraceae were segregated from the Magnoliaceae in 1933, part of a trend towards smaller plant families.

Pseudowintera axillaris

(J. R. et G. Forst.) Dandy

Pepper tree

Horopito

BOTANICAL NOTES: The name 'horopito' is applied to *P. axillaris* but the notes probably refer to both it and the closely allied *P. colorata* (Raoul) Dandy. These two aromatic shrubs were referred to *Drimys* and *Wintera* before being placed in *Pseudowintera*.

MEDICAL USE: The leaves were bruised, steeped in water, and used for paipai, a skin disease, and venereal diseases. The extract is aromatic and a stimulant and the bark was used as a substitute for quinine.[294][485] It was used by the Maori for various diseases and was the 'Winter's bark' of New Zealand.[17] It was also used by the Maori for driving out evil spirits[45] and the leaves were occasionally used by settlers who were suffering from diarrhoea.[304] The sap was used for skin disease and gonorrhoea. A decoction of the leaves was taken for stomach-ache and was known as 'Maori painkiller'[54][233] and 'Bushman's painkiller'. The leaves were chewed for toothache and were rubbed on the breasts when weaning infants.[2] A decoction made by boiling the leaves in water strongly desensitises human subjects to sweet tastes and possibly to bitter taste sensations without affecting sensitivity to salty and sour qualities.[455]

RELATED PHARMACOLOGY: *Drimys winteri* and *D. chilensis* were medicinal plants of the Araucanos Indians.[243] *Drimys winteri* furnished Winter's bark of commerce, a tonic, antiscorbutic, and stimulant.[178] A decoction of *Drimys* is used in New Guinea as an abortifacient.[403] The bark of the tulip-tree (*Liriodendron tulipifera*) yields a stimulant tonic which is useful in dyspepsia[178] and which has been used in southern USA to relieve toothache.[330]

CHEMISTRY: Briggs and co-workers[80] have identified 29 components of the essential oil including eugenol, which is a dental analgesic.[521] In a search for the active principle of the leaves of *Pseudowintera colorata* Walker and co-workers[339] isolated the sesquiterpenoid dialdehyde polygodial, which has strong antibiotic activity against *Candida albicans*. It is also an insect anti-feedant.[339]

ILLUSTRATION: See page 232

References

References are also given to *Chemical Abstracts (CA)* where the original papers were not available.

1. Abraham, E. P. *et al.* 'An antibacterial substance from *Onopordon tauricum*.' *Nature* 158: 744, 1946.
2. Adams, Olga L. G. *Maori medicinal plants*. Auckland Botanical Society, Auckland, 1945 (Auck. Bot. Soc. Bull. 2).
3. Adhikari, S. *et al.* 'Cyclitols from the heartwood of *Phyllocladus trichomanoides*.' *J. Chem. Soc.* 2829-31, 1962.
4. Agarwal, J. S., Rastogi, R. P. and Srivastava, O. P. 'In vitro toxicity of constituents of *Rumex maritimus* Linn. to ringworm fungi.' *Curr. Sci.* 45: 619-20, 1976. (*CA* 1976, 85: 137975.)
5. Aliev, R. K., 'A wound-healing preparation from the leaves of the large plantain.' *Amer. J. Pharm.* 122: 24-26, 1950. (*CA* 1950, 4203.)
6. Aliotta, G. and Pollio, A.' Vitamin A and C contents of some edible wild plants of Italy.' *Riv. Ital. EPPOS* 63: 47-48, 1981. (*CA*, 1981, 94: 173071.)
7. Allan, H. H., 'Notes on New Zealand floristic botany, including descriptions of new species.' *Trans. Roy. Soc. N.Z.* 65: 221-31, 1935.
8. Allan, H. H. *A handbook of the naturalised flora of New Zealand*. Government Printer, Wellington, 1940 (DSIR Bull. No. 83).
9. Allan, H. H. *Flora of New Zealand*, Vol. 1, Government Printer, Wellington, 1961.
10. Andersen, J. C. *Maori life in Ao-tea*. Whitcombe & Tombs Ltd., Christchurch, 1907.
11. Andersen, J. C. 'Popular names of New Zealand plants.' *Trans. N.Z. Inst.* 56: 659-714, 1926.
12. *Annual Report*, 1951. New Zealand Department of Agriculture.
13. Anon. *The New Zealanders*. Charles Knight, London, 1830.
14. Anon. 'In Memoriam: William Skey.' *Trans. Proc. N.Z. Inst.* 34: 554, 1902.
15. Anon. Unpublished notes, Botany Division, DSIR, Christchurch, 1940-41.
16. Anon. Unpublished notes in the Botany Section, Auckland Museum, 1964.
17. Armstrong, J. F. 'On the vegetation of the neighbourhood of Christchurch, including Riccarton, Dry Bush, etc.' *Trans. Proc. N.Z. Inst.* 2: 118-28, 1870.
18. Arora, R. B., Dandiya, P. C. and Sharma, V. N. 'Preliminary laboratory investigations of *Piper aurantiacum*.' *Univ. Rajputana Studies. Med. Sec.* 30-35, 1953-54. (*CA* 1956, 5238.)
19. Aston, B. C. 'The alkaloids of the pukatea.' *Trans. Proc. N.Z. Inst.* 41 (Proc.): 56-58, 1909.
20. Aston, B. C. 'Alkaloids of the pukatea.' *J. Chem. Soc.* 97: 1381, 1910.
21. Aston, B. C. 'Indigenous tans and vegetable dyestuffs of New Zealand.' *N.Z. J. Agric.* 15: 55-62, 117-28, 1917. 16: 358-65, 1918. 17: 136-39, 1919.
22. Aston, B. C. 'Preliminary note on the tinctorial properties of the genus *Coprosma* (Family Rubiaceae).' *N.Z. J. Sci. Tech.* 1: 3-4, 1918.
23. Aston, B. C. 'The genus *Coprosma* as a source of dyes.' *N.Z. J. Sci. Tech.* 1:264-67, 346-51, 1918.
24. Aston, B. C. 'The poisonous, suspected and medicinal plants of New Zealand.' *N.Z. J. Agric.* 16: 324-28, 1918. 17: 6-9, 1918. 26: 78-80, 149-56, 230-32, 1923.

25 Atkinson, N. and Brice, H. E. 'Antibacterial action of essential oils from some Australian plants.' *Aust. J. Exp. Biol. Med. Sci.* 33: 547-54, 1955. (*CA* 1956, 4462.)
26 Aubert, J. M. Letter to Director-General of Health. In Health Department files, 1924.
27 Baber, J. 'The medicinal properties of some New Zealand plants.' *Trans. Proc. N.Z. Inst.* 19: 319-22, 603, 1887.
28 Babulka, P. 'Feasibility of utilization of *Rumex* species in therapy.' *Gyogyszereszet.* 25: 81-87, 1981. (*CA* 1981, 94: 185150.)
29 Bagnall, A. G. and Petersen, G. C. *William Colenso.* Reed, Wellington, 1948.
30 Bailey, R. W. and Pain, V. 'Polysaccharide mannose in New Zealand ferns.' *Phytochem.* 10: 1065-73, 1971.
31 Baker, C. Journals. Typescript copies in the Auckland Museum Library. 1827-67.
32 Baker, M. 'Maori herbal medicine.' *Craccum*, Auckland University Students Association, 30 April 1985.
33 Barger, G. and Girardet, A. 'Constitution de la pukateine et de la laureline.' *Helv. Chim. Acta* 14: 481-504, 1931.
34 Barger, G. and Schlittler, E. 'Synthese von l-pukatein-methylather.' *Helv. Chim. Acta* 15: 381-94, 1932.
35 Barrau, J. 'Review of New Zealand medicinal plants.' *J. Polynesian Soc.* 71: 416, 1962.
36 Barton, B. H. and Castle, T. *The British flora medica.* Chatto & Windus, London, 1877. (New ed. rev. by J. R. Jackson.)
37 Basu, N. K. and Singh, G. B. 'Investigations on Indian medicinal plants: *Vitex negundo*.' *Quart. J. Pharm. & Pharmacol.* 20: 136-37, 1947. (*CA* 1948, 1025.)
38 Bathory, M. *et al.* 'Determination and isolation of ecdysteroids in goosefoot species.' *Herba Hung.* 23: 131-45, 1984. (*CA* 1985, 102: 182421.)
39 Baylis, G. T. S. 'Chromosome number and distribution of *Solanum aviculare* Forst. and *S. laciniatum* Ait.' *Trans. Roy. Soc. N.Z.* 82: 639-43, 1954.
40 Beattie, H. 'Nature-lore of the Southern Maori.' *Trans. Proc. N.Z. Inst.* 52: 53-77, 1920.
41 Beever, J. 'The origin of the name cabbage tree for *Cordyline* species in New Zealand. *Wellington Bot. Soc. Bull.* No. 41, 50-58, 1981.
42 Belen'kii, N. and Sakharova, E. 'Orach as a source of vitamin A.' *Sovet. Ptitsevodstov.* 27-28; *Khim. Referat. Zhur.* 12: 40, 1939. (*CA* 1941, 581.)
43 Belkin, M., Fitzgerald, Dorothea B. and Cogan, G. W. 'Tumour-damaging capacity of plant materials: I. Plants used as cathartics.' *J. Nat. Cancer Inst.* 13: 139-55, 1952. (*CA* 1953, 1851.)
44 Bell, Muriel E. 'Toxicology of karaka kernel, karakin, and β-nitropropionic acid.' *N.Z. J. Sci.* 17: 327-34, 1974.
45 Bell, T. W. 'Medical notes on New Zealand.' *N.Z. Med. J.* 3: 65-83, 129-45, 1890.
46 Benigni, R., Capra, C. and Cattorini, P. E. *Piante Medicinali.* Vol. 1. Inverni and Beffa, Milan, 1962.
47 Bennett, Dr Quoted in Bell (1890) (possibly from Bennett G., *Gatherings of a naturalist in Australasia . . .* John van Voorst, London, 1860).
48 Bennett, G. 'Nachrichten von Neuseelandischen Pflanzen, mitgetheilt von G. B. in der London Medical Gazette. Nov. u Dec. 1831.' *Annalen der Pharmacie.* 8: 332-35, 1833.
49 Bennett, W. D. 'Isolation of the cyanogenetic glucoside prunasin from bracken fern.' *Phytochem.* 7: 151-52, 1968.
50 Bergeron, J. M. and Goulet, M. 'Study on phytoestrogenic and phytotoxic effects of open-land plants on a laboratory mouse.' *Can. J. Zoo.* 58: 1575-81, 1980. (*CA* 1980, 93: 232070.)
51 Berghan, F. Personal communication.
52 Bernauer, K. 'Über alkaloide aus *Laurelia novae-zelandiae* A. Cunn.' *Helv. Chim. Acta* 50: 1583-88, 1967.
53 Berüter, J. and Somogyi, J. C. *7th Int. Congress of Nutrition* 5: 543, 1966. Quoted by Connor (ref. 156).
54 Best, E. 'Maori medical lore . . .' *J. Polynesian Soc.* 13: 213-37, 1905. 14: 1-23, 1906.
Best, E. 'Maori forest lore . . . Part I.' *Trans. Proc. N.Z. Inst.* 40. 185-254, 1908.
55 Best, E. Correspondence with T. F. Cheeseman. Auckland Museum Library.
56 Best, E. *The Maori.* Government Printer, Wellington, 1924. (Polynesian Soc. Mem. 5).
57 Bick, I. R. C. *et al.* 'Aristotelinone and serratoline: New indole alkaloids from

Aristotelia serrata W. R. B. Oliver.' *Tetrahedron Lett.* 21: 545–46, 1980.

58. Bick, I. R. C. and Hai, M. A. In *The alkaloids*, ed. A. Brossi, Vol. XXIV Academic Press, New York, 1985: 113–51.
59. Birch, A. J. *et al.* 'Ipomeamarone and ngaione.' *Chem. & Ind.* 902–3, 1954.
60. Blackman, J. G. and Sumich, M. *Proc. Univ. Otago Med. Sch.* 44: 25, 1966. Quoted by Connor (ref. 156).
61. Blake, S. T. 'Critical notes on the Gramineae and Cyperaceae of South Australia with descriptions of new species.' *Trans. Roy. Soc. S. Aust.* 67: 42–61, 1943.
62. Blunden, G. *et al.* 'Steroidal sapogenins from the leaves of *Cordyline* spp.' *J. Nat. Products.* 44: 441–47, 1981.
63. Bohlmann, F. and Zdero, C. 'Weitere acetylenverbindungen aus der familie Pittosporaceae.' *Chem. Ber.* 108: 2541–46, 1975.
64. Brandt, C. W. 'Chemistry of *Phormium tenax* (New Zealand Flax). Part I. The leaf and fibre of "Ngaro".' *N.Z. J. Sci. Tech.* 18: 613–27, 1937.
65. Brandt, C. W. and Neubauer, L. G. 'Miro resin I. Ferruginol. *J. Chem. Soc.* 1031–37, 1939.
66. Brandt, C. W. and Ross, D. J. 'Podocarpic acid as a source of an estrogenic hormone.' *Nature* 161: 892, 1948.
67. Brandt, C. W. and Ross, D. J. 'Constitution of ngaione.' *J. Chem. Soc.* 2778–81, 1949.
68. Brasch, D. J., Chuah, C-T. and Melton, L. D. 'A^{13}C. N.M.R. study of some agar related polysaccharides from some New Zealand seaweeds.' *Aust. J. Chem.* 34: 1095–1105, 1981.
69. Briggs, L. H. 'Plant products of New Zealand.' *J. Roy. Soc. N.S.W.* 80: 151–77, 1947.
70. Briggs, L. H. *et al.* 'Chemistry of the *Coprosma* genus. Part XIV. Constituents of five New Zealand species.' *J. C. S. Perkin I.* 1789–92, 1976.
71. Briggs, L. H. and Cambie, R. C. 'The constituents of *Phebalium nudum*. Hook: 1, The bark.' *Tetrahedron* 2: 256–70, 1958.
72. Briggs, L. H. and Cambie, R. C. 'Solanum alkaloids: Part XIII. The examination of alkaloids from seven *Solanum* species.' *J. Chem. Soc.* 1422–25, 1958.
73. Briggs, L. H., Cambie, R. C. and Couch, R. A. F. 'Triterpenes from some New Zealand dicotyledons.' *N.Z. J. Sci.* 10: 1076–82, 1967.
74. Briggs, L. H., Cambie, R. C. and Couch, R. A. F. 'Lirioresinol-C dimethyl ether, a diaxially substituted 3, 7-dioxabicyclo [3,3,0] octane lignan from *Macropiper excelsum* (Forst.f.) Miq.' *J. Chem. Soc. C.* 3042–45, 1968.
75. Briggs, L. H. *et al.* '*Sophora* alkaloids: Part VI. The alkaloids of the bark and flowers of *S. microphylla* and the isolation of diosmin from the flowers.' *J. Chem. Soc.* 1955–56, 1960.
76. Briggs, L. H. *et al.* 'Constituents of *Eugenia maire* A. Cunn.: Part I. A trimethyl ether of ellagic acid and mairin, a new triterpene.' *J. Chem. Soc.* 642–45, 1961.
77. Briggs, L. H., Cambie, R. C. and Montgomery, R. K. 'New Zealand phytochemical survey: 13. Constituents of the wood and bark of *Sophora microphylla* and *S. tetraptera*.' *N.Z. J. Sci.* 18: 555–58, 1975.
78. Briggs, L. H. and Cebalo, T. P. 'Chemistry of the Podocarpaceae: Part II. The isolation of genistein from *Podocarpus spicatus* and the constitution of podospicatin.' *Tetrahedron* 6: 145–47, 1959.
79. Briggs, L. H., Hassall, C. H. and Short, W. F. 'Leptospermone II.' *J. Chem. Soc.* 706–9, 1945.
80. Briggs, L. H. *et al.* 'A New Zealand phytochemical survey: 12. The essential oils of some New Zealand species.' *N.Z. J. Sci.* 18: 549–54, 1975.
81. Briggs, L. H. and Locker, R. H. 'Flavonols from the bark of *Melicope ternata*: Part I. The isolation of four new flavonols, meliternatin, meliternin, ternatin and wharangin.' *J. Chem. Soc.* 2157–62, 1949.
82. Briggs, L. H. and Locker, R. H. 'Chemistry of New Zealand *Melicope* species: Part IV. Constituents of the bark of *Melicope simplex*.' *J. Chem. Soc.* 2376–79, 1950.
83. Briggs, L. H. and Nicholls, G. A. 'Chemistry of the *Coprosma* genus: Part VIII. The occurrence of asperuloside.' *J. Chem. Soc.* 3940–43, 1954.
84. Briggs, L. H., Penfold, A. R. and Short, W. F. 'Leptospermone I.' *J. Chem. Soc.* 1193–95, 1938.
85. Briggs, L. H. and Ricketts, J. '*Sophora* alkaloids I: The alkaloids of the seeds

of *S. microphylla* Ait.' *J. Chem. Soc.* 1795-98, 1937.
86 Briggs, L. H. and Taylor, A. R. 'Chemistry of the *Coprosma* genus: Part X.' *J. Chem. Soc.* 3298-99, 1955.
87 Briggs, L. H. and Taylor, W. I. 'The occurrence of methyl salicylate in a fern, *Asplenium lamprophyllum.*' *Trans. Roy. Soc. N.Z.* 76: 597, 1947.
88 Briggs, L. H. and Taylor, W. S. '*Sophora* alkaloids II: The alkaloids of the seeds of *S. tetraptera.*' *J. Chem. Soc.* 1206-7, 1938.
89 *British pharmaceutical codex*, ed. C. E. Corfield. The Pharmaceutical Press, London, 1934.
90 Brooker, S. G. 'A note on the oil extracted from titoki berries (*Alectryon excelsum*).' *Trans. Roy. Soc. N.Z.* 84: 935, 1957.
91 Brooker, S. G. 'New Zealand plant fats: Part II. The oil of *Dysoxylum spectabile* Hook.' *Trans. Roy. Soc. N.Z.* 88: 157-58, 1960.
92 Brooker, S. G. 'New Zealand plant fats: Part III. The oil of *Tetrapathaea tetranda* Cheesem.' *Trans. Roy. Soc. N.Z.* 88: 158-59, 1960.
93 Brooker, S. G., Cambie, R. C. and Cooper, R. C. *New Zealand medicinal plants*. 2nd ed. Heinemann, Auckland, 1981.
94 Brooker, S. G., Cambie, R. C. and Cooper, R. C. 'Economic native plants of New Zealand.' Unpublished manuscript, 1985.
95 Brooker, S. G. and Cooper, R. C. *New Zealand medicinal plants*. Unity Press, Auckland, 1961 (Handbook of the Auckland Museum).
96 Brown, T. E. and Eyster, H. C. 'Carbonic anhydrase in certain species of plants.' *Ohio J. Sci.* 55: 257-62, 1955. (*CA* 1956, 5099.)
97 Brownsey, P. J., Given, D. R. and Lovis, J. D. 'A revised classification of New Zealand pteridophytes with a synonymic checklist of species.' *N.Z. J. Bot.* 23: 431-89, 1985.
98 Bruckner, B. H. *et al. J. Clin. Invest.* 28: 894-98, 1949. (*CA*, 1950, 44: 10796.)
99 Buchanan, J. 'Sketch of the botany of Otago.' *Trans. Proc. N.Z. Inst.* 1: (pt. 3 — essays) 22-53, 1869. 2nd ed. 1875: 181-212.
100 Buck, P. (Te Rangi Hiroa). *The coming of the Maori*. Whitcombe & Tombs Ltd., Christchurch, 1949.
101 Bulmer, R. N. H. Personal communication.
102 Burkill, I. H. *A dictionary of the economic products of the Malay Peninsula*. Crown Agents for the Colonies, London, 1935.
103 Burn, J. H. and Withell, E. R. 'A principle in raspberry leaves which relaxes uterine muscle.' *Lancet* (2): 1-3, 1941.
104 Burton, J. F. and Cain, B. F. 'Antileukaemic activity of polyporic acid.' *Nature* 184: 1326-27, 1959.
105 Butt, P. H. *et al. Proceedings, 4th Asian symposium on medicinal plants and spices*. Bangkok. 1980: 30-39.
106 Bylicka, H., *et al*. 'Antibiotics of lichens.' *Acta microbiol. Polon.* 1: 185-92, 1952. (*CA* 1955, 6364.)
107 Cain, B. F. 'Note on partition chromatography of ellagic acid ethers.' *N.Z. J. Sci.* 5: 390-92, 1962.
108 Cain, B. F. 'The water soluble phenolics of bark extracts of *Leptospermum scoparium* Forst.' *N.Z. J. Sci.* 6: 264-68, 1963.
109 Cain, B. F. and Cambie, R. C. 'Leaf extractives from *Pomaderris elliptica* Labill.' *N.Z. J. Sci.* 2: 240-43, 1959.
110 Caius, J. F. 'Medicinal and poisonous plants of India: Flacourtiads, Pittosporads, etc.' *J. Bombay Nat. Hist. Soc.* 41: 369-83, 1939.
111 Calder, A. J. and Carter, C. L. 'The essential oil of *Pittosporum tenuifolium.*' *J. Soc. Chem. Ind. Lond.* 68: 355-56, 1949.
112 Cambie, R. C. 'The extractives of *Dysoxylum spectabile* Hook.' *J. Chem. Soc.* 468-69, 1959.
113 Cambie, R. C. 'The constituents of *Phebalium nudum* Hook: 2. Alkaloids of the wood.' *N.Z. J. Sci.* 2: 254-56, 1959.
114 Cambie, R. C. 'The extractives of *Vitex lucens* T. Kirk. Part 2. The leaves and bark.' *N.Z. J. Sci.* 2: 230-36, 1959.
115 Cambie, R. C. 'Wood extractives of *Aristotelia serrata.*' *N.Z. J. Sci.* 2: 257-59, 1959.
116 Cambie, R. C. 'Utilization of New Zealand natural products.' *Chemistry in New Zealand* 35: 69-76, 1971.
117 Cambie, R. C. 'Obituary: Lindsay Heathcote Briggs.' *Proc. Roy. Soc. N.Z.* 103: 100-110, 1975.
118 Cambie, R. C. 'A New Zealand phytochemical register: Part III.' *J. Roy. Soc. N.Z.* 6: 307-79, 1976.
119 Cambie, R. C. Unpublished results.
120 Cambie, R. C. and Cain, B. F. 'Bark extractives of *Dacrydium cupressinum.*'

N.Z. J. Sci. 3: 121-26, 1960.
121 Cambie, R. C. and Couch, R. A. F. 'Extractives of some *Myrsine* species.' N.Z. J. Sci. 10: 1020-29, 1967.
122 Cambie, R. C. and De la Mare, P. B. D. 'Organic Chemistry'. In *Chemistry in a young country*, ed. P. P. Williams. N.Z. Institute of Chemistry Inc. Christchurch, 1981.
123 Cambie, R. C. and Parnell, J. C. 'A New Zealand phytochemical survey: Part 7. Constituents of some dicotyledons.' N.Z. J. Sci. 12: 453-66, 1969.
124 Cambie, R. C. and Parnell, J. C. 'A New Zealand phytochemical survey: Part 8. Constituents of some New Zealand plants.' N.Z. J. Sci. 13: 108-16, 1970.
125 Cambie, R. C. and Potter, G. J. 'Utilization of solasodine as a potential ecdysone antagonist.' *Chemistry in New Zealand* 43: 91-93, 1979.
126 Cambie, R. C. and Seelye, R. N. 'Note on the identification of manuka manna.' N.Z. J. Sci. 2: 498, 1959.
127 Cambie, R. C. and Seelye, R. N. 'Constituents of the flowers of *Metrosideros excelsa* Sol. ex Gaertn.' N.Z. J. Sci. 4: 189-93, 1961.
128 Cambie, R. C., Simpson, W. R. J. and Colebrook, L. D. 'Chemistry of the Podocarpaceae: VII. Podototarin and the constituents of the heartwood of *Podocarpus hallii* Kirk.' *Tetrahedron* 19: 209-17, 1963.
129 Campbell, W. P. and Todd, D. 'Structure and configuration of resin acids: Podocarpic acid and ferruginol.' *J. Amer. Chem. Soc.* 64: 928-35, 1942.
130 Carlomagno, J. 'Etiopina, a nitrogenated organic base extracted from calla *Zantedeschia aethiopica* (L.) Spreng: Araceae.' *Rev. univ. nacl. Cordoba (Arg.).* 35: 211-14, 1948. (CA 1949, 43: 1156.)
131 Carter, C. L. 'Karakin, the glucoside of *Corynocarpus laevigata* and hiptagenic acid.' *J. Soc. Chem. Ind. Trans.* 62: 238-40, 1943.
132 Carter, C. L. 'The constitution of karakin.' *J. Sci. Fd. Agric.* 2: 54-55, 1951.
133 Carter, C. L. and Heazlewood, W. V. 'The essential oil of *Pittosporum eugenoides*.' *J. Soc. Chem. Ind. Lond.* 68: 34-36, 1949.
134 Cashmore, A. R. *et al.* 'The structure of prostratin: A toxic tetracyclic diterpene ester from *Pimelea prostrata*.' *Tetrahedron Lett.* 1737-38, 1976.
135 Chapman, G. T. *Chapman's centenary memorial of Captain Cook's description of New Zealand one hundred years ago.* G. T. Chapman, Auckland, 1870.
136 Chapman, T. Letters and journals, 1830-69. Typescript copy in Auckland Museum Library.
137 Chapman, V. J. and Chapman, D. J. *Seaweeds and their uses.* 3rd ed. Chapman & Hall, London, 1980.
138 Cheeseman, T. F. *Illustrations of the New Zealand flora.* Government Printer, Wellington, 1914.
139 Cheeseman, T. F. *Manual of the New Zealand flora.* 2nd ed. Government Printer, Wellington, 1925.
140 Chemistry Division, DSIR Report, 1979.
141 Chopra, R. N., Nayar, S. L. and Chopra, I. C. *Glossary of Indian medicinal plants.* Council of Scientific and Industrial Research, New Delhi, 1956.
142 Chumbalov, T. K. and Fedeeva, O. V. 'Antineoplastic preparations from some plants of Kazakhstan.' *Tezisy Dokl.* 58-60, 1974. (CA 1977 86: 136339.)
143 Church, A. H. 'Further report on the chemistry of *Phormium tenax*.' *Trans. Proc. N.Z. Inst.* 6: 260-71, 1874.
144 Churchward, F. Personal communication.
145 Ciulei, I. and Istudor, V. 'Chemical studies of the species *Rumex wallachii*.' *Farmacia* (Bucharest) 21: 85-88, 1983. (CA 1973, 79: 102756.)
146 Clare, N. T. *Photosensitization in diseases of domestic animals.* Commonwealth Bureau of Animal Health, 1952. (Rev. series No. 3.)
Clare, N. T. 'Photosensitization in animals.' *Advances in Veterinary Science* 2: 182, 1955.
147 Cockayne, L. *Report on the sand dune areas of New Zealand.* Government Printer, Wellington, 1909.
148 Cockayne, L. and Allan, H. H. 'Notes on New Zealand floristic botany, including descriptions of new species, etc. (No. 5).' *Trans. Proc. N.Z. Inst.* 57: 48-72, 1927.
149 Colenso, W. Quoted from a letter to W. J. Hooker. *London J. Bot.* 3: 45, 1844.
150 Colenso, W. 'On the botany of the North Island of New Zealand.' *Trans. Proc. N.Z. Inst.* 1: (pt. 3 — essays), 1-58, 1869. 2nd ed: 233-83, 1875.
151 Colenso, W. 'On the Maori races of

New Zealand.' *Trans. Proc. N.Z. Inst.* 1 (pt. 3 — essays): 1-76, 1869. 2nd ed.: 339-424, 1875.

152 Colenso, W. 'On the vegetable food of the ancient New Zealanders before Cook's visit.' *Trans. Proc. N.Z. Inst.* 13: 3, 1881.

153 Colenso, W. Quoted in Aston, 1917 (ref. 21).

154 Collier, S. Unpublished notes on the files of Botany Division, DSIR, Christchurch, 1941.

155 Conn, B. J. 'A taxonomic revision of *Geniostoma* subs. *Geniostoma* (Loganiaceae).' *Blumea.* 26: 245-364, 1980.

156 Connor, H. E. *The poisonous plants in New Zealand.* 2nd rev. ed. Government Printer, Wellington, 1977.

157 Cook, J. *A voyage towards the South Pole and round the world.* Strahan & Cadell, London, 1777.

158 Corbett, R. E. and McDowall, M. A. 'Extractives from the New Zealand Myrtaceae: Part III.' *J. Chem. Soc.* 3715-16, 1958.

159 Cowan, J. *The Maori yesterday and today.* Whitcombe & Tombs Ltd., Christchurch, 1930.

160 Cranwell, Lucy M. 'Medicinal Plants of the New Zealand Maori,' 1941. Manuscript notes, Auckland Museum.

161 Cranwell, Lucy M. *The botany of Auckland.* 3rd ed. Auckland Museum, 1981.

162 Cranwell, Lucy M. and von Post, L. 'Post Pleistocene pollen diagrams from the Southern Hemisphere.' *Geogr. Annalen* 3-4: 308-47, 1936.

163 Craven, B. M. 'The molecular structure of tutin.' *Nature* 197: 1193-94, 1963.

164 Craven, B. M. 'The crystal structure and absolute configuration of α-bromoisotutin.' *Acta Cryst.* 17: 396-403, 1964.

165 Crawford, J. C. 'On New Zealand coffee.' *Trans. Proc. N.Z. Inst.* 9: 545-46, 1877.

166 Cribb, A. B. and Cribb, J. W. *Wild medicine in Australia.* Collins, Sydney, 1981.

167 Crookes, M. *New Zealand Herald,* 7 October, 1974.

168 Cruise, R. A. *Journal of a ten months' residence in New Zealand (1820).* 2nd ed. Longman, Hurst, London, 1824.

169 Culpeper, N. *Culpeper's complete herbal.* W. Foulsham and Co., London, 1652.

170 Cunningham, G. H. *The Gasteromycetes of Australia and New Zealand.* McIndoe, Dunedin, 1942.

171 Czapek, A. 'Phytoncides of spices.' *Prumysl Potravin* 6: 433-35, 1955. *(CA* 1956, 504.)

172 Czetsch-Lindenwald, H. v. '*Rumex alpinus* and *Rumex hydrolapathum* as raw materials for the preparation of galenicals.' *Dtsch. Heilpfl.* 9: 99-101, 1943. *(CA* 1945, 2847.)

173 Dacre, J. C. Personal communication.

174 Daniel, K. 'Further communciations on the photodynamic substance hypericin.' *Hippokrates* 20: 526-30, 1949. *(CA* 1952, 9721.)

175 D'Arcy, P. F. and Howard, E. M. 'A new anti-inflammatory test, using the chlorio-allantoic membrane of the chick embryo.' *Brit. J. Pharmacol. Chemother.* 29: 378-87, 1967. *(CA* 1967, 66: 114278.)

176 Dawson, J. W. 'New Zealand Umbelliferae. *Lignocarpa* Gen. Nov. and *Scandia* Gen. Nov.' *N.Z. J. Bot.* 5: 400-17, 1967.

177 Dieffenbach, E. *Travels in New Zealand; with contributions to the geography, geology, botany and natural history of that country.* J. Murray, London, 1843.

178 *The dispensatory of the United States of America.* 21st ed. Lippincott, Philadelphia, 1926.

179 Drury, D. G. 'A broadly based taxonomy of *Lagenifera.*' *N.Z. J. Bot.* 12: 365-96, 1974.

180 Dumkow, K. and Pohl, R. 'The isolation and identification of flavonol glycosides of *Euphorbia exigua* and *Euphorbia peplus.*' *Planta Medica* 24: 145-47, 1973.

181 Dzhumagalieva, F. D. and Seidakhanova, T. A. 'Various aspects of the pharmacological action of polyphenol compounds.' *Tr. Inst. Fiziol, Akad. Nauk Kaz. SSR.* 16: 33-38, 1971. *(CA* 1972, 76: 94605.)

182 Easterfield, T. H. 'Studies on the chemistry of the New Zealand flora.' *Trans. Proc. N.Z. Inst.* 43: 53-55, 1911. J. Bee is the joint author of a note on the matai (*Podocarpus spicatus*) on pp. 54-55.

183 Easterfield, T. H. and Aston, B. C. Tutu: Part I. Tutu: Part II. N.Z. Dept. Agric. Chemical Div. Bulletins, 1900, 1901.

184 Easterfield, T. H. and Aston, B. C. 'Studies on the chemistry of the New Zealand flora: Part I. The tutu plant.' *Trans. & Proc. N.Z. Inst.* 33: 345-55 and

550, 1901. 'Part II. The karaka-nut.' Ibid. 34: 495–97, and 566–67, 1902. 'Part III. Rimu-resin.' Ibid. 36: 483–86, 526. 1904.

185 Easterfield, T. H. and McDowell, J. C. 'Studies on the chemistry of the New Zealand flora: Part V. The chemistry of *Podocarpus totara* and *Podocarpus spicatus*.' *Trans. Proc. N.Z. Inst.* 48: 518–20, 1916.

186 Easterfield, T. H. Bibliography of the papers of Professor Easterfield. *Trans. Roy. Soc. N.Z.* 78: 383–84, 1950.

187 Eckey, E. W. *Vegetable fats and oils* . Reinhold, New York, 1954.

188 Edgar, E. 'Nomina nova plantarum Novae-Zelandiae, 1960–1969: Gymnospermae, Angiospermae.' *N.Z.J. Bot.* 9: 322–30, 1971.

189 Edgar, E. and Connor, H. E. 'Nomina nova II 1970–1976.' *N.Z.J. Bot.* 16: 103–18, 1978.

190 Edgar, E. and Connor, H. E. 'Nomina nova III 1977–1982.' *N.Z.J. Bot.* 21: 421–41, 1983.

191 Eglinton, G., Hamilton, R. J. and Martin-Smith, M. 'The alkane constituents of some New Zealand plants and their possible taxonomic implications.' *Phytochem.* 1: 137–45, 1962.

192 Eldridge, Joan. 'Bush medicine in the Exumas and Long Island, Bahamas: A field study.' *Economic Botany* 29: 307–32, 1975.

193 Emboden, W. A. *Bizarre plants*. Studio Vista, London, 1974.

194 *The extra pharmacopoeia*. 22nd ed. The Pharmaceutical Press, London, 1941.

195 *The extra pharmacopoeia*. 27th ed. The Pharmaceutical Press, London, 1972.

196 Embrey, H. 'The antiscorbutic vitamin in some oriental fruits and vegetables.' *Phil. J. Sci.* 22: 77–82, 1923. (*CA* 1922, 17: 1273.)

197 Evans, I. A. 'The radiomimetic nature of bracken toxins.' *Cancer Research* 28: 2252–61, 1968.

198 Evans, I. A. *Proceedings 10th International Cancer Congress* (Houston). 1970: 178. Quoted by Connor (ref. 156).

199 Evans, I. A. and Osman, M. A. 'Carcinogenicity of bracken and shikimic acid.' *Nature* 250: 348–49, 1974.

200 Eyres, L. and Brooker, S. G. 'Lipids of the New Zealand species of the Sapindaceae.' Handbook of 10th International Symposium on the Chemistry of Natural Products. Dunedin (B33), 1976.

201 Fankhauser, B. L. and Brasch, D. J. 'The preparation of high fructose syrup from the New Zealand cabbage tree *Cordyline australis*.' *N.Z.J.Tech.* 1: 27–31, 1985.

202 Fany, Z. and Yu, J. 'Study on hemostatic constituent of Xue Dang Gui *Rumex chalerpensis* Mill.' *Jiangxi Inst. Pharmacol. Peoples' Repub. China Zhongcaoyao* 138: 6–7, 1982. (*CA* 1982, 97: 133423.)

203 Fastier, F. N. 'Tutu poisoning.' In *Research in Physiology*, F. F. Kao, K. Koizumi and M. Vassalle. Aulo Gaggi, Bologna, 1971.

204 Fastier, F. N. and Laws, G. F. 'Drugs from New Zealand plants?' *Search* 6: 117–20, 1975.

205 Faulkner, A. E. Address to Registered Nurses' Association, Tauranga. 'Medical lore of old-time Maori.' *Dominion* , Wellington, 23 May 1959.

206 Field, H. C. *The ferns of New Zealand*. Griffith, Farren, London, 1890.

207 Firth, R. W. 'The kauri gum industry, some economic aspects.' Thesis, University of New Zealand, 1922.

208 Fitzpatrick, Florence K. 'Plant substances active against *Mycobacterium tuberculosis*.' *Antibiotics and Chemotherapy* 4: 528–36, 1954. (*CA* 1954, 13800.)

209 Fleming, C. A. 'The geological history of New Zealand.' *Tuatara* 2: 79–90, 1949.

210 Fleming, C. A. 'The history of life in New Zealand forests.' *Forest and Bird* 210:2–10, 1978.

211 Fleming, C. A. *The geological history of New Zealand and its life*. Auckland University Press, 1979.

212 Flück, H., Jaspersen-Schib, Rita and Rowson, J. M. *Medicinal plants*. 1st English translation. Foulsham, Hong Kong, 1976.

213 Fogg, W. S. 'The pharmacological action of pukateine.' *J. Pharmacol.* 54: 167–87, 1935.

214 Fukuoka, M. 'Chemical and toxicological studies on bracken fern, *Pteridium aquilinum* var. *latiusculum*: VI. Isolation of 5-0-caffeoylshikimic acid as antithiamine factor.' *Chem. Pharm. Bull. Japan* 30: 3219–24, 1982.

215 Fukuoka, M. *et al.* 'Chemical and toxicological studies on bracken fern, *Pteridium aquilinum* var. *latiusculum*: II. Structures of pterosins,

sesquiterpenes having 1-indanone skeleton.' *Chem. Pharm. Bull. Japan* 26: 2365-85, 1978.
216 Fulton, R. *Medical practice in Otago and Southland in the early days*. Otago Daily Times and Witness Newspapers Co. Ltd., Dunedin, 1922.
217 Galanti, M. and Manil, P. 'Antibiotic action of extracts of higher plants: Some experimental observations on the genus *Geranium*.' *C.R. Soc. Biol.* 148: 1892-94, 1954. (CA 1955, 13594.)
218 Galloway, D. J. *Flora of New Zealand: Lichens*. Government Printer, Wellington, 1985.
219 Gardner, C. A. and Bennetts, H. W. *The toxic plants of Western Australia*. West Australian Newspapers, Perth, 1956.
220 Gardner, R. 'Notes on the chemistry of the New Zealand flora.' *N.Z.J. Sci. Tech.* 6: 147-51, 1923.
Gardner, R. 'Further notes on the chemistry of the New Zealand flora.' *N.Z.J. Sci. Tech.* 7: 220-21, 1924.
221 Gardner, R. 'The essential oils of *Metrosideros*.' *J. Soc. Chem. Ind.* 50: 141-44T, 1931.
222 Gardner, R. O. 'Six plants whose nativity to New Zealand has been doubted.' *Auckland Bot. Soc. Newsletter* 40 (2):'41-44, 1985.
223 Garg, S. K. and Mathur, V. S. 'Effect of chromatographic fractions of *Polygonum hydropiper* (roots) on fertility in female albino rats.' *J. Reprod. Fert.* 29: 421-23, 1972. (CA 1972, 77: 97314.)
224 Gatty, H. 'The use of fish poison plants in the Pacific.' *Fiji Soc. Sci. Ind.* 3: 152-59, 1947.
225 Georgadze, V. N. 'Pharmacology of the *Sophora* alkaloids.' *J. Physiol. USSR* 25: 179-95, 1947. (CA 1939, 2994.)
226 Gerritsen, F. B. J. *Belg. Pat. B. E.* 890671, 1982. (CA 1982, 96: 129815.)
227 Girven, A. Letter on the files of the Auckland Museum, 1961.
228 Given, D. R. 'A register of rare and endangered indigenous plants in New Zealand.' *N.Z. J. Bot.* 14: 135-49, 1976.
229 Given, D. R. 'A taxonomic revision of *Celmisia coriacea* (Forst.f.) Hook.f. and its immediate allies.' *N.Z. J. Bot.* 18: 127-43, 1980.
230 Given, K. Unpublished notes on the files of Botany Division, DSIR, Christchurch, 1940.
231 Glenn, R. *The botanical explorers of New Zealand*. Reed, Wellington, 1950.

232 Gluckman, L. K. *Tanigiwai, a medical history of New Zealand prior to 1860*. Published by the author, Auckland, 1976.
233 Goldie, W. H. 'Maori medical lore . . .' *Trans. Proc. N.Z. Inst.* 37: 1-120, 1905.
234 Goodyear, J. *'Dioscorides' Greek Herbal Trans*. 'Englished' by J. Goodyear, 1655. Hafner, New York, 1959.
235 Gotta, H., Opferkuch, H. J. and Hecker, E. 'On the active principles of the Euphorbiaceae: IX. Ingenane type diterpene esters from five *Euphorbia* species.' *Z. Naturforsch.* 39B: 683-94, 1984.
236 Gower, A. A. Unpublished notes on the files of Botany Division, DSIR, Christchurch, 1940.
237 Grange, L. I. 'Diatomite: principal New Zealand occurrences and uses.' *N.Z. J. Sci. Tech.* 12: 94-99, 1930.
238 Gregory, B. C. *et al.* 'Debate on introduction of Maori Affairs Amendment Bill.' *Hansard* 444: 868-82, 1982.
239 Greville, R. P. (Chairman). *Report of a commission to inspect and classify kauri-gum reserves in the Land District of Auckland*. Government Printer, Wellington, 1914.
240 Gunter, M. J. *et al.* 'Choleretic potencies of some synthetic compounds.' *J. Pharmacol. Exp. Therap.* 99: 465-78, 1950 (CA 1951, 263.)
241 Gurevich, A. I. *et al.* 'Hyperforin, an antibiotic from *Hypericum perforatum*.' *Antibiotiki* 16: 510-13, 1971. (CA 1971, 75: 95625.)
242 Guseva, A. 'Determination of aucubin in Eucommia.' *Dokl. Ak. Nauk. S.S.S.R.* 85: 1353-56, 1952. (CA 1953, 1243.)
243 Gusinde, M. 'Plantas medicinales que los indios Araucanos recomiedan.' *Anthropos* 31: 555-71, 850-73, 1936.
244 Hagenstrom, U. 'The occurrence of an antibacterial fraction in the capsules of some species of *Hypericum*.' *Anzneimittel-Forsch.* 5: 155, 1952. (CA 1955, 8389.)
245 Hall, R. B. Private communication, 1985.
246 Hamilton, E. *The flora homoeopathica*. Leath & Ross, London, 1852.
247 Hamilton, W. D. *et al.* '(-)-Epingaione, (-)-dehydrongaione, (-)-dehydroepingaione, and (-)-deisopropylngaione, toxic furanoid sesquiterpenoid ketones from *Myoporum deserti*.' *Aust. J. Chem.* 26:

375-87, 1973.
248 Hamlin, B. G. 'A new name in *Sonchus* for New Zealand.' *N.Z. J. Bot.* 14: 279, 1976.
249 Han, D. S. and Cho, H. J. 'Studies in the naphthaquinones of the root of *Polygonum ciliinerve*.' *Owi. Saengyak Hakhoe Chi.* 12: 221-26, 1981. *(CA* 1982, 97: 20714.)
250 Handy, E. S. C., Pukui, Mary K. and Livermore, Katherine. 'Outline of Hawaiian physical therapeutics.' *Bull. Bishop Mus.* 126: 1-51, 1934.
251 Harvey, H. Private communication, 1985.
252 Hashimoto, Y. and Maeda, Y. 'Animal protein factor and vitamin B_{12} in marine products: 11. Seaweeds.' *Bull. Jap. Soc. Sci. Fish.* 19: 141-44, 1953. *(CA* 1955, 5697.)
253 Healy, A. J. *Identification of weeds and clovers, with a chapter on aquatic weeds by R. Mason.* Editorial Services, Wellington, 1970.
254 Healy, A. J. and Edgar, E. *Flora of New Zealand*, Vol. 3. Government Printer, Wellington, 1980.
255 Hector, J. *Phormium tenax as a fibrous plant.* Col. Museum & Geol. Survey Dept., Wellington, 1872.
256 Hegarty, B. F. *et al.* '(-)-Ngaione, a toxic constituent of *Myoporum deserti*. The absolute configuration of (-)-ngaione.' *Aust. J. Chem.* 23: 107-17, 1970.
257 Hegnauer, R. *Chemotaxonomie der Pflanzen.* Birkhauser Verlag, 1962-73.
258 Hei, H. Unpublished notes on the files of Botany Division, DSIR, Christchurch, 1941.
259 Hemsley, W. B. 'On the genus *Corynocarpus* Forst., with descriptions of two new species.' *Ann. Bot.* 17: 743-60, 1903.
260 Herler, M. 'Ointment for treating inflammatory or septic processes.' Austrian Patent 172, 670, 1952. *(CA* 1952, 11592.)
261 Herz, W. *et al.* 'The antimicrobial principle of *Clematis dioscoreifolia*.' *Science* 114: 206, 1951.
262 Hill, R. and Heyningen, Ruth van. 'Ranunculin, the precursor of the vesicant substance of the buttercup.' *Biochem. J.* 49: 332-35, 1951.
263 Hirono, I. *et al. J. Nat. Cancer Inst.* 48: 1245, 1972. Quoted by Connor (ref. 156).
264 Ho, L-Y., Chen, B-Z. and Xiao, P-G. 'Survey, identification and constituent analysis of Chinese herbal medicines from the genus *Rumex*.' *Yao Hsueh Hsueh Pao.* 16: 289-93, 1981. *(CA* 1981, 95: 175626.)
265 Hodge, W. H. *American Fern Journal* 63: 77, 1973. Quoted by Connor (ref. 156).
266 Hofmann, A. and Tscherter, H. 'Isolierung von Lysergsaure — Alkaloiden aus der mexakanischen Zauberdroge Ololiugui [*Rivea corymbosa* (L.) Hall f.]' *Experientia* 16: 414, 1960.
267 Honana, H. Unpublished notes on the files of Botany Division, DSIR, Christchurch, 1941.
268 Hooker, J. D. *Handbook of the New Zealand flora.* Reeve, London, 1864-67.
269 Hooker, J. D. (Ed.) *Journal of the Right Hon. Sir Joseph Banks, Bart., KB, PRS, during Captain Cook's first voyage in HMS Endeavour in 1768-71 to Terra Del Fuego, Otahite, New Zealand, Australia and the Dutch East Indies, etc.* Macmillan, London, 1896.
270 Hosking, J. R. and Brandt, C. W. 'Contributions to the chemistry of the genus *Dacrydium*.' *N.Z. J. Sci. Tech.* 17: 750-58, 1936.
271 Hughes, G. K. *et al.* 'Alkaloids of the Australian Rutaceae.' *Nature* 162: 223-24, 1948.
272 Humphreys, F. R. 'Drugs from Australian plants have medicinal uses.' *Forest and Timber* (Forestry Commission of NSW) 14: 2-4, 1978.
273 Hunt, P. (daughter of Rev. E. Ward) Personal communication.
274 Hunter, J. A. 'New Zealand *Todea* fibre and orchid growing.' *J. Roy. N.Z. Inst. Hort.* 2: 342-45, 1958.
275 Hutchins, R. F. N. *et al.* 'Toxicity of nitrocompounds from *Lotus pedunculatus* to grass grub (*Costelytra zealandica*) (Coleoptera — Scarabaeidae).' *J. Chem. Ecol.* 10: 81-93.
276 Hutchinson, Amy H. *Plant dyeing.* The Daily Telegraph Co., Napier, 1941.
277 Imperato, F. 'Two new kaempferide 3, 7-diglycosides from the fern *Asplenium bulbiferum*.' *Chem. & Ind.* (London): 186-87, 1984.
278 Ironside, S. Diary. 1841. Published in *N.Z. Methodist*, 7 February 1981. (In Kinder Library, St. John's College, Auckland.)
279 Ito, H. and Hikada, H. *Jap. Pat.* 80, 157, 516, 1980 *(CA* 1981, 94: 71478.)
280 Jensen, S. R. and Nielsen, B. J. 'Iridoid alkaloids in *Griselinia, Aralidium* and

281 Jogia, M. K., Vakamoceae, V., and Weaver, R. T. 'Synthesis of some furfural and syringic acid derivatives.' *Aust. J. Chem.* 38: 1009-16, 1985. *Toricella*.' *Phytochem.* 19: 2685-88, 1980.

282 Johannesson, J. K. Personal communication through M. Martin-Smith.

283 Johns, Barbara. 'The ascorbic acid content of some New Zealand products.' *N.Z. J. Sci. Tech.* 27A: 188-97, 1945.

284 Johns, R. B., Slater, S. N. and Woods, R. J. 'Picrotoxin and tutin: Part VIII.' *J. Chem. Soc.* 4715-27, 1956.

285 Johnson, J. 'Colonial surgeon.' 1847. Typescript manuscript in Auckland Museum Library.

286 Kahaki, Hirini. Unpublished notes, Botany Division, DSIR, Christchurch, 1941.

287 Kahaki, Kiri. Unpublished notes, Botany Division, DSIR, Christchurch, 1941.

288 Kang, S. S. and Woo, W. S. 'Anthraquinones from the leaves of *Polygonum sacchalinense*.' *Saengyak Hakhoe Chi.* 13: 7-9, 1982. (CA 1982, 97: 141734.)

289 Kariyone, T., Kasiwagi, K. and Mizutani, S. 'The constituents of *Coriaria japonica* V.' *J. Pharm. Soc. Japan* 57: 182-83, 1937. (CA 1939, 6279.)

290 Kariyone, T. and Sato, T. 'The poisonous principle of *Coriaria japonica* A. Gray II.' *J. Pharm. Soc. Japan* 50: 659-60, 1930. (CA 1930, 5109.) Kariyone, T. and Sato, T. 'Poisonous constituents of *Coriaria japonica* A. Gray III.' *Ibid.* 51: 988-93, 1931. (CA 1932, 1936.)

291 Kato, M. et al. 'Studies in the structure of the polysaccharide from *Tetragonia tetragonioides*.' *Chem. Pharm. Bull. Japan.* 33: 3675-80, 1985.

292 Kauri Deposit Surveys Ltd. 'Report on project concept and environmental assessment.' Lodged with Lands and Survey Dept., 1979.

293 Kerry-Nicholls, J. H. *The King Country*. 3rd ed. Sampson Low, Marston, London, 1884.

294 Kerry-Nicholls, J. H. 'The origin, physical characteristics, and manners and customs of the Maori race, from data derived during a recent exploration of the King Country, New Zealand.' *J. R. Anthrop. Inst.* 15: 187-209, 1886.

295 Kesteven, L. Quoted in Bell (ref. 45).

296 Kezeli, T. A. and Dzhaparidze, L. I. 'Ascorbic acid content of some higher fungi.' *Bull. Acad. Sci. Georgian SSR.* 5: 993-96, 1944. (CA 1947, 3172.)

297 Kezeli, T. A. and Tarasashvili, K. M. 'Content of vitamin C in hay from high mountain plants.' *Soobshch. Akad. Nauk Gruz. SSR.* 13: 407-11, 1952. (CA 1954, 6520.)

298 Kilgore, L. B., Ford, J. H. and Wolfe, W. C. 'Insecticidal properties of 1,3-indandiones.' *Industr. Engng. Chem.* 34: 494-97, 1942.

299 King, R. O. C. '*Chenopodium atriplicinum* (lamb's tongue), a plant toxic for sheep in the immature stages of growth.' *NSW Dept. Agric. Research Rept.* 7: 95-100, 1937. (CA 1939, 3424.)

300 Kinghorn, A. D., Balandrin, M. F. and Lin, L-J. 'Alkaloid distribution in some species of the Papilionaceous tribes Sophoreae, Dalbergieae, Loteae, Brongniartieae and Bossiaceae.' *Phytochem.* 21: 2269-75, 1982.

301 Kingzett, C. T. *Chemical encyclopaedia.* Gresham, London, 1928.

302 Kinoshita, K. 'Constituents of *Coriaria japonica* Gray II. Coriarine.' *J. Chem. Soc. Japan* 51: 99-105, 1930. (CA 1932, 731.) Kinoshita, K. 'Constituents of *Coriaria japonica* Gray III. Catalytic reduction of tutin.' *Ibid.* 52: 171-76, 1931. (CA 1932, 5100.)

303 Kirk, T. 'On the export of fungus from New Zealand.' *Trans. Proc. N.Z. Inst.* 11: 454-56, 1879.

304 Kirk, T. *The forest flora of New Zealand.* Government Printer, Wellington, 1889.

305 Kirk, T. 'Plants indigenous to New Zealand, available for food, medicine, and other economic purposes.' Unpublished notes, Auckland Museum.

306 Klinkowski, M. 'The inactivation of tobacco-mosaic virus by fungal metabolic products.' *Mitt. Biol. Zent. Anst. Berl.* 80: 162-68, 1954. (CA 1955, 8375.)

307 Kloosterman, J. 'Development of steroid synthesis from natural products.' *Chemistry in New Zealand.* 43: 146-47, 1979.

308 Koedam, A. '*Plantago* — History and use.' *Pharm. Weekbl.* 112: 246-52, 1977. (CA 1977, 86: 136269.)

309 Kofod, H. and Eyjolfsson, R. 'The

310. isolation of the cyanogenic glycoside prunasin from *Pteridium aquilinum* (L.) Kühn.' *Tetrahedron Lett.* 1289-91, 1966.
310. Kora, T. Unpublished notes, Botany Division, DSIR, Christchurch, 1941.
311. Kozuka, M. *et al.* 'The granulation-inhibiting principles of *Euphorbia peplus*: II, The structures of euglobal-Ia$_1$, -Ia$_2$, -Ib, -Ic, -IIa, -IIb and -IIc.' *Chem. Pharm. Bull. Japan.* 30: 1952-63, 1982.
312. Krayer, O. and Briggs, L. H. 'Antiaccelerator cardiac action of solasodine and some of its derivatives.' *Brit. J. Pharmacol.* 5: 118, 517, 1950.
313. Kreitmair, H. 'Pharmacological trials with some domestic plants.' *E. Merck's Jber.* 50: 102-10, 1936. (*CA* 1937, 3149.)
314. Kubo, M. *Jap. Pat.* 7, 856, 310, 1978. (*CA* 1978, 89: 117792.)
315. Kudo, Y. *et al.* 'Action of picrotoxin and related compounds on the frog spinal cord: the role of a hydroxyl group in the 6-position in antagonising the actions of amino acids and presynaptic inhibition.' *Brit. J. Pharmacol.* 81: 373-80, 1984. (*CA* 1984, 100: 204748.)
316. Kupchan, S. M., Meshulam, H. and Sneden, A. T. 'New curcubitacins from *Phormium tenax* and *Marah oreganus*.' *Phytochem.* 17: 767-69, 1978.
317. Kuroyanagi, M. *et al.* 'Chemical and toxicological studies on bracken fern, *Pteridium aquilinum* var.*latiusculum*: III. Further characterisation of pterosins and pterosides, sesquiterpenes and the glucosides having 1-indanone skeleton, from the rhizomes.' *Chem. Pharm. Bull. Japan* 27: 592-601, 1979.
318. Kururangi, T. Unpublished notes, Botany Division, DSIR, Christchurch, 1941.
319. Laing, R. M. and Blackwell, E. W. *Plants of New Zealand.* 6th ed. Whitcombe & Tombs, Christchurch, 1957.
320. Lambev, I., Markov, M. and Pavlova, N. 'Study of the anti-inflammatory and capillary restorative activity of a dispersed substance from *Plantago major* L' *Probl. Vutr. Med.* 4: 162-69, 1981. (*CA* 1983, 98: 65216.)
321. Lantz, Edith M. and Smith, Margaret. 'The carotene and ascorbic acid values of some wild plants used for food in New Mexico.' *New Mexico Agr. Expt. Station Bull.* 989, 1944. (*CA* 1945, 1695.)
322. Lassak, E. V. and McCarthy, T. *Australian medicinal plants.* Methuen, Sydney, 1983.
323. Leclerc, H. '*Centaurea cyanus* L. and *Euphrasia officinalis* L. in opthalmology.' *Pr. Med.* 44: 1216, 1936. (*CA* 1937, 4398.)
324. Leclerc, H. 'Kawa-kawa: *Piper methysticum* Forst.' *Pr. Med.* 45: 164, 1937. (*CA* 1937, 8114.)
325. Leclerc, H. 'Pharmacology of *Urtica dioica* L. et *urens* L.' *Pr. Med.* 46: 480, 1938. (*CA* 1938, 5924.)
326. Lee, W-Y. and Lee, Y-F. 'The vitamin C content of Shanghai vegetables.' *Chinese J. Nutrition* 2: 22-30, 1948. (*CA* 1950, 4602.)
327. Le Strange, R. *A history of herbal plants.* Angus & Robertson, London, 1977.
328. Letham, D. S., Shannon, J. S. and McDonald, I. R. C. 'Regulators in cell division in plant tissues: III. The identity of zeatin.' *Tetrahedron* 23: 479-86, 1967.
329. Levitt, D. *Plants and people: Aboriginal use of plants on Groote Eylandt.* Aust. Inst. Aboriginal Studies, Canberra, 1981.
330. Lewis, W. H. and Elvin-Lewis, M. P. F. *Medical botany: Plants affecting man's health.* John Wiley & Sons, New York, 1977.
331. Leys, T. W. (ed). *Brett's colonists' guide and cyclopaedia of useful knowledge.* Auckland Evening Star Office, 1883. Reprinted by Capper Press, Christchurch, 1980.
332. L'Horne, P. de. Extracts from the journal of. In McNab, R. *Historical records of New Zealand* 2: 296-347, 1914.
333. Lin, Y. L. 'Studies on the constituents of the antihypertensive plant *Polygonum perfoliatum* L.' *Kuo Li Chung-kuo I. Yao Yen Chiu So Yen Chiu Pao Kao.* (July) 103-29, 1983. (*CA* 1984, 100: 117811.)
334. Lindsay, W. L. 'The toot-poison of New Zealand.' *Pharm. J.* 2 (5): 371-73, 1864.
   Lindsay, W. L. 'On the toot plant and poison of New Zealand.' *British & Foreign Medico-Chirurgical Review* 36: 153-78, 1865.
335. Lindsay, W. L. *Contributions to New Zealand botany.* Williams & Norgate, London, 1868.
336. Lowry, J. B. 'The distribution and potential taxonomic value of alkylated ellagic acids.' *Phytochem.* 7: 1803-13, 1968.
337. Lowry, J. B. *Rhabdothamnus solandri*: some phytochemical results.' *N.Z. J. Bot.* 11: 555-60, 1973.
338. Lundius, O. C. D. Personal communication.

339 McCallion, R. F., *et al.* 'Antibiotic substances from New Zealand plants: II, Polygodial, an anti-candida agent from *Pseudowintera colorata*.' *Planta Medica* 44: 134–38, 1982.

340 McCormick, I. R. N., Nixon, P. E. and Waters, T. N. 'On the structure of prostratin: an X-ray study.' *Tetrahedron Lett.* 1735–36, 1976.

341 Macdonald, Christina. *Medicines of the Maori*. Collins, Auckland, 1973.

342 McDowall, F. H. 'Constituents of *Myoporum laetum* Forst. (the 'ngaio'): Part I.' *J. Chem. Soc.* 127: 2200–2207, 1925. 'Part II.' Ibid. 130: 731–40, 1927. 'Part III.' Ibid. 131: 1324–31, 1928.

343 McIlroy, R. J. '*Phormium* gum.' *J. Chem. Soc.* 1372–73, 1951.

344 McIntosh, H. W. 'Flax may save calves.' *N.Z. Dairy Exporter* 35 (5): 47, 1959.

345 McLintock, A. H. (ed.). *An encyclopaedia of New Zealand*. Government Printer, Wellington, 1966.

346 MacMillan, D. *Byways of history and medicine*. Willis & Aiken, Christchurch, 1946.

347 Makereti (Maggie Papakura). *The old-time Maori*, ed. T. K. Penniman, Gollancz, London, 1938.

348 Maksyutina, N. P. *et al.* 'Chemical composition and hypocholesteropemic action of some drugs from *Plantago major* leaves: Part I. Polyphenolic compounds.' *Farm. Zh. (Kiev)* 4: 56–61, 1978. (*CA* 1979, 90: 48400.)

349 Mansour, R. M. A., Saleh, A. M. and Boulos, L. 'A chemosystematic study of the phenolics of *Sonchus*.' *Phytochem.* 22: 489–92, 1983.

350 Marker, R. E. *et al.* 'Sterols CLVII. Sapogenins 69. Isolation and structures of thirteen new steroidal sapogenins. New sources of known sapogenins.' *J. Amer. Chem. Soc.* 65: 1199–1209, 1943.

351 Markham, K. R. 'Flavonoids and the chemotaxonomy of three *Sophora* species.' *Phytochem.* 12: 1091–94, 1973.

352 Markham, K. R. and Godley, E. J. 'Chemotaxonomic studies in *Sophora*: I. An evaluation of *Sophora microphylla* Ait.' *N.Z. J. Bot.* 10: 627–40, 1972.

353 Martin, Mary Ann. *Our Maoris*. Society for Promoting Christian Knowledge, London, 1884.

354 Martiu, K. Unpublished notes, Botany Division, DSIR, Christchurch, 1941.

355 Mathis, C. and Ourisson, G. 'Étude chimio-taxonomique du genre hypéricum: I. Répartition de l'hypéricine.' *Phytochem.* 2: 157–71, 1963.

356 Mei, M-Z. 'Rapid screening method for hypocholesterolemic agents.' *Yao Hsueh Hsueh Pao.* 14: 8–11, 1979. (*CA* 1980, 92: 33601.)

357 *Merck index*. 6th ed. Merck & Co., Rahway, N.J., 1952.

358 *Merck index*. 9th ed. Merck Rahway, N.J., 1976.

359 Miller, Winifred E. Unpublished notes, Botany Division, DSIR, Christchurch, 1940.

360 Mironov *et al.* 'Physiologically active alcohols of *Plantago major*.' *Khim-Farm. Zh.* 17: 1321–25, 1983. (*CA* 1984, 100: 32223.)

361 Mokomoko, A. Unpublished notes, Botany Division, DSIR, Christchurch, 1941.

362 Monckton, F. A. '*Phormium tenax* and its therapeutic value.' *Gardeners' Chron.* 24 (NS): 411; *Australian Med. Gaz.* IV: 84, 1885.

363 Moore, Beryl. Unpublished notes, Botany Division, DSIR, Christchurch, 1940.

364 Moore, Lucy B. 'New Zealand seaweeds.' *Post-primary school bulletin* 2 (13): 257–49, 1948.

365 Moore, Lucy B. Quoted in *Rodney and Waitemata Times*, 26 September, 1979: 34.

366 Moore, Lucy B. and Edgar, Elizabeth. *Flora of New Zealand*, Vol. II. Government Printer, Wellington, 1970.

367 Morice, Isobel M. 'Seed fats of the New Zealand Agavaceae.' *J. Sci. Food Agric.* 13: 666–69, 1962.

368 Morice, Isobel M. 'Two potential sources of linoleic acid in New Zealand.' *N.Z. J. Sci.* 8: 446–49, 1965.

369 Morice, Isobel M. 'Seed fats of some New Zealand and Australian monocotyledons.' *Phytochem.* 9: 1829–33, 1970.

370 Morice, Isobel M. 'Fruit-coat and seed fats of *Rhopalostylis*, *Elaeocarpus*, and *Nestigis* species.' *Phytochem.* 14: 765–67, 1975.

371 Mortimer, P. H. and White, E. P. 'Hepatotoxic substance in *Brachyglottis repanda*.' *Nature* 214: 1255–56, 1967.

372 Moss, Betty and Naylor, Margaret. 'The chemical composition of the two New Zealand species of *Durvillea*.' *Trans. Roy. Soc. N.Z.* 81: 473–78, 1954.

373 Moyer, B. M. et al. '3-Nitropropanoyl-D-glucopyranoses of *Corynocarpus laevigatus.*' *Phytochem.* 18: 111–13, 1979.

374 Muir, A. D., Cole, A. L. J. and Walker, J. R. L. 'Antibiotic compounds from New Zealand plants: I. Falcarindiol, an antidermatophyte agent from *Schefflera digitata.*' *Planta Medica* 44: 129–33, 1982.

375 Muir, A. D. and Walker, J. R. L. 'Antibiotics from New Zealand plants: a re-evaluation of some Maori folk medicine.' *Chemistry in New Zealand* 43: 94–95, 1979.

376 Murray, J. *An account of the Phormium tenax or New Zealand flax, printed on paper made from its leaves.* Renshaw, London, 1836.

377 Murray, J. 'Contributions of New Zealand workers to the chemistry of plants: Part II.' *J. N.Z. Inst. Chem.* 13: 128–35, 1949. 14: 44–52, 1950.

378 Murray, J. and Stanley, B. G. 'The essential oil of *Nothopanax simplex.*' *J. Appl. chem.* 2: 5–7, 1952.

379 Nakamura, M. 'Phosphorylase of sweet potatoes.' *J. Agric. Chem. Soc. Japan* 25: 413–17, 1952. (*CA* 1923, 46: 11266.)

380 Neil, J. F. *The New Zealand family herb doctor.* Mills, Dick, Dunedin, 1889. (2nd ed. 1891.)

381 Neil, S. Unpublished notes, Botany Division, DSIR, Christchurch, 1941.

382 Nepia, G. and McLean, T. P. *I, George Nepia.* Reed, Wellington, 1963.

383 Newman, A. K. 'New Zealand from a physician's point of view.' *Trans. N. Z. Inst.* 12: 433–38, 1879.

384 Newton, Lily. *Seaweed utilisation.* Sampson Low, London, 1951.

385 *New Zealand Herald,* 17 May 1980.

386 Nicholas, J. L. *Narrative of a voyage in New Zealand,* 1817. Vol. I: 340. Quoted by Aston (ref. 21).

387 Nicholl, R. Private communication.

388 Nishida R. and Bowers, W. S. *Insect biology of the future,* ed. M. Locke and D. S. Smith. Academic Press, 1980.

389 Northwood, W. Personal communication.

390 O'Carroll, P. J. O'N. 'Medical botany of New Zealand.' In *Taranaki Almanac,* 1884. (Reprinted in Skinner, W. H. *Pioneer medical men of Taranaki, 1834 to 1880,* 1933.)

391 Ohnel, R. F. 'Effect of piperidine and allied substances on mammalian skeletal muscle.' *Acta Physiol. Scand.* 11: 361–72, 1946. (*CA* 1946, 6673.)

392 Oliver, W. R. B. 'The New Zealand species of *Metrosideros* with a note on *Metrosideros collina* (Forst.) Gray.' *Trans. Proc. N.Z. Inst.* 59: 419–23, 1928.

393 Oliver, W. R. B. 'The genus *Coriaria* in New Zealand.' *Rec. Dom. Mus.* 1: 21–43, 1942.

394 Palmer, G. B. 'Tohungaism and makutu — some beliefs and practices of the present day Maori.' *J. Polynes. Soc.* 63: 147–63, 1954.

395 Palmer-Jones, T. 'A recent outbreak of honey poisoning: Part I. Historical and descriptive.' *N.Z. J. Sci. Tech.* 29A: 107–114, 1947.

396 Palmer-Jones, T. and White, E. P. 'A recent outbreak of honey poisoning: Part VII. Observations on the toxicity and toxin of the tutu (*Coriaria arborea* Lindsay).' *N.Z. J. Sci. Tech.* 31A (2): 46–56, 1949.

397 Panin, M. and Grisha, G.Ya. 'Sulfur content of some plants in the Semiplatinsk region of the Kazak SSR.' *Rastit, Resur.* 11: 473–83, 1975. (*CA* 1976, 84: 71411.)

398 Panosyam, A. G. et al. 'Search for substances with prostaglandin-like activity in plants.' *Khim. Prir. Soedin.* (6): 825–26, 1980. (*CA* 1981, 94: 180557.)

399 Papy, H.-René and L'Herbier, L. 'Nouveau catalogue des plantes medicinales de Tahiti.' *Trav. Lab. For. Toulouse,* t. V, 2 section, Vol. I, art. IV, 1–28, 1957.

400 Parham, H. B. Richenda. *Fiji native plants ... with an introduction by J. C. Andersen.* The Polynesian Society, Wellington, 1943. (Polynes. Soc. Mem. 16).

401 Parker, W., Raphael, R. A. and Wilkinson, D. I. 'The structure and synthesis of bullatenone.' *J. Chem. Soc.* 3871–75, 1958.

402 Perez-Llano, G. A. 'Lichens — their biological and economic significance.' *Bot. Rev.* 10: 1–65, 1944.

403 Perry, L. M. *Medicinal plants of South and Southeast Asia.* MIT Press, Cambridge, Mass., 1980.

404 Petard, P. *Raau Tahiti: The use of Polynesian medicinal plants in Tahitian medicine.* South Pacific Commission, Noumea, 1972.

405 Peterson, P. J. 'Non-protein amino acid distinctions between Aspleniaceae and Athyriaceae in New Zealand.' *N.Z.J. Bot.* 10: 3–7, 1972.

406 *Philippine National Formulary.* 2nd. ed. National Sci. & Tech. Authority,

Manila, 1982.
407 Philpott, H. G. *A history of the New Zealand dairy industry 1840-1935*. Government Printer, Wellington, 1937.
408 Pickmere, Katie. Unpublished notes, Botany Division, DSIR, Christchurch, 1940-41.
409 Pilgrim, R. L. C. 'Some properties of the sting of the New Zealand nettle *Urtica ferox*.' *Proc. Roy. Soc. London* 151B: 48-56, 1959.
410 Plakhova, N. B. 'Comparative effect of tannins from Siberian plants on bacteria of the dysentery group.' *Farmakol. i. Toksikol.* 17(4): 39-42, 1954. (*CA* 1954, 13820.)
411 Plouvier, V. 'Nouvelles recherches sur le quebrachitol des Sapindacees...' *C. R. Acad. Sci. Paris* 228: 1886-88, 1949.
412 Polack, J. S. *New Zealand*. Bentley, London, 1838.
413 Polack, J. S. *Manners and customs of the New Zealanders*. Madden, London, 1840.
414 Poverty Bay Federation of Women's Institutes. *Cookery calendar* (includes special Maori section). Gisborne, 1935?
415 Puckey, W. G. Letters and journals, 1831-68. Typescript copy, Auckland Museum Library.
416 Radcliffe, C. B. and Short, W. F. 'The essential oil of *Phebalium nudum*.' *J. Soc. Chem. Ind.* 47: 324T, 1928.
417 Raeside, J. D. 'Some post-glacial climatic changes in Canterbury and their effect on soil formation.' *Trans. Roy. Soc. N.Z.* 77: 153-71, 1948.
418 Rafter, P. M. *Never let go! The remarkable story of Mother Aubert*. Reed, Wellington, 1972.
419 Rageau, J. *Plantes medicinales de la Nouvelle-Calédonie*. Institut Francaise d'Océanie, Noumea, 1957.
420 Rageau, J. *Plantes medicinales de la Nouvelle Calédonie*. Office de la Récherche Scientifique et Technique Outre-Mer (ORSTOM), Paris, 1973.
421 Raoul, E. *Choix de plantes de la Nouvelle-Zélande, recueillies et décrites par M. E. Raoul ... Ouvrage publié sous les auspices de M. le baron de Makau ...* Fortin, Masson, Paris, 1846.
422 Reed, A. H. (ed.) *More Maoriland adventures of J. W. Stack*. Reed, Dunedin, 1936.
423 *Auckland almanac, provincial handbook, and strangers' vade mecum*. Reed & Brett, Auckland, 1874.
424 Reports on DSIR files, Christchurch.

425 Rimington, E. and Roets, G. C. S. 'The isolation of the alkaloidal constituent of the drug 'channa' or 'kougoed' (*Mesembryanthemum anatomicum* and *M. tortuosum*).' *Onderstepoort J. Vet. Sci.* 9: 187-91, 1937. (*CA* 1938, 4279.)
426 Rizk, A. M. *et al.* 'Constituents of Egyptian Euphorbiaceae: Part VIII. Phytochemical investigation of *Euphorbia peplus*.' *Fitoterapia* 51: 223-27, 1980. (*CA* 1981, 95: 76860.)
427 Roi, J. *Traité des plantes médicinales Chinoises*. Lechevalier, Paris, 1955.
428 Rorke, J. (ed.) *A Marist missionary in New Zealand 1843-1846*, by Fr. J. A. M. Chouvet. Trans. P. Berry. Whakatane and District Hist. Soc., Whakatane, 1985.
429 Rout, Ettie A. *Native diet, with numerous practical recipes*. Heinemann, London, 1926.
430 Rowan, D. D., MacDonald, P. E. and Skipp, R. A. 'Antifungal stress metabolites from *Solanum aviculare*.' *Phytochem.* 22: 2102-104, 1983.
431 Rowan, D. D. and Newman, R. H. 'Noroleanane saponins from *Celmisia petriei*.' *Phytochem.* 23: 639-44, 1984.
432 Russell, G. B. *et al.* '2-Deoxy-3-epiecdysone from the fern *Blechnum vulcanicum*.' *Phytochem.* 20: 2407-10, 1981.
433 Russell, G. B. and Fenemore, P. G. 'Insect moulting hormone activity of some New Zealand gymnosperms.' *N.Z. J. Sci.* 13: 61-68, 1970.
434 Russell, G. B. and Fenemore, P. G. 'Insect moulting hormone activity in some New Zealand ferns.' *N.Z. J. Sci.* 14: 31-35, 1971.
435 Russell, G. B. and Fenemore, P. G. 'New lignans from leaves of *Macropiper excelsum*.' *Phytochem.* 12: 1799-1803, 1973.
436 Russell, G. B. and Frazer, J. C. 'Identification of isoboldine as the major alkaloid from berries of *Bielschmiedia tawa*.' *N.Z. J. Sci.* 12: 694-95, 1969.
437 Russell, G. B. and Reay, P. F. 'The structures of tetraphyllin A and B, two new cyanoglucosides from *Tetrapathaea tetrandra*.' *Phytochem.* 10: 1373-77, 1971.
438 Ryburn, H. J. *Te Hemara, James Hamlin 1803-1865: Friend of the Maoris*. Published by the author, Dunedin, 1979.
439 Saleh, N. *et al.* 'Vitamin content of fruits

440   and vegetables in common use in Egypt.' *Z. Ernahrungsm.* 16: 158-62, 1977. (*CA* 1978, 88: 4998.)
440   Sannié, C. 'Sur la composition des algues des Iles Kerguelen.' *C.R. Acad. Sci. Paris.* 232: 2040-41, 1951.
441   Santesson, C. G. 'Piule, a Mexican narcotic.' *Arch. Pharm.* 275: 532-37, 1937. (*CA* 1938, 722.)
442   Savage, J. *Some account of New Zealand.* Murray, London, 1807. Reprinted by J. McIndoe, Dunedin, 1966.
443   Schauenberg, P. and Paris, F. *Guide to medicinal plants.* Lutterworth Press, Guildford, 1977.
444   Schenk, H. R. *et al.* 'Diterpenes LXII. A new productive partial synthesis of ambreinolide.' *Helv. Chim. Acta* 35: 817-24, 1952.
445   Schiffer, A. P. and Kovacs, A. 'Tetragonin: a yeast growth regulating substance from *Tetragonia expansa*.' *Nature* 183: 988-89, 1959.
446   Schreiber, K. 'Steroid alkaloids: the *Solanum* group. In *The alkaloids*, ed. R. H. E. Manske. Vol. 10. Academic Press, New York, 1968.
447   Sharaf, A. E. A. 'Chemical investigations of the Egyptian plant *Euphorbia peplus*.' *Brit. Vet. J.* 105: 128-35, 1949.
448   Sharma, V. N. 'Chemical examination of *Vitex peduncularis*.' *J. Sci. Ind. Res. (India)* 14B: 267-70, 1955. (*CA* 1956, 5649.)
449   Shearer, G. D. 'Some observations on the poisonous properties of buttercups.' *Vet. J.* 94: 22-32, 1938. (*CA* 1938, 4669.)
450   Shedlock, W. Personal communication.
451   Sherwani, M. R. K. *et al.* 'Reinvestigation of the seed oil of *Dodonea viscosa* (Sapindaceae).' *Chem. & Ind.* 523-24, 1979.
452   Shibata, S. *et al.* 'Relation between chemical constitution and antibacterial effects, of usnic acid and its derivatives.' *J. Pharm. Soc. Japan.* 68: 298-300, 1948. (*CA* 1951, 6691.)
453   Shibata, S. 'Pharmacology of coriamyrtin. A supplement.' *Folia Pharm. Jap.* 51: 229-35, 1955. (*CA* 1956, 14975.)
454   Shortland, E. *The southern districts of New Zealand.* Longman, London, 1851.
455   Simmonds, M. B. Personal communication to L. H. Briggs, 1974.
456   Simmons, D. R. (ed.) *Customs and habits of the New Zealanders 1838-1842.* By Fr. C. Servant, Marist missionary in the Hokianga. Trans. J. Glasgow. Reed, Wellington, 1973.
457   Skey, W. 'On extract of towai bark.' *Trans. Proc. N.Z. Inst.* 1: 28, 1869. 2nd ed.: 431, 1875.
458   Skey, W. 'On the examination of the bark of *Coprosma grandifolia* for alkaloids.' *Trans. Proc. N.Z. Inst.* 2: 152, 1870.
459   Skey, W. 'On the extraction of the poisonous principle of the tutu plant (*Coriaria ruscifolia*).' *Trans. Proc. N.Z. Inst.* 2: 153-55, 1870.
460   Skey, W. 'Preliminary notes on the isolation of the bitter substance of the nut of the karaka tree (*Corynocarpus laevigata*).' *Trans. Proc. N.Z. Inst.* 4: 316-21, 1872.
461   Skey, W. 'Notes on the presence in certain fibres of a substance susceptible of some striking colorific changes when chemically treated.' *Trans. Proc. N.Z. Inst.* 4: 370, 1872.
462   Skey, W. 'On a search for the poisonous principle of *Brachyglottis repanda* and *B. rangiora*.' *Trans. Proc. N.Z. Inst.* 14: 400-402, 1882.
463   Skinner, W. H. *Pioneer medical men of Taranaki, 1834 to 1880.* Thomas Avery & Sons, New Plymouth, 1933. (Including an article on the medical botany of New Zealand by Dr P. J. O'N. O'Carroll.)
464   Slater, S. N. 'Tutin.' *J. Chem. Soc.* 50-51, 1943.
465   Smith, A. C. *Flora Vitiensis nova. A new flora of Fiji.* (Spermatophytes only). Pacific Tropical Botanic Garden, Hawaii, 1975-85.
466   Smith, J. A. 'On two indigenous productions — manganese and *Zostera marina* — which might be made fair articles of export.' *Trans. Proc. N.Z. Inst.* 10: 568-69, 1878.
467   Smith, L. Unpublished notes, Botany Division, DSIR, Christchurch, 1940.
468   Sohn, C. E. *Dictionary of the active principles of plants.* Balliere, Tindall & Cox, London, 1894.
469   Somogyi, J. C. In *Toxicants occurring naturally in foods.* 2nd ed. National Academy of Sciences, Washington D.C., 1973.
470   Sparrman, A. *A voyage round the world with Captain James Cook in HMS Resolution.* The Golden Cockerel Press, London, 1944.
471   Spencer, K. C., Seigler, D. S. and

Domingo, J. L. 'Tetraphyllins A and B, Deidaelin and epitetraphyllin B from *Tetrapathea tetranda* (Passifloraceae).' *Phytochem.* 22: 1815–16, 1983.

472 Spenser, D. M. *Disease, religion and society in the Fiji Islands.* University of Washington Press, Seattle, 1966.

473 Squire, P. W. *Squire's companion to the British pharmacopoeia.* 19th. ed. Churchill, London, 1916.

474 Steenis-Kruseman, M. J. van *Select Indonesian medicinal plants.* 1953. (Organization for Scientific Research in Indonesia Bull. 18).

475 Steinmetz, E. F. *Piper methysticium (kava) famous drug plant of the South Sea Islands.* Published by the author, Amsterdam, 1960.

476 Stevens, M. Unpublished notes, Botany Division, DSIR, Christchurch, 1941.

477 Stone, R. C. J. *The Young Logan Campbell.* Oxford/Auckland University Presses, 1982.

478 Sutherland, M. D. 'The odour of *Coprosma foetidissima.*' *N.Z. J. Sci. Tech.* 29B: 94-95, 1947.

479 Sutherland, M. D. and Palmer-Jones, T. 'A recent outbreak of honey-poisoning: Part II. The toxic substances of the poisonous honey.' *N.Z. J. Sci. Tech.* 29A: 114–20, 1947.

480 Sutherland, M. D. and Park, R. J. In *Terpenoids in plants*, ed. I. B. Pridham, Academic Press, London, 1967.

481 Tapper, B. A. and Reay, P. F. In *Chemistry and biochemistry of herbage*, ed. G. W. Butler and R. W. Bailey, Vol. 1. Academic Press, London, 1973.

482 Tanimoto, T. *(Report on) ti investigation.* Printed Repts. Ann. meeting Hawaiian Sugar Planters' Assoc. Rept. Comm. in charge Expt. Sta. 60: 126–29, 1941. (CA 1941, 7750.)

483 Tarle, D., Petricic, J. and Kupinic, M. 'Antibiotic effects of aucubin, saponins and extract of plantain leaf — herbe or folium *Plantaginis lanceolate.*' *Farm. Glas.* 37: 351–54, 1981. (CA 1982, 96: 40797.)

484 Taylor, R. Journals, 1833–73. Typescript copies in Auckland Museum Library.

485 Taylor, R. *A leaf from the natural history of New Zealand.* Stokes, Wellington, 1848, 2nd ed. 1870.

486 Taylor, R. *Te Ika a Maui.* Wertheim & MacIntosh, London, 1855.

487 Tehon, L. R. *The drug plants of Illinois.* Illinois Natural History Survey, Urbana, 1951. (Nat. Hist. Surv. Circ. 44.)

488 Thompson, R. H. *Naturally occurring quinones.* Butterworths, London, 1957.

489 Thomson, A. S. *The story of New Zealand.* Murray, London, 1859. Reprinted by Capper Press, Christchurch, 1974.

490 Thomson, W. A. R. (ed.) *Healing plants: a modern herbal.* MacMillan, London, 1978.

491 Thorpe, J. F. and Whitely, M. A. *Thorpe's dictionary of applied chemistry.* 4th ed. Vol. 5. Longmans, London, 1941. (Article on furfural.)

492 Toth, I. *et al.* 'Ecdysteroids in Chenopodiaceae: *Chenopodium album.*' *Fitoterapia* 52: 77–80, 1981. (CA 1982, 96: 159355.)

493 Tregear, E. *The Maori-Polynesian comparative dictionary.* Lyon & Blair, Wellington, 1891.

494 Tseng, C. K. and Chang, C. F. 'Chinese seaweeds in herbal medicine.' In *Proceedings XI International Seaweed Symposium* (Quindao: 1953), ed. C. F. Bird and M. A. Ragan. Dr. W. Junk, Pubs., Dordrecht, 152–54, 1984.

495 Urzúa, A. and Cassels, B. K. 'Additional alkaloids from *Laurelia phillipiana* and *L. novazelandiae.*' *Phytochem.* 21: 773–76, 1982.

496 Valenzuela, P., Concha, J. A. and Santos, A. C. 'List of some Philippine medicinal plants . . .' *J. Philipp. Pharm. Ass.* 34: 1–57, 1947.

497 Van der Berghe, D. A. *et al.* 'Screening of higher plants for biological activities: II. Anti-viral activity.' *Lloydia* 41: 463–71. (CA 1978, 89: 204192.)

498 Veen, A. G. van. 'The isolation of the soporific substance from kawa-kawa or wati.' *Proc. Acad. Sci. Amst.* 41: 855–58, 1938. (CA 1939, 1445.)
Veen, A. G. van. 'Isolation and constitution of the narcotic substance from kawa-kawa *(Piper methysticum).*' *Rec. Trav. Chim.* 58: 521–27, 1939. (CA 1939, 6271.)

499 Vincent, M. 1848. Quoted in Church (ref. 143).

500 Virtanen, A. I. and Linko, P. 'The occurrence of free ornithine and its N-acetyl derivative in plants.' *Acta Chem. Scand.* 9: 531–32, 1955.

501 Visser, F. R. 'Variation in the vitamin C content of some New Zealand grown fruit and vegetables.' *N.Z. J. Sci.* 27: 105–12, 1984.

502 Voitenko, G. N., Lipkam, G. N. and Maksyutina, N. P. 'Effect of plantaglucide from *Plantago asiatica* L. on the induction of experimental gastric dystrophy.' *Rastit. Resur.* 19: 103-07, 1983. (CA 1983, 98: 119454.)

503 Walker, J. R. L. Botany Department, University of Canterbury. 'Notes given by a bushman,' 1979.

504 Walker, R. 'Tohunga territory.' *Listener* 93: 51, 1979.

505 Walker, W. Unpublished notes, Botany Division, DSIR, Christchurch, 1941.

506 Wall, A. and Cranwell, Lucy M. *The botany of Auckland.* Wilson & Horton, Auckland, 1943.

507 Walt, S. J. van der and Steyn, D. G. 'Recent investigations into the toxicity of known and unknown poisonous plants in the Union of South Africa XII.' *Onderstepoort J. Vet. Sci.* 17: 211-23, 1941. (CA 1944, 1029.)

508 Watt, A. H. Personal communication.

509 Watt, J. M. and Breyer-Brandwijk, M. G. *The medicinal and poisonous plants of Southern and Eastern Africa.* 2nd ed. Livingstone, Edinburgh, 1962.

510 Webb, L. J. *Guide to the medicinal and poisonous plants of Queensland.* Government Printer, Melbourne, 1948. (CSIRO Bull. 232.)

511 Weiner, M. A. *Secrets of Fijian medicine.* N.p., 1984.

512 Weiss, E., Bernauer, K. G. and Girardet, A. 'Notiz zur Konstitution des Laurepukins.' *Helv. Chim. Acta* 54: 1342-45, 1971.

513 Wharton, W. J. L. (ed.) *Captain Cook's journal during his first voyage round the world* . . . Eliot Stock, London, 1893.

514 White, E. P. 'Alkaloids of the Leguminosae . . .' *N.Z. J. Sci. Tech.* 38B: 707-25, 1957 (and preceding papers).

515 White, J. *Te Rou; or the Maori at home.* Sampson Low, Marston, London, 1874.

516 Williams, H. W. *A dictionary of the Maori language.* 6th ed. Government Printer, Wellington, 1957.

517 Williams, H. W. *A dictionary of the Maori language.* 7th ed. Government Printer, Wellington, 1975.

518 Williment, T. M. I. *John Hobbs 1800-1883: Wesleyan Missionary to the Ngapuhi tribe of Northern New Zealand.* Government Printer, Wellington, 1985.

519 Wilson, D. H. *Stewart Island plants.* Field Guide Publications, Christchurch, 1982.

520 Wilson, R. D. 'Chemotaxonomic studies in the Rubiaceae: 1. Methods for the identification of hybridisation in the genus *Coprosma* J. R. et G. Forst. using flavonoids.' *N.Z. J. Bot.* 17: 113-16, 1979.

521 Wilson, C. O., Gisvold, O. and Doerge, R. F. *Textbook of organic medicinal and pharmaceutical chemistry.* 6th ed. Lippincott, Philadelphia, 1971.

522 Winiata, M. Personal communication.

523 Withers, Mihi. Unpublished notes, Botany Division, DSIR, Christchurch, 1941.

524 Wren, R. C. *Potter's new cyclopaedia of botanical drugs and preparations.* 7th ed. Health Science Press, Wellingborough, Northamptonshire, 1973.

525 Xu, G. 'Preliminary study on active constituents of *Polygonum aubertii* Henry.' *Yaoxue Tongbao* 16: 55-56, 1981. (CA 1982, 96: 100898.)

526 Yamazaki, M. 'Extraction of cerebrosides as anti-ulcer agents from *Tetragonia expansa.*' *Jap. Pat.* 82, 122, 018, 1982. (CA 1982, 97: 150720.)

527 Yang, H-C., Chang, H-H. and Weng, T-C. 'Influence of several Chinese drugs on the growth of some pathologic organisms: preliminary report.' *J. Formosan Med. Ass.* 52: 109-12, 1953. (CA 1953, 8175.)

528 Yate, W. *An account of New Zealand.* Seeley & Burnside, London, 1835.

529 Yun, H-S. *et al.* 'Plants with liver-protecting activities: IV. Chemistry and pharmacology of *Plantaginis Semen et Folium.*' *Soul Taehakkyo Saengyak Yonguso Opjukjip.* 19: 69-72, 1980. (CA 1981, 95: 91122.)

530 Zayed, S. *et al.* 'New tigliane and daphnane derivatives from *Pimelea prostrata* and *Pimelea simplex.*' *Experientia* 33: 1554-55, 1977.

531 Zechner, L. and Wohlmuth, H. 'Anemonin and protoanemonin II: Vermicidal action.' *Sci. Pharm.* 22: 90-95, 1954. (CA 1954, 13169.)

532 Zepernick, B. *'Arzneipflanzen der Polynesier.'* Reimer, Berlin, 1972.

533 Zotov, V. D. 'Grasses of the subantarctic islands . . .' *Rec. Dom. Mus. Wellington* 5: 101-46, 1965.

534 Zotov, V. D. *'Heirochloe* R. Br. (Gramineae) in New Zealand.' *N.Z. J. Bot.* 11: 561-80, 1973.

Glossary

ABORTIFACIENT   Anything used to cause an abortion.
AGUE   A periodic or intermittent fever.
ALKALOID   A basic organic nitrogenous compound of plant origin that is pharmacologically active and bitter tasting.
ALLERGEN   A substance capable of inducing an allergic response.
ALTERATIVE   A vague term to indicate an agent presumed to correct a disordered bodily function.
AMENORRHOEA   An abnormal suppression or non-occurrence of menstruation.
ANALGESIC   Pain reliever that does not induce loss of consciousness; anodyne.
ANGIOSPERMS   Flower-bearing plants; ovules are enclosed in an ovary that forms the fruit after fertilisation.
ANKYLOSTOMIASIS   (ancylostomiasis) A hookworm disease common in tropical countries.
ANODYNE   Pain-easing.
ANOREXIA   Loss of appetite.
ANTHELMINTIC   Causing death or removal of worms in the body.
ANTIHAEMOLYTIC   Agent preventing the dissolution or breakdown of red blood corpuscles.
ANTINEOPLASTIC   Anti-tumour.
ANTIPERIODIC   Preventing the return of those diseases which recur, such as malaria.
ANTIPYRETIC   Agent relieving or reducing fever.
ANTIRHEUMATIC   Agent that prevents or relieves the pain of rheumatism.
ANTISCORBUTIC   Preventing scurvy.
ANTISEPTIC   Preventing infection or putrefaction.
ANTISPASMODIC   Preventing or curing spasms, as in epilepsy, etc.
APERIENT   Producing a natural movement of the bowels.
APHRODISIAC   Exciting sexual desire.
ARIL   An accessory covering of a seed.
ASTRINGENT   Binding; causing contraction of the tissues.
BITTER   Applied to bitter-tasting drugs which are used to stimulate the appetite.
BLENNORRHOEA   An inordinate discharge of mucous; gonorrhoea.
CARCINOGEN   A substance which causes cancer.
CARDIAC   Products which have an effect upon the heart.
CARIES   Bacterial infection of the enamel and dentine of the tooth leading to decalcification and cavities.
CATAPLASM   A soothing poultice.
CATARRH   Excessive secretion from an inflamed mucous membrane.
CATHARTIC   Producing evacuation of the bowels.
CHEMOTHERAPY   The treatment of diseases by the use of drugs, usually synthetic, whose action is specific against certain pathogenic micro-organisms but non-toxic to the patient.
CIRRHOSIS   An abnormal formation of connective tissue, with wasting of the proper tissue of the liver.
CONTACT DERMATITIS   Local allergic reaction provoked by skin contact with chemical substances that act as antigens or haptens.

CONTUSIONS   Bruises.
CYANOGENIC   Capable of producing hydrocyanic acid (HCN).
CYTOTOXIC   Having a specific destructive action on particular cells.

DEMULCENT   Applied to drugs which sooth and protect the alimentary canal.
DEOBSTRUENT   Clearing away obstructions by opening the natural passages of the body.
DERMATIC   Applied to drugs with an action on the skin.
DETERGENT   Cleansing.
DIAPHORETIC   Drugs which promote perspiration.
DIARRHOEA   Abnormal frequency and fluidity of stool discharges.
DICOTYLEDON   An angiosperm having two cotyledons (seed leaves); usually the leaves are net-veined and floral parts in fours or fives.
DIGESTIVE   Aiding digestion.
DIURETIC   Agent that increases urine flow, by acting on the kidneys.
DROPSY   Abnormal accumulation of fluid between cells.
DRUPE   A soft fleshy fruit enclosing a hard-shelled stone or seed.
DYSMENORRHOEA   Difficult or painful menstruation.

ECZEMA   Noncontagious, itching, inflammatory skin eruption characterised by papules, vesicles, and pustules that may also be associated with oedema, scaling, or exudation.
ELEPHANTIASIS   A skin disease causing the affected part to resemble an elephant's hide.
EMETIC   Applied to drugs which cause vomiting.
EMMENAGOGUE   Applied to drugs which have the power of exciting the menstrual discharge.
EMOLLIENT   Used in relation to substances which have a softening and soothing effect.
EMPHYSEMA   Distension of the lung tissues by gas.
EPIPHYTE   A plant growing non-parasitically upon another.
EPISPASTIC   A drug which raises blisters.

ESSENTIAL   Applied to the volatile oils of plants, marked by characteristic odour. Also applied to fatty acids believed by nutritionists to be necessary for health.
ESTROGENIC   A generic term for compounds which induce sexual excitement in females.
EXPECTORANT   Promoting expectoration and removing secretions from the bronchial tubes.

FEBRIFUGE   Reducing fever.

GLAUCOMA   Group of diseases characterised by increased intraocular pressures causing defects in vision.
GLYCOSIDE   Naturally occurring substance consisting of sugars combined with nonsugars (aglycones).
GOITROGENIC   Capable of initiating or promoting a goitre.
GRAVEL   A disease characterised by formation of granular concretions in the kidneys.
GYMNOSPERM   A cone-bearing vascular plant; the seeds are exposed and the endosperm is formed before fertilisation.

HAEMOPHILIA   A disorder characterised by profuse and excessive bleeding even from slight injuries.
HAEMOSTATIC   Drugs used to control bleeding.
HALLUCINOGEN   Agent inducing false perceptions that occur without true sensory stimuli.
HEPATOTOXIC   Used in connexion with substances having an effect upon the liver.
HYDRAGOGUE   Having the property of removing accumulations of water or serum; causing water evacuations.
HYPERTENSION   Abnormally high constrictive tension in blood vessels, usually revealed as high blood pressure.
HYPOCHOLESTEROLAEMIA   A deficiency of cholesterol in the blood.
HYPOGLYCEMIA   Deficiency of normal glucose levels in the body; low blood sugar.

INOTROPIC   Interference with the contractility of muscle.

259

LAXATIVE   A gentle bowel stimulant.
LECTIN   Protein that effects agglutination, precipitation, or other phenomena resembling the action of a specific antibody.
LEUCORRHOEA   A whitish morbid discharge from the vagina.

MENORRHAGIA   Excessive menstruation.
MICTURITION   The act of urination.
MITOGEN   Substance that stimulates cell division and transformation.
MONOCOTYLEDON   Angiosperms having one cotyledon (seed leaf); usually the leaves are parallel-veined and floral parts in threes.
MUTAGEN   Agent that elicits a genetic change.

NERVINE   Applied to drugs used to restore the nerves to their natural state.

OEDEMA   An accumulation of fluid in various organs or tissues of the body.

PARTURIENT   Applied to substances used during childbirth.
PHOTODERMATITIS   Inflammation of the skin resulting from activation of chemicals on the skin by light.
PHTHISIS   A wasting disease of the lungs; difficulty in breathing.
PHYTOALEXIN   An antimicrobial compound produced in a plant in response to fungal infection.
PITYRIASIS   A skin disease in which the epidermis sheds thin scales as dandruff.
POST-PARTUM   After childbirth.
PRURITUS   Itching.
PSORIASIS   A noncontagious inflammatory skin disease characterised by reddish patches and white scales.
PURGATIVE   Drugs which evacuate the bowels. More drastic than a laxative or aperient.
PYORRHOEA   Inflammation of the lining membrane of the teeth associated with pus, and looseness of teeth.

QUINSY   Inflammation of the tonsils and adjoining tissue.

RHIZOME   Horizontal underground stem distinguished from a root by scale-like leaves and axillary buds.
RUBEFACIENT   Applied to counter irritants to the skin. Substances which produce blisters or inflammation.
RUDERAL   A plant which usually grows on rubbish heaps or waste places.

SAPONIN   A substance characterised by the ability to form emulsions and soapy lathers.
SCABIES   The itch.
SCROFULOUS WENS   A tuberculous condition occurring commonly on the scalp.
SOPORIFIC   Inducing sleep.
SPRUE   A disease of tropical regions marked by anaemia, emaciation, and gastrointestinal disturbances.
STIPE   (bot.) A stalk or support.
STOMACHIC   Applied to drugs given for disorders of the stomach.
STYPTIC   Substances which clot the blood and thus stop bleeding.
SUDORIFIC   Producing copious perspiration.

TETTER   A vesicular skin disease, as eczema.
THROMBOCYTOPENIA   Deficiency of blood platelets.
THRUSH   A fungal disease of the mouth, lips, and throat.
TUBERCULOSIS   Primary pulmonary infection caused by *Mycobacterium tuberculosis*; may also be found within the skin, lymphatics, and kidney.

URETHRITIS   Inflammation of the duct by which urine is discharged from the bladder.

VASOPRESSOR AGENT   A substance which reduces blood pressure.
VENOUS STASIS   Stoppage of the circulation of blood through the capillaries and blood vessels.
VERMICIDE   Substance which kills worms.
VERMIFUGE   Substance which expels worms from the body.
VULNERARY   Used in healing wounds.

Index

Bold numbers indicate principal references.

Abutilon 162, 163
Acaena 140, **206**, 207
Agathis 29, **78**, 87
Agave 84
Ageratum 101
Agrimonia 208
Agrimony, common 208
Agropyron 144
Aka 174, 176
Aka kura 176
Akatawhiwhi 176
Akatea 174
Akeake 218
Alectryon 22, 213, **218**, 219
Aloe 224
Alphitonia 205
Althaea 162
Anabaena 67
Anacyclus 194
Anaphalioides 102
Angelica 17, 233, 234
Angiangi 62
Antennaria 103
Apium 17, 136, 137, **229**, 230
Apple of Sodom 226
Arctostaphylos 131
Areca 182, 183
Aristotelia 29, **125**, 126, 128
Arthropodium 37, 153, **156**, 157
Arum lily 91
Arundo 144
Aspidium 73
Asplenium **65**, 66, **67**, 95
Astelia 119
Atherosperma 166
Atriplex **96**, 97, 98

Atropa 226
Avens, common 207
Azolla **67**, 68

Baptisia 154
Bearberry 131
Bed-straw, New Zealand 215
Beech, native 20
Beilschmiedia 80, **149**, 150
Betel (nut) 85, 183
Bidi-bid 206
Bindweed 109
Bittersweet 226
Black maire 179
Black mustard 117
Black pepper 187
Black pine 83
Black tree-fern 72
Blackberry 209
Blechnum **68**, 69, 73
Blue gum 48, 169
Bourreria 180
Brachycome 145
Brachyglottis 29, 37, **99**, 104
Bracken 16, 74, 75, 77
Brassica 35, **117**, 118
Broadleaf 115
Brooklime 222
Bull kelp 57, 58
Bullibulli 224
Bulrush 37, 229
Bush lawyer 208
Bushman's painkiller 240
Buttercup 202, 203

Cabbage tree 24, 84
Cabbage, wild 117
Calvatia **60**, 61
Calystegia **109**, 110

261

Candida   240
Cardaria   119
Cardiomanes   **71**, 191
Carex   23
Cat's-foot   103
Cedar, native   163
Celery   32, 136
Celery-leaved pine   81, 146
Celmisia   **100**, 101, 123
Century-plant   84
Cephaelis   212
Chenopodium   97, 98
Christmas tree   175
Cinchona   212
Cinnamomum   149
Cinnamon   149
Cirsium   **101**, 102
Clathrus   60
Clematis   37, 163, **200**, **201**, 202, 212, 214
Clove   180
Clover   24, 107, 191
Coltsfoot   101
Common agrimony   208
Common avens   207
Common mallow   162
Common nettle   235
Common nightshade   225
Common orache   96
Common speedwell   222
Cook's scurvygrass   118, 137
Coprosma   20, 22, 27, 30, 34, 37, 38, 158, 176, 200, **210**, 211, 212, 215, 216
Cordyline   24, 65, **84**, 85, 86, 171
Coriaria   26, 29, 58, 80, **112**, 113, 114, 124
Cornus   114
Corokia   **114**, 208
Cortaderia   **144**, 159
Corynocarpus   26, **115**, 116, 163
Cotton plant   100
Cotton thistle   102
Cranesbill   138
Cuckoopint   92
Cudweed   103
Cusparia   216
Cut-leaved cranesbill   138
Cut-leaved nightshade   25, 29, 224
Cutty grass   122
Cyathea   21, 35, 69, **71**, **72**
Cyathodes   16, **128**, 129
Cyclosorus   73
Cyperus   **122**, 141

Dacrycarpus   **79**, 87, 170
Dacrydium   25, 79, **80**, 81, 87, 149
Dactylanthus   35
Daisy, native   104
Dandelion   108
Dandelion, native   22, 108
Danthonia   24
Dewberry   209, 210
Diarrhena   145
Dicksonia   23
Dioscorea   25
Disphyma   **133**, 142
Dock   197
Dock, swamp   197
Dodonaea   218, 219
Dogwood   114
Dove's-foot cranesbill   139
Dracaena   84, 85, 86
Dragon tree   84
Drimys   239, 240
Dryopteris   73, 74
Durvillaea   51, **57**, 58
Dysoxylum   87, **163**, 164, 172, 177, 202, 223, 238

Ecklonia   58
Edwardsia   37, 155
Elaeocarpus   **127**, 128
Embelia   169
Eucalyptus   **169**, 170
Eugenia   179, 180
Euphorbia   **131**, 132, **133**, 142
Euphrasia   38, **220**
Eyebright   220
Eyebright, New Zealand   220

False laurel   149
Fat-hen   96, 97
Fern, black tree   72
Fern, gully   73
Fern, hen and chickens   65
Fern, horseshoe,   72
Fern, kidney   71
Fern, king   72
Fern, silver tree   71
Fern, tree   23, 71
Fern, water   67
Flax, mountain   86
Flax, New Zealand   18, 22, 36, 37, 38, 41, 48, 86, 89, 90, 91, 162, 183, 229
Flea seed   193
Forget-me-not   191
Fuchsia   **181**, 182
Fuchsia, tree   181

262

Fungus, Jew's ear   21

Galium   **215**, 216
Gardenia   212
Gaultheria   130
Geniostoma   17, **157**, 158
Geranium   **138**, **139**
Geum   **207**
Giant puffball   60
Gigartina   24
Ginseng   93, 94
Gnaphalium   **102**, 103
Goniopteris   73
Goose grass   215
Green celery   229
Grindelia   101
Griselinia   **115**, 141, 158, 212
Gully fern   73
Gum plant   101
Gumdigger's soap   204

Haloragis   **146**, 147
Hangehange   17, 157
Harakeke   37, 86, 93
Hebe   16, 59, 214, **220**, 221, 222
Hebenstreitia   220
Hedera   95
Hedycarya   **164**, 165
Hemp, New Zealand   86
Hen and chickens fern   65
Herb-bennet   207
Hibiscus   **158**, 161, 162, 177
Hibiscus, starry   158
Hierochloe   **144**, 145, 159
Hinau   20, 127
Hioi   148
Hirneola   21
Hohere   162
Hoheria   34, 37, 89, **162**, 163, 177
Holy grass   144
Honeysuckle   199
Horokaka   133
Horopito   239
Horse daisy   100
Horseshoe fern   72
Houhere   37, 162
Huainanga   97
Hutiwai   206
Hymenophyllum   65
Hypericum   30, **147**, 148, 160
Hypnum   62

Ice plant   133, 134
Ice plant, New Zealand   133
Indian corn   145

Ipomoea   **110**, 111, 112, 167
Ivy   95
Ixora   215

Jew's-ear fungus   21

Kahakaha   119
Kahikatea   19, 79, 170
Kahikatoa   79, 163, 170
Kaikai aruhe   140
Kaikaiatua   133, 140
Kakaho   144
Kamahi   119
Kanga   145
Kanuka   170
Kapeti   117
Kapuka   115
Karaka   8, 26, 27, 29, 56, 113, 115, 116, 163
Karamu   27, 176, 210, 212
Karamuramu   38
Kareao   164, 223
Karengo   58
Karerarera   67, 68
Karetu   144
Karo   189
Kauri   19, 20, 35, 78, 217
Kawakawa   41, 185, 186
Keketuwai   38, 62
Kidney fern   71
King fern   72
Kiwikiwi   68
Knightia   **196**, **199**
Knot weeds   194
Kohekohe   37, 163, 164
Kohepiro   233
Koheriki   233
Kohia   89, 183, 189, 191
Kohoho   37, 224
Kohukohu   39, 64, 90, 190, 191
Kohutuhutu   181
Kokihi   134
Kokomuka   220, 221
Kopakopa   71, 107, 191
Kopata   140, 207
Kopukapuka   202
Korare   163
Korari   86
Korau   35
Korokio   114, 208
Korokio taranga   114
Koromiko   16, 36, 41, 53, 59, 204, 220, 221, 222
Kotimana   101

263

Kotukutuku   181, 182
Kowhai   10, 37, 151, 154, 155, 156, 171, 172
Kowhitiwhiti   119
Kumara   19, 22, 110, 111, 186
Kumarahou   176, 204, 205
Kunzea   22, **170**, 171, 172, 212
Kyllinga   122

Lacebark   162
Lagenifera   **104**, 123
Lake scirpus   122
Lamb's quarters   97
Lamb's tongue   98
Laminaria   57, 58
Lastrea   73
Laurelia   29, 115, **166**, 178
Lembophyllum   52, **62**
Lemonwood   188
Lepidium   **118**, 119, 136
Lepidosperma   122
Leptopteris   23
Leptospermum   29, 33, 79, 82, 151, 164, **170**, 171, 172, 173, 178
Leucopogon   16, **129**
Lilium   157
Liriodendron   240
Litsea   **150**, 151, 152, 182
Lizard's tail   184
Lomaria   73
Lophomyrtus   **173**, **174**
Lycoperdon   37, 60
Lygodium   85

Maawe   215
Macrocystis   58
Macropiper   41, 42, **185**, 186, 187, 188, 234
Mahoe   238
Maika ka   156
Maikaika   37, 156
Maire   179
Maire tawake   179
Mairehau   29, 217
Maize   145, 146
Maki   126
Makomako   29, 125
Mallow, common   162
Malva   162
Mamaku   21, 72
Manakura   163, 238
Mangeao   150, 182
Manono   210, 212
Manuka   20, 21, 22, 29, 41, 82, 151, 156, 170, 172, 212
Maori celery   137, 229
Maori mint   148
Maori painkiller   240
Maori privet   157
Maori spurge   131
Mapau   168
Marattia   65, 70, **72**, 73
Mariscus   122
Marohi   74
Marsh mallow   162
Maruru   202
Matai   83
Mate Maori   48
Matipo, red   168
Matoutou   90
Matuakumara   138
Mauku   65
Mauru   113
Mawe   215
Melaleuca   172, 173
Melicope   **216**, 217
Melicytus   163, 232, **238**, 239
Mentha   37, **148**, 149, 160
Meryta   90, **93**, 209
Mescal bean   155
Mesembryanthemum   133, 134
Metrosideros   22, **174**, **175**, **176**, 179, 195
Mexican yam   25
Micrococcus   193
Milkweed   133
Mingimingi   128, 129
Mint   148
Miro   19, 82, 83
Mistletoe   157, 158, 212
Mitchella   216
Mouku   65, 95
Mountain flax   86
Mussaenda   212
Mycobacterium   148
Myoporum   37, 112, **166**, 167, 168
Mysotidium   191
Myrsine   **168**, 169, 178
Myrtle, native   173
Myrtus   173, 174

Namunamu   139
Nani   35
Napahuite   164
Nasturtium   **119**, 137
Native beech   20
Native cedar   163
Native daisy   104

264

Native dandelion   108
Native myrtle   173
Nau   118
Nemuaron   166
Neomyrtus   174
Nephrodium   73
Nettle, European   235
Nettles, stinging   197
Nettle, tree   186, 234
New Zealand bed-straw   215
New Zealand eyebright   220
New Zealand flax   18, 22, 37, 41, 54, 86, 90, 91, 183, 229
New Zealand hemp   84, 86
New Zealand ice plant   133
New Zealand passion fruit   29, 183
New Zealand spinach   21, 134
Ngaio   36, 37, 48, 166, 167
Ngaro   91
Nightshade, common   225
Nightshade, cut-leaved   25, 224
Nikau   182, 183

Old man's beard   63
Ongaonga   186, 234
Onopordon   101, 102
Orache, common   96

Paewhenua   197
Panax   93
Pansy   238
Papa   157
Papa-aumu   157, 158, 212
Papapa   130, 204
Papauma   115, 158, 210, 212
Para   72
Parani   104
Parerarera   191
Paretao   67
Paretau   67
Parsley   136, 137, 230
Passiflora   29, **183**, 184, 191
Passion flower   183
Passion fruit   183
Patete   66, 94
Pelargonium   **140**, 142
Pepper-tree (Macropiper)   185
Pepper-tree (Pseudowintera)   239
Peppermint   148
Petroselinum   230
Peu   73
Phebalium   29, 213, **217**
Phegopteris   73
Phormium   18, 22, 26, 30, 36, 37, 38, **86**, 90, 91, 93, 106, 162, 163, 183, 191, 209, 229
Phyllocladus   **81**, 88, 146
Pia   172, 173
Picrorhiza   222
Pigeon wood   164
Pikiarero   37, 200
Pilocarpus   216
Pimelea   29, 30, **228**, 229
Pinatoro   228
Pink pine   25
Piper   41, 93, 185, 187, 188
Piripiri   206
Pirita   223
Pitau   112
Pittosporum   39, 62, 90, **188**, 189, **190**, 196
Piupiu   73
Planchonella   214, **219**
Plantago   71, 107, **191**, 192, 193
Plantain   191, 193, 197
Pneumatopteris   70, 73
Poa   **145**
Podocarpus   79, **82**, 83, 88, 172
Pohata   117
Pohatu   108, 118
Pohue   109
Pohuhe   109
Pohutukawa   175
Polygonum   **193**, 194, 195, 197
Polypodium   73, 74
Polystichum   73
Pomaderris   130, 176, **204**, 205, 206, 222
Ponga   71
Poporokaiwhiri   164
Porokaiwhiria   164
Poroporo   25, 29, 37, 224
Pororua   104, 107
Porphyra   51, **58**, 59
Potato   19, 35, 36, 227
Poverty weed   204
Prince of Wales feathers   23
Privet, Maori   157
Prostrate parsley   229
Prumnopitys   30, **82**, **83**, 105
Prunus   207
Pseudocyphellaria   64
Pseudopanax   **94**, 123
Pseudowintera   16, 232, **239**, 240
Pteridium   16, 38, **74**, 75, 76, 77
Pteris   37, 74, 77
Pterocladia   24

Puapuatea   102
Puarangi   158
Puatawhiwhi   176
Puatea   102
Puawananga   163, 201
Pue   35
Puffball   60
Puha   39
Puhou   112
Puka   93
Pukapuka   37, 99
Pukatea   27, 29, 115, 166
Pukurau   37, 60
Pukuvau   60
Pumpkin   46
Puriri   236
Puwha   39, 104, 108, 114, 191

Radiata pine   20
Ragwort   100
Rahurahu   74
Ramarama   173
Rangiora   27, 29, 37, 99
Ranunculus   201, **202**, **203**, 204
Raorika   47
Raoriki   203
Rapanea   168
Rarahu   74
Rarauhe   38, 74
Raspberry   209, 210
Rata   22, 41, 174, 176
Raukawa   94
Raupo   229
Raurekau   66, 94, 210
Rauriki   104
Red manuka   170
Red matipo   168
Red pine   80
Rengamutu   134
Rengarenga   36, 37, 156
Rewarewa   199
Rhabdothamnus   **140**, 143
Rhamnus   205, 206
Rhopalostylis   **182**
Rhubarb   43, 45
Ribbon-wood   36
Rimu   10, 19, 21, 27, 80, 112
Rimurapa   57, 58
Rimuroa   57, 58
Ripogonum   164, **223**
Rivea   111
River cudweed   102
Rock lily   156

Rohutu   174
Roniu   145
Rorippa   **119**, 137, 141
Rose-leaved anise   233
Rosemary   22
Round-leaved pigface   133
Rubus   90, 93, 182, **208**, 209, 210, 229
Ruerueke   133
Rumex   **197**, 198, 199
Runa   197
Ruruhau   35
Rye grass   218

Sapindus   218
Sassafras   149
Scammony   111
Scandia   17, **233**
Schefflera   13, 31, 66, **94**, 95
Scirpus   **122**, 125, 141
Scleranthus   62
Scolypopa   114
Scotch thistle   101, 102
Scurvygrass, Cook's   118, 137
Seagrass   23
Sedge   23, 122
Senecio   29, 99, 100, **104**
Senna   208
Seven finger   94
Sideroxylon   219
Silver tree-fern   71
Silver tussock   145
Sisal   22
Slippery elm   162
Smartweed   194
Smilax   224
Snowberry   130
Solanum   25, 29, 33, 36, 37, **224**, 225, 226, **227**, 228, 231
Sonchus   **104**, 107, 108, 124, 136, 189, 191
Sophora   29, **151**, 152, 153, 154, **155**, 156, 169, 171, 172
Sopubia   220
Sorrel   197
Sour kroutt   135
Sow thistle   104, 108, 118, 189
Sphagnum moss   24
Speedwell, common   222
Spinach, New Zealand   21, 134
Spruce   80
Spurge, Maori   131
St John's wort   30, 147, 148
Staphylococcus   148, 154, 172

Starry hibiscus   158
Stellaria   62
Sticta   52, 64
Stinging nettle   197
Strathmore weed   29, 228
Strychnos   157
Supplejack   223
Suttonia   168
Swamp dock   197
Sweet potato   110, 186
Sweet-scented grass   145
Syzygium   **179**, 196

Taewa   227
Takaka   74
Tanekaha   81
Tarakupenga   210
Tarata   188, 189
Taraxacum   22, **108**, 109, 124
Tarenna   212
Tatarahake   200, 210
Tataraheke   37, 210
Tataramoa   93, 182, 208, 229
Taumingi   128
Tawa   80, 149
Tawapou   219
Taweke   104
Tawheke   104
Tawhero   120, 121
Tea-tree   20, 170, 171
Terminalia   180
Tetragonia   21, 107, **134**, 135, 136, 137
Tetrapathaea   89, 183
Thelypteris   73
Thistle, cotton   102
Thistle, Scotch   101, 102
Thistle, sow   104
Ti   84, 171
Ti awe   84
Ti kauka   84
Ti kouka   84
Ti pua   84
Ti rakau   84
Ti whanake   84
Tikumu   100
Titoki   22, 189, 191, 218, 238
Titongi   218
Toa   172
Toatoa   146
Todea   23
Toetoe   41, 122, 144
Toetoe upokotangata   122
Toetoe whatumanu   122

Toetoe whatupakau   122
Toot   112
Toromiro   82
Totara   19, 37, 82, 113, 172
Towai   27, 119, 120
Tree fern   23
Tree fuchsia   181
Tree manuka   170
Tree nettle   186, 234
Trichilia   164
Trichomanes   71
Tulip-tree   240
Tulipa   157
Tumingi   128
Tupakihi   112
Turnip, wild   108, 117
Tussilago   101
Tussock ('tussac') grass   145
Tutae kehua   60
Tutae koau   229
Tutae whetu   60
Tutu   8, 26, 56, 58, 80, 112
Tutumako   38, 220
Tutunawai   193
Typha   90, 209, **229**, 231

Ulmus   162
Urostemon   29, 30
Urtica   197, **234**, 235
Usnea   62, 63

Veronica   16, 41, 220, 221, 222
Viola   238
Violet   238
Vitex   **236**, 237

Waiuatua   131
Waiuokahukura   131
Waoriki   203
Warrigal cabbage   134
Water fern   67
Water smartweed   194
Watercress   119, 136
Wati   187
Wawa   122
Weinmannia   **119**, 120, **121**
Wharangi   99, 216
Wharariki   86
Whawhakou   179
White-flowered rata   174
White manuka   170, 212
White pine   79
Whitey wood   238
Wi   145

Wild cabbage   117
Wild celery   136, 230
Wild parsley   136, 137
Wild turnip   108, 117
Wineberry   125
Winter's bark   240
Wintera   239
Wormseed   98

Yam, Mexican   25
Zantedeschia   **91,** 92
Zea   **145**, 146, 160
Ziziphus   206
Zostera   23